escape the writer's web

Untangle Your Procrastination Type,
Discover Personalized Solutions, and
Transform Your Writing Life

ESCAPE
THE
WRITER'S
WEB

" Should not only be on the reading lists of
would-be creative writers, but on the radars of
anyone prone to procrastination... "

~Midwest Book Review

COLLEEN M. STORY

Books may be ordered through booksellers or by contacting the publisher at:

Midchannel Press
P.O. Box 131
Iona, ID 83427 www.midchannelpress.com
Email: publisher@midchannelpress.com

To receive a free weekly email newsletter delivering the tools to break through self-doubt, procrastination, and fear so you can write consistently, publish confidently, and build a thriving creative career, register directly at www.masterwritermindset.com/newsletter.

Cover Design: Miblart

ISBN 13: 979-8-9926172-4-5 (Paperback edition)
ISBN 13: 979-8-9926172-3-8 (eBook edition)

Library-of-Congress Control Number: 2025907044

First Edition: August 2025, printed in the U.S.A.

also by colleen m. story

THE MIDAS LEGACY

The Curse of King Midas (Book I)
The Gimirri Invasion (Book II)

STAND-ALONE FICTION

Rise of the Sidenah
Loreena's Gift
The Beached Ones

NONFICTION

Overwhelmed Writer Rescue
Writer Get Noticed!
Your Writing Matters

For more information, please see:

colleenmstory.com

masterwritermindset.com

author's note

Before you dive in, I wanted to let you know: if you'd like extra support as you work through the ideas in this book, I've created a companion workbook you may want to check out.

The *Escape the Writer's Web Workbook* gives you space to personalize your journey, work through practical exercises for your procrastination type, and build real momentum toward the writing life you want.

It also contains new material you won't find here — including targeted action steps, mindset shifts, troubleshooting tools, and exercises for blended types. It's designed to walk beside you as you read, helping you move from awareness to real, lasting change.

You certainly don't have to use the workbook. The insights here stand on their own. But if you'd like a place to take action as you go, the workbook can help you create steady, powerful shifts in your writing life.

Look for the *Escape the Writer's Web Workbook* wherever books are sold.

contents

introduction
The Curse of Tomorrow

"I'll do it tomorrow."

These words seem harmless enough when they roll off the tongue. We assume we have plenty of tomorrows. We'll get to it then.

But in the creative writer's world, that's like saying, *I'm not going to make my dreams come true, and that's okay with me.*

When you say, *I'll do it tomorrow,* you might as well be saying, *I've given up on this dream.*

It's that serious.

We all know what's going to happen. Tomorrow will come, and we'll be just as busy, tired, frustrated, drained, or uninspired as we were today.

No biggie, we tell ourselves. *I'll just do it tomorrow. Tomorrow, I'll be better. I'll get more sleep tonight, and I'll have more energy. My brain will be sharper. My creativity? Sure to be firing on all cylinders. I just need more rest and a better day, and then . . . and then . . .*

It's amazing how easily we deceive ourselves. A few simple words, and we let ourselves off the hook. No need to work a little harder today. No reason to put in just a few more minutes of effort toward the one thing we can't stop thinking about—our creative work.

But we're not really fooling ourselves. We know we're putting it off. We know we're shrinking in fear from the dream we hold in our hearts.

Deep down, we understand that we have more potential inside us, and by failing to at least try, we're shortchanging ourselves.

That's why we feel guilty.

The moment we turn away from our work, the guilt crawls over us like a shadow—heavy, sticky, and nauseating. We shake it off with the reassurance that tomorrow, the feeling will fade, because tomorrow, we'll magically but assuredly be better, stronger, smarter, and more disciplined.

Tomorrow, we'll work on that dream.

But tomorrow won't be our salvation. It will be a repeat of today, and the day before that, and the day before that. The shadow will grow until it darkens the sky above us. We'll get caught in the dark web of procrastination, and sadly, many of us will never escape its grip.

Meanwhile, our dreams—our true artistic selves—will remain forever out of reach.

The Curse of Tomorrow

When I first started writing this book, the introduction above poured out of me. I worried it might be too negative—after all, books like this are supposed to be positive, motivating, and uplifting.

And that's exactly what I intend this book to be.

But as we begin tackling the subject of procrastination, I can't help but be real. I've seen far too many dreams shattered by the curse of tomorrow, and I know there's only one way to break free—by taking a clear-eyed look at exactly what we're up against.

Too many of us believe that procrastination is just a pesky bad habit, an occasional bump in the road, or an unavoidable part of human nature. And while it *can* be those things at times, far more often, it's a chronic condition that brings pain, guilt, and regret.

That's why I call it a curse. Look up the word and you'll find several definitions. The one I'm referring to comes from Merriam-Webster: "a cause of great harm or torment."

Yep. That's procrastination.

Procrastination is about tomorrow and the regrets that will inevitably follow if we don't find a way to break free.

Scientists have even found evidence of this regret. In a 2009 study of nearly 3,000 people—some chronic procrastinators, some not—researchers discovered that non-procrastinators reported significantly *less* regret at the end of their lives than those who regularly put things off.

Darius Foroux, author of *The Stoic Path to Wealth*, writes on his blog:

> "We all know that putting off our dreams for one week turns into a month, then into a year, and then into decades, and finally, we die with regret. If that sounds harsh, it's because it is harsh. When you keep procrastinating, you become one of those people who never do what they say."

I meet *those people* all the time—attendees at writers' conferences who say they want to get back to writing their novel but just "haven't had time" yet. Book buyers at my signings who tell me they've always wanted to write a book, but they never got around to it. Artists who say, *If only I could quit my day job, maybe I could finally pursue my dreams.*

I see the guilt in their eyes, the haunting desire. And I know that when they walk away, most of them will carry that guilt to their deathbeds.

It's one thing to think about writing a book once or twice and then forget about it. It's an entirely different thing to *intend* to write that book and never do it. That kind of regret can haunt a person for life.

Timothy A. Pychyl, Ph.D., author of *Solving the Procrastination Puzzle: A Concise Guide to Strategies for Change*, once attended a conference on personal meaning. In an article for *Psychology Today,* he recalled asking Dr. Grafton T. Eliason—co-editor of *Existential and Spiritual Issues in Death Attitudes*—what people tend to regret when facing the loss of a loved one.

Dr. Eliason explained that people regret many things, including not doing what they believe their loved one would have wanted. But the deepest regret he encountered in his work was this: the sorrow over things people *meant to do* but never did—regrets born from procrastination.

While losing a person is undeniably more profound, Pychyl noted that the regrets people express in those moments can, in some ways, mirror the regrets we experience when we lose a dream:

> "While it may be possible to forgive oneself for an act of commission, as we all make mistakes, realizing too late in life that you simply failed to take action when you could have, is unbearable in many instances."

Neglecting Our Own Agency in Life

Procrastination, ultimately, is about failing to act according to our values. When we're talking about failing to go after our creative dreams, we're not talking about putting off doing our taxes or waiting to vacuum the house until next weekend.

We're talking about setting aside *the* thing—or at least *one* of the things—we believe will help us find meaning in our lives. The thing we believe will help us rise above all the humdrum, less-important stuff.

Think about it: Way down deep in your soul, what do you feel called to do?

Is it your writing? Your art? Your music?

If you're not doing it—and by "doing it," I mean incorporating it into your daily life—you're not living authentically. You're not honoring yourself and who you are.

That means you're allowing procrastination to do nothing less than separate yourself from yourself. You're allowing procrastination to turn you into someone you don't intend to be.

Curse, indeed.

Imagine if you live your entire life this way, focused more on things that matter less to you. Imagine yourself on your deathbed explaining to those you love why you regret failing to nurture that one dream that never left your heart.

Imagine being *out of tomorrows*, with no more chances remaining to change course.

Your Procrastination Type is Unique to You

I know there are a lot of reasons *why* we procrastinate. I'm going to help you understand them so you can finally break your own procrastination curse.

I also know you've probably tried to overcome this before. For years, we've been fed the idea of "one-size-fits-all" when it comes to defeating procrastination. We just need to have more self-discipline, they say, avoid our impulses, set goals, create schedules, have accountability partners, install reminder apps, and get with it already and all will be well.

But in my research, I've learned that procrastination differs from person to person. How you experience it—and why you experience it—will be different from how and why I experience it.

That means your solutions should look different from mine. And that's important because until you find the right solution, you can't help but continue to fall victim to procrastination's tempting allure.

It's also true that procrastination can show up for different reasons at different times in our lives, sparked by different events.

It used to be we blamed people for their lack of discipline and will. Today, we know that procrastination is more complicated than that. Hardworking people procrastinate. Smart people procrastinate. Determined people procrastinate. Clever people procrastinate.

This is not about character weakness. It's about identifying the true source of a psychological phenomenon so that we can finally turn around and address it successfully and live the lives we were meant to live.

And ultimately, become the artists we were meant to become.

You may be frustrated that this demon is still clinging to your back, and that despite your efforts, you haven't been able to exorcise it. If that's the case, I'm so glad you picked up this book. I believe you'll find ideas here you haven't encountered before, presented in a way that clears the fog around procrastination and makes addressing it feel a little more inviting, and even a little fun.

Think of this as a choose-your-own-adventure book. Start with Chapters 1-3, where you'll be introduced to the big picture of procrastination—what it really is, why it happens, and what we've come to understand about it so far. Then take the quiz in Chapter 4. Once you've completed it, you'll be able to identify which of the 13 procrastination types most affect your life. From there, you can turn to the chapters that speak directly to your experience and learn how to manage those patterns more effectively.

Because many people have more than one type that applies to them, I've also included guidance to help you identify your unique "procrastination blend" and create a personalized mix of solutions to help you break free from it.

In the final chapters, you'll discover practical tips for overcoming fear, moving through apathy, and creating lasting change in your writing life.

The Information In This Book is Part Science, Part Intuition

To give you a sense of where all this comes from, it's grounded in my research into the scientific literature on procrastination and the types identified by experts. But that's only the beginning. After gathering the research, I developed the quiz myself and invited writers and other artists to take it. They offered helpful feedback on whether their results felt accurate and how well the suggested solutions worked for them.

I didn't run this quiz through a panel of scientists or publish it in a scientific journal—that's outside the scope of my work as a writer and researcher. Instead, what I offer here is based on extensive study, years of working with hundreds of writers, and my own personal experience with procrastination. While it's not peer-reviewed, I believe it to be highly accurate, grounded in research and real-world feedback. I offer it to you as a practical tool to support your creative practice. Use it in whatever way serves you best.

So if you're ready, take a deep breath and turn the page. What lies ahead is a journey through the tangled web of procrastination—one that can lead you back to clarity, momentum, and the creative life you're meant to live.

one
the origin of the
procrastination
curse

NO ONE really knows when procrastination first appeared in human nature, but it seems to have been with us for a long time.

Author Eric Jaffe, for instance, writing for the Association for Psychological Science, notes that people have struggled with it since ancient times:

> "The Greek poet Hesiod, writing around 800 B.C., cautioned not to 'put your work off till tomorrow and the day after.' The Roman consul Cicero called procrastination 'hateful' in the conduct of affairs....For all we know, the dinosaurs saw the meteorite coming and went back to their game of Angry Pterodactyls."

Similarly, author Sarah Stodola, writing for Mental Floss, notes that the Ming Dynasty poet and painter Wen Jia, living in the 1500s, wrote his *Poem of Today* as a warning to procrastinators:

> Today follows today, how few todays one has!
> If he doesn't do today, when can it be done!
> How many todays one will have for a hundred years of
>   life, what a pity if there is no action today!

1

If you say just wait until tomorrow, you will have something else for tomorrow.
I'm writing the Poem of Today for you, please just
working hard from today.

Diving deeper into the word itself, we find that "procrastinate"
comes from the Latin *procrastinare*, meaning "to put off until tomorrow." It also shares an etymology with the Greek term *akrasia,* which
refers to acting against one's better judgment. (That's an interesting one
—in other words, procrastination is a reflection of our worst judgment!)

My guess? The problem has existed since humans first walked the
earth. Over the past several decades, however, scientists have been
studying it more intently with the goal of understanding "why" we
procrastinate—and, ultimately, how we can stop.

Is Procrastination a Failure to Discipline Ourselves?

Initially, the prevailing belief was that people procrastinate due to a
failure of self-regulation—the scientific term for self-discipline. Scientists and psychologists seemed to suggest that these "slackers" simply
lacked the ability or willpower to reign in their impulses and "make"
themselves get things done.

Recent research, however, has shown that the issue is far more
complex. Just as we now understand that being overweight can result
from a myriad of factors—including biology, physiology, diet, activity
level, and emotional health—we now recognize that procrastination is
about much more than just time management or self-regulation.

The Difference Between Procrastinating and Being a Chronic Procrastinator

Before we dive into what we know so far about why we procrastinate,
it's important to understand the difference between occasional procrastination and chronic procrastination.

Most of us would admit to procrastinating now and then—that's
occasional procrastination. We may simply put things off sometimes

because we just don't feel up to them for whatever reason. Particularly when we're faced with tasks we don't want to do—like filing our taxes—we're likely to experience delays. (Scientists call this act of avoiding distasteful tasks "task aversion.")

I might procrastinate on mopping the kitchen floor, for example, letting stains and dirt accumulate until I finally force myself to clean it. That might be because I'm too tired to mop that day, or because I really despise mopping. Someone else might procrastinate on doing the dishes, allowing them to pile up in the sink until there's nothing left to eat on but the table itself.

These are examples of everyday types of procrastination that can affect anyone. Usually, the consequences are minor. My floor may stay dirty for longer than it should, and that reluctant dishwasher may have to eat off paper plates one night, but in the grand scheme of things, it's not a big deal.

That doesn't mean life wouldn't be better if we learned to avoid even these more "surface-level" delays. I always feel better when my kitchen floor is clean (especially once it's done!), and washing dishes right after use is certainly more sanitary. This book can help with this kind of procrastination too, so even you "surface dwellers" can sharpen your follow-through and get more done with ease.

But then there's the more serious, chronic type of procrastination—the kind where our delay tactics take root and begin to truly torment us.

What is Chronic Procrastination?

Chronic procrastination is an ongoing, long-term habit of putting things off, even when it causes stress, missed opportunities, or harm to your goals. This isn't a now-and-then thing—it's a "happens regularly" type of thing.

Chronic procrastination can affect people in two ways:

1. Chronic procrastination on a specific type of task
2. Pervasive chronic procrastination

Often, writers and other creative artists fall into the first category. In general, you may be good at getting things done—your dishes are clean, your errands are completed, and your employer is satisfied with your work.

But when it comes to your art—a specific type of task—you hesitate. You try to establish a regular writing practice but then make excuses. You dream of publishing a novel, yet it never becomes a reality because whenever you try to take action, your procrastination takes the lead.

This isn't "task aversion" because you don't dislike writing. On the contrary, it's probably very important to you. And it's also not just one task, like writing a synopsis–it's anything related to your writing dream. You're procrastinating on a specific type of task in your life.

Does this sound familiar? If you're not sure, ask yourself how many stories or books you've started but never finished, or how many times you've intended to write but haven't followed through. If your answer to either question is more than one, then you probably fit into the first group: a chronic procrastinator when it comes to your creative work.

Then there's the second group: pervasive chronic procrastinators. These individuals struggle to complete almost *any* task on time. They are consistently late with work assignments, their household chores often go undone, their writing dreams are on hold, and they feel perpetually overwhelmed by trying to keep up.

Whether you chronically procrastinate in just one area of your life—like writing—or in most areas, you're certainly not alone. Scientists estimate that about 20 percent of the population are chronic procrastinators, defined as "persons intentionally delaying as a self-sabotaging strategy decisions and tasks that need to be done."

That's one-fifth of the population, so if you fall into this group, don't despair. Clearly, chronic procrastination isn't rare, but it does raise an important question.

Why do some people suffer from this affliction while others don't?

Scientists are still looking for answers. Here's a general overview of what they've discovered so far.

There May be a Biological Component

In their book *Procrastination: Why You Do It and What to Do About It Now*, authors Burka and Yuen examine the many possible reasons why a person may become a chronic procrastinator.

One chapter is devoted to the idea of a biological component. While no single gene is linked to procrastination, studies suggest that certain brain functions can contribute to it.

The authors write:

"For example, if you have some degree of attention deficit disorder, executive dysfunction, seasonal affective disorder, depression, obsessive-compulsive disorder, chronic stress, or sleep deprivation, what's going on in your brain is likely to be closely tied to your procrastination."

The good news is that the brain is far more flexible and capable of change than we once believed. So even if you struggle with some of these issues, that doesn't mean you can't overcome procrastination—it may just help you to understand its roots.

Personally, I know I'm more vulnerable to procrastination when I'm tired or discouraged—yet another reason it's always wise to take care of yourself!

You May Have a Skewed Relationship to Time

Burka and Yuen also explore the idea that our sense of time develops as we go through life, starting in childhood. What time means to us as infants—when want to be fed or changed *now*—is often different from what it means to us when we start school or become teenagers. As we grow into adults with schedules and deadlines, our relationship with time shifts again.

At any stage of this process, it's possible to develop a difficult relationship with time. Some people avoid thinking about the future for various reasons, which can lead to procrastination. Others may feel constrained by time and choose to ignore it altogether.

One interesting study found that procrastinators often feel disconnected from their future selves. While productive people complete tasks today to avoid dealing with them tomorrow, procrastinators may not relate to their future selves at all, making it easier to push tasks onto that distant version of themselves.

This disconnect can make overcoming procrastination particularly challenging unless the procrastinator finds a way to bridge the gap and recognize that their future self is *still* them, equally subject to the consequences of delayed action. If this sounds familiar, you'll find more information about it—as well as some tips to help—in Chapter 2.

You May Have Trouble Self-Regulating

As mentioned earlier, the lack of self-regulation theory is one of the earliest explanations for procrastination, and it still applies in many cases today.

According to this theory, we procrastinate because we don't want to force ourselves to do something when we're not in the mood. In essence, it's a struggle with self-discipline. If this is a recurring challenge in your life, it may be a key factor behind your procrastination.

For example, let's say you're trying to lose weight. Choosing ice cream for dessert instead of fruit is a failure of self-regulation. The desire for ice cream is an immediate impulse that arises in your brain, and your ability to self-regulate determines how well you can resist that impulse.

People who struggle with substance abuse are often vulnerable to this type of procrastination, but they're not the only ones. If you find it hard to self-regulate in other areas—like spending, sleeping, eating, or screen time—you may also tend to prioritize short-term comfort over long-term goals.

It's still unclear why some people struggle more than others with this type of procrastination, but research suggests that individuals who score high on impulsiveness on personality tests are more likely to be affected.

You Could Be Anxious

Some people struggle with procrastination due to an underlying sense of anxiety or fear, often tied to feelings of self-doubt or a sense of inadequacy. You might think, *I'm not good enough to complete this task the way it should be done.* This feeling can become especially intense when facing something deeply meaningful, like writing the story you've always dreamed of telling.

For some, the fear goes even deeper: *If I fail at this one project, I'll never reach my lifelong dream.* That kind of pressure only amplifies the anxiety and makes it even harder to begin.

Procrastination can also stem from feeling overwhelmed by the amount of work a task will take. Writing a book, for instance, can take a year or more to complete. When you don't know how the writing will go or how the final result will turn out, that can also create enough anxiety to cause you to delay taking the first step.

Anxiety often creates a vicious cycle because procrastinating on a task typically makes us even more anxious about it. As a deadline approaches, if there is one, panic increases. In a 2024 study of university students, researchers found that procrastination led to depression and anxiety over time.

For employees, anxiety and procrastination may also be linked, particularly if the job is stressful. Researchers theorized that when a person feels anxious about many things, they may be more likely to procrastinate to help themselves feel better.

I won't worry about that now, they might say, essentially letting themselves off the hook and improving their mood—for the moment, at least.

Other Possible Reasons

There are several other reasons why a person may procrastinate, and we'll continue exploring them in this book. There are also other existing theories in the scientific world, with researchers actively developing new ones at the time of this writing.

I will be discussing some of the unique reasons why *you* may procrastinate as we progress from chapter to chapter. Understanding your tendency to delay is a big part of successfully breaking free of this curse, as then you can focus on the approaches that will work best for you.

It's not my intention, however, to dive too deeply into the science. While I've done extensive research, to be frank, I don't want to bore you with it. There are plenty of other books that cover the scientific side of procrastination in far more detail.

And in the end, that wouldn't help you much, anyway.

Despite all the research, scientists have yet to reach a consensus on exactly what procrastination is or why we struggle with it. The reasons likely vary from person to person, which is one of the key motivations behind my desire to write this book. No two people are the same when it comes to their reasons for putting things off. That's why a more personal approach is critical to finding solutions.

I want to make this heavy issue of procrastination feel lighter and more manageable. Scientific research is valuable for improving our understanding and developing better strategies. But if you're struggling to get your creative work done right now, you probably don't care much about all the whys and wherefores.

You just want to find a way to overcome this thing so you can make your dreams come true!

So practical solutions are key. I am going to pause here, though, to recognize just how much procrastination can not only undermine your creative dreams, but reduce your overall quality of life. Did you know that scientists have been researching this too? And they've found some alarming results.

How Procrastination Destroys Your Life

Unfortunately, procrastination affects us in many negative ways, with the consequences running deeper than most of us realize. It reaches into every area of life, undermining our health, clouding our mental well-being, and limiting our ability to live with purpose and joy.

In a 2023 study of over 3,500 students, researchers found that procrastination was associated with worse mental health, upper extremity pain, unhealthy lifestyle habits (such as poor sleep and lack of physical activity), increased loneliness, and greater economic difficulties.

These findings align with those of an earlier study, which showed that people struggling with severe procrastination were more likely to report symptoms of tension, anxiety, depression, pain, sleep disturbances, and an overall lower quality of life.

German researchers analyzed data from 1,350 women and 1,177 men between the ages of 14 and 95. Across all age groups, they found that procrastination was associated with the following:

- higher levels of stress
- depression and anxiety
- fatigue
- reduced satisfaction with life as a whole, including work and income levels

Researchers have even found that habitual procrastination may increase the risk of heart disease! In a 2003 study titled "I'll Look After My Health, Later," scientists linked procrastination to poor health, higher stress levels, and a lower engagement in behaviors that promote wellness.

Clearly, procrastination is a destructive habit. Not only can it keep your writing dreams out of reach, but it can harm your health and, if severe enough, derail your entire life. While this book focuses on how procrastination blocks your creative goals, it may help you to know that if you can break free of procrastination in even one area of your life, the benefits will likely bleed into other areas, as well.

Procrastination Can Kill Your Dreams

Others often encourage us to get things done in various areas of our lives. Your boss or supervisor, for example, may provide the motivation you need to get your work done. Family and friends offer another form of accountability in your home and community life, making it harder to drop the ball on tasks that affect them.

When it comes to writing your book or building your author platform, though, no one is there to make sure you do the work. If you have even one person who cares about it, count yourself lucky! But even then, it's hard to believe the world will end if you don't write that book, so the urgency is often lacking.

And you're right—the world won't end. For the most part, life will go on as usual, which is why this is a unique type of problem. You can keep putting off your writing indefinitely without any serious consequences to your daily life.

But what about *your inner* world? What about how you see yourself?

Strangely, most of us consider those low priorities . . . until our lives are nearly over. When we're staring death in the face, we finally realize that we were supposed to make ourselves happy in this life. We were supposed to fulfill our purpose. We were supposed to make our dreams come true.

If I can accomplish anything with this book, it will be to impress upon you *how important* your creative work is. I'm not talking about what it might do for others, though it may have a significant impact. I'm talking about what it will do for *you*. And there's no way to fully understand that until you've done it—until you're looking back.

That's where I am now. There was a time in my life when I wanted nothing more than to write a novel and have it traditionally published. I eventually reached that goal, but in the many years between deciding I wanted it and finally achieving it, self-doubt, procrastination, worry, anxiety, discouragement, and even despair threatened to stop me.

I wanted to reach this goal. The drive was so strong within me that I couldn't deny it.

But I never realized how *important* it was, not just to my growth as a writer, but as a human being. Today, I am a much better person in many ways than I was before I achieved my dream. I'm smarter, more skilled, and more experienced. But beyond that, I'm also more at peace, more in touch with my inner spirit, and more "whole" as a person.

I often wonder what I would be like if I *hadn't* been so stubborn about making this creative dream a reality. Whenever I think about it, all I can see is *less*—as if, somehow, I would be less than I am now.

I want you to have *more*. I want you to feel the fullness of who you are. I want you to experience that incredible sense of growth as you engage in your creative work day by day, letting it shape and mold you.

Never doubt it—this creative dream of yours is *extremely* important. I know that because you cared enough about it to pick up this book in the first place. And that means if procrastination is stopping you, you must find a way to overcome it so it no longer holds you back.

To that end, we'll move on to more practical, actionable strategies you can start using today. But first, I want to help you tackle the two most common reasons writers and other creative artists procrastinate.

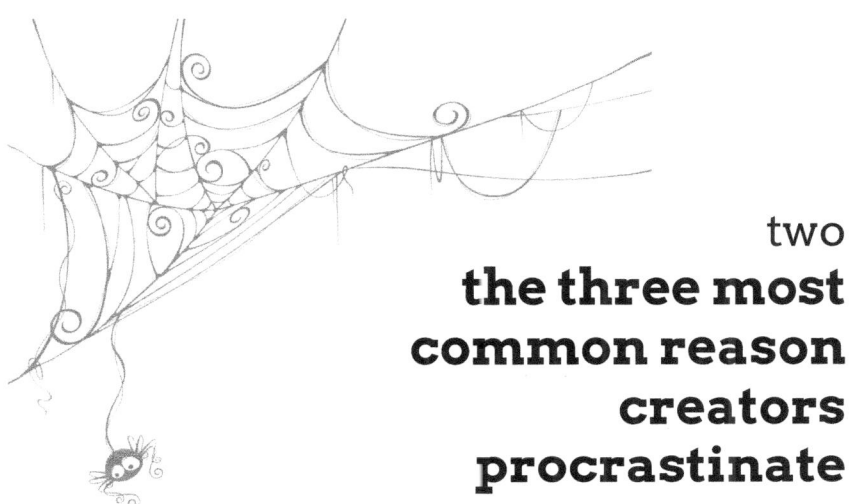

two
the three most common reason creators procrastinate

ONE OF THE questions we often ask ourselves is: *Why do we procrastinate?* We know it's not good for us, and we understand that we'll eventually pay the price for it. So why do we give in to it anyway?

In this chapter, we'll explore the three most common reasons behind this puzzling behavior.

Writing Can Create a Battle in the Brain

Whenever we're faced with a difficult or unpleasant task—and writing or writing-related projects can be either or both—the brain launches a kind of civil war. The limbic system, which is responsible for emotions and sensations of pleasure, wants us to enjoy ourselves *now,* not later. This is the "older" part of the brain. It's been around for centuries of human evolution, and it's incredibly powerful.

On the other hand, the prefrontal cortex, which governs planning and decision-making, wants us to get the project done. This "newer" part of the brain knows what's best for us in the long run and urges us to buckle down and do the work we intended to do.

The problem is that the limbic system often possesses the stronger army. It's the part of the brain that makes you jerk your hand out of a fire or run when you come face-to-face with a tiger. Automatic and commanding, it's difficult to resist. This is why, when you think about your writing project, you may instead give in to the temptation to watch an hour of television. Your limbic system is compelling you to choose immediate pleasure over long-term rewards.

The prefrontal cortex, by contrast, has weaker defenses, partly because, evolutionarily speaking, it hasn't had as much time to build up its power in our brains. Located right behind the forehead, it developed later and functions differently. Unlike the instinctive, reflex-driven limbic system, the prefrontal cortex needs more time to act. It has to gather information from other parts of the brain, analyze it, and then decide what to do.

It's as if the limbic system has a machine gun fully loaded and ready to fire, while the prefrontal cortex has a rifle stored in the back closet that needs to be unpacked. So when you think about writing chapter three of your novel, your limbic system jumps into action, urging you to watch those funny YouTube videos instead.

By the time the prefrontal cortex has analyzed the situation, determined what's best, and spoken up to encourage you to write instead, it's already too late—you've started watching the videos and you're unlikely to stop. You may promise yourself that you'll do better next time without realizing that the same process will repeat itself, leaving your story unfinished.

#1 Reason Writers Procrastinate: The Project is Difficult

The key to getting past your brain's tendency to drop you in front of YouTube or the video game console is to address the first common reason we writers procrastinate: we see the project we want to work on as *difficult*. Most of us would rather do something easy or fun—exactly what the limbic system prefers.

Researchers confirmed this in a study published in *Transactions of the Kansas Academy of Science*. They varied the difficulty of tasks assigned to participants and then watched how they responded. Not surprisingly, difficult and boring tasks led to more procrastination than easier and more engaging ones.

A more recent study published in *Learning and Instruction* reinforced this finding, showing that perceived difficulty significantly impacts the tendency to procrastinate.

This wouldn't be a problem if we could view everything we do as easy or straightforward. But most of the accomplishments we take pride in—earning a degree, mastering a skill, raising a family, nurturing relationships, running a successful business, or writing and publishing a book—are anything but simple. They're tough, arduous, and often demanding, which means we tend to procrastinate on *the things that matter most in our lives*.

And that's not good news.

The solution? We need to shift our mindset so that the tasks that truly matter seem easier to tackle. The goal is to convince yourself that the project in front of you isn't too taxing or overwhelming. Instead, you want to see the time you spend on it as enjoyable, partly because it feels easy to you.

1. MAKE THE START OF THE PROJECT FUN.

Remember, your limbic system wants you to enjoy yourself, so try giving in a little. Find a way to make this project you have to do fun, at least in the beginning.

Maybe you promise yourself a favorite cup of coffee when you sit down to write, or treat yourself to something else that motivates you. Put on your favorite music, or let calming sounds like ocean waves or a babbling creek fill the background. You might even read a short poem or a page from a favorite book to ease you into the creative flow before your fingers touch the keyboard.

The more often you do this, the less procrastination will trouble you because your brain will start associating the beginning of any writing project with pleasure.

2. SHRINK THE PROJECT.

Often, the reason we perceive a project as difficult is because we're looking at it as a whole. Writing an entire story or book-length manuscript is challenging. The solution is to break the project down by 80–95 percent. Ask yourself: Can I complete just five percent of this project today?

Maybe you'll write only 50 words instead of 500 or spend just ten minutes researching new ways to market your work. The key is to make it easy to *get started*. Once you begin, you'll probably want to keep going. All you have to do is trick your brain into thinking that what you want to do is a piece of cake.

3. Set a timer.

Decide that you'll work on whatever it is for just 5–10 minutes. Set your timer and go. Get as much done in those few minutes as you can. Apply your focus and attention to your highest ability, and then you're done! If you want to keep going, feel free, but you don't have to.

This approach not only makes the project seem easier, but it also gives you something crucial for overcoming procrastination: *progress*. Every time you make progress on your project, it feels good, and your brain likes it. That means the next time you think about working on that project, your brain is more likely to see it as fun rather than difficult.

4. Get together with another writer.

What may seem difficult and unpleasant when you have to do it by yourself can become fun if you're doing it with someone else. Some writers invest in shared office spaces for this reason. It's simply easier to get things done when you're surrounded by others who are also working. But you don't have to rent a space to benefit from this effect. Instead, get together with another creator at someone's house, a café, a library, or a coffee shop. You can also connect virtually via Zoom or even livestream on YouTube. Make it a weekly or twice-weekly appointment, and you'll likely accomplish more while enjoying the process.

5. Make your writing environment more inviting.

Take another look at where you do your creative work. Is it inviting and comfortable? Do you enjoy working there? If not, consider upgrading it. Paint the walls with fresh colors, put up new artwork, invest in a comfortable chair, and make sure your computer equipment meets your needs.

6. USE REWARDS.

Remember—your limbic system is holding you hostage. If you've been procrastinating on your writing project, it's because your emotions are dictating your actions.

This can be especially challenging for writers and other creators since we often believe we work best when we're "in the mood." But take a moment to consider how often you actually feel that way. If you're being honest, it's probably not very often. Emotions are constantly shifting, and they aren't reliable.

If you want to achieve your writing goals, you have to ignore how you feel on any given day and simply get to work. Use the other techniques on this list, and make it a habit to reward yourself when you push past procrastination and get some writing done.

7. CHANGE HOW YOU TALK TO YOURSELF.

Think about what you say to yourself before getting to work. "I have to finish this chapter," is a common one. "I need to" is another. These phrases are often spoken with a resigned tone of voice.

If you want to convince your brain that this is something worth looking forward to, change your words. "I want to" is a good alternative: *I want to finish this chapter* or *I want to create a new freebie for my newsletter subscribers.*

To take it even further, try *I can't wait to finish this chapter!* or *I'm so excited to get a new freebie up on the website!* Even if you don't genuinely feel that excited, statements like these can shift your perspective.

That little change might be all you need to get started, and from there, it's all downhill.

#2 Reason Writers Procrastinate: The Project is Important

The second most common reason writers procrastinate is that they view the project in front of them as important, which often translates to difficult and demanding.

Think about it. If you don't usually procrastinate on doing the dishes, it's probably because a) you see the task as necessary but not particularly *important*, and b) you know you could wash them in your sleep. It doesn't demand your full focus or your best self, so it's easy to get it done.

But when it comes to something you truly care about—like the book you're writing or the new website you're creating—it feels much more significant. That makes it easier to believe you're not up to the task at the moment.

The more important a project is to you, the more likely you are to procrastinate. This ties back to the infamous fear of failure that most of us have. When something matters, you want to succeed at it. But in daily life, few of us feel like bestselling authors or brilliant creators. We tell ourselves that maybe tomorrow we'll feel more like that person—the kind who can write a masterpiece.

The solution? Change your mind about the project. Convince yourself that it's not *that* important. But how do you do that when this is your dream? Here are some ideas.

I. EXPAND YOUR DREAM

When I first started out as a writer, all I wanted was to write and publish a novel. I focused on that one goal for years. But now, after publishing multiple books, I realize how shortsighted that was. If I had envisioned a long writing career filled with many books, that first one wouldn't have felt so monumental. Believing there was more to come might have taken some of the pressure off and made the process feel a little lighter.

Think about how you might expand your dream. Make it bigger. If you want to be a lifelong writer, picture all the books you'll write.

Maybe you'd like to become a public speaker, sharing insights on the topics you write about, or perhaps you're interested in building an online community around a central theme.

Even if you think you have only one book in you—perhaps a memoir—you can still take this approach. Imagine what may develop after completing the memoir and how it will shape your life. See yourself becoming more than who you are today. Maybe the memoir will lead to other ventures, such as speaking, further writing, or even starting a nonprofit organization. Try to view every step you're taking right now —not just writing this story—as a contribution to the future self you are becoming.

2. Keep Your Perspective

When the project begins looms large before you, its perceived importance can feel overwhelming. Remind yourself that this is only one part of who you are. Yes, becoming a writer or getting this book out into the world matters to you, but your life is so much more than that.

You may be a mother or father, a daughter or son, a sibling, a community member, an employee or business owner, a church member, a pet owner, a volunteer . . . the list is nearly endless. Many facets make up who you are, and while this project is important, it's not everything.

Yes, you want to get it done, but it won't be the end of the world if it's not perfect. It's just one part of your life. When it's time to work on it, try to keep that in mind.

3. Stop Thinking About Everyone Else

I think the best way to get past the feeling that this project is too important to work on today is to do it solely for yourself.

"But Colleen," you may say, "I want to publish this book!"

I get that. But right now, when you think about publishing, you think about other people reading your story. And because this book matters to you, you want them to like it. So, when you sit down to work on it, you start worrying—will others enjoy it? Will it be good enough?

Then doubt creeps in. You convince yourself you're not clever enough today to tackle the difficult task of pleasing readers with your words. You don't feel up to writing that really important story—the one you dream of others praising once it's published—so instead, you go play video games.

I mean, who wouldn't?

When we put that kind of pressure on ourselves—*this project is important, I want it to be good, and I want everyone to love it and admire me for it*—it's impossible to live up to it in the moment. We're tired. We've had a long day at work or a long week with a sick child. It's just too high a hurdle to clear.

But imagine for a moment that you're writing this book only for yourself. You can decide *after* it's finished whether to publish it or not. For now, take that pressure off. No one else is going to see it, so you can just enjoy writing it without worrying whether "they" will like it. Right now, the only thing that matters is finishing it so you can finally get the darn monkey off your back.

4. REDEFINE YOURSELF

Who are you in your mind? Be honest. Are you a bestselling author? A genius? A celebrity who writes? Do you imagine that when this book is published, everyone will finally recognize you as these extraordinary things?

We all like to imagine such things about ourselves. They make us feel good, and we enjoy indulging in these daydreams. "I'm going to be like Stephen King," you might say to yourself. "I write better than he does anyway."

But these kinds of self-aggrandizing thoughts—while typically harmless—can be dangerous when it comes to actually doing creative work. Suddenly, we have to put up or shut up. Are we really a bestselling author? We'd better prove it on the page. Truly a genius? If it doesn't show up when the book is published, we'll have to face humiliation. Worse, we'll have to admit that maybe we're not all those amazing things we believed ourselves to be. For many of us, that realization can be devastating, as it might make us feel like we're not much of anything at all.

The solution is to redefine yourself in the most mundane and ordinary way possible. Forget being a genius or a bestseller. You're just a regular person who enjoys writing. You do it because you love creating stories or because you like putting words together. When you write, you lose track of time, and you feel great afterward. It's just something you do, nothing more.

The less pressure you put on yourself to be someone special, the less important your project will seem and the easier it will be to work on it. It's okay to be an ordinary person. There's absolutely nothing wrong with not having anything remarkable about you.

Imagine your project isn't special, either. It's just something you enjoy working on, like when you were a kid drawing pictures or building snow forts. Back then, you didn't worry about being special. You certainly weren't concerned about whether your picture or fort proved you were a genius. You just created for the joy of it.

Wouldn't you like to get back to that place? You can, with a small mindset shift. Set aside those grandiose images of yourself for a little while—just long enough to allow yourself to work on your project in an easy, flowing way.

#3 Reason Writers Procrastinate: You Think Your Future Self Will Handle It Better

Sticking to a daily writing or marketing routine isn't easy. It takes real discipline to work on your novel when you're not in the mood, or write a guest blog post or set up a book giveaway when you're already exhausted from a long day at the computer.

Occasional procrastination won't hurt—you deserve a break now and then. But if procrastination is a regular demon in your writing life, there's one more common reason behind it: you're believing its lie.

Procrastination convinces you that your future self—the one who exists days, weeks, months, or even years from now—will be better equipped to handle everything you're avoiding today.

When it's time to write (or complete another writing-related task), you may feel one or more of the following:

- Too tired
- Afraid that you're not feeling motivated enough to write well
- Distracted by something else that's going on
- Pulled to do something easier (because writing is hard)
- Doubtful about your abilities to be able to make this story work
- Worried that your story will not succeed on the market
- Anxious about being humiliated once the book comes out

Procrastination convinces you that tomorrow, you'll be better equipped to handle all these thoughts and emotions. Tomorrow, you'll be stronger, more confident, more determined, more motivated, and more energized. Tomorrow, you'll be the person you want to be, and writing will become easier.

The problem is, this is a *big lie*. It creates a dangerous illusion for writers—the belief that simply waiting until tomorrow will make everything better. But when tomorrow comes and you feel the same as you did today, the lie resurfaces, convincing you once again that your future self will do better.

It's time to pull back the curtain on this deceptive wizard. How do you do that?

A WRITER MUST CLEARLY SEE THE TRUE FUTURE SELF

Your future self isn't here yet. Today, you have only your present self and the echoes of your past self. That person you will become in the future? They're just a figment of your imagination.

Some people naturally relate to their future selves and are considered "future-oriented." They take their vitamins, save money from each paycheck, and make choices that benefit their future selves.

Others are more present-oriented, focused on making their current selves happy. That person in the future? She can take care of herself.

Research shows that people who procrastinate tend to view their present and future selves as entirely separate individuals rather than as two versions of the same person.

Didn't get your writing done today? That "other person"—the stronger, more capable one—can handle it tomorrow. The consequences belong to them, not you. You have full confidence in that future person, which means that today, you can relax and not worry about not getting your creative work done.

If You Can Relate, You Won't Procrastinate

For a study published in the scientific journal, *Personality and Individual Differences*, scientists tested nearly 600 undergraduate students, and found that those who viewed their future selves as an extension of their present selves were less likely to procrastinate than those who saw fewer similarities between the two. Additionally, students who could better visualize their future selves were more likely to complete their work on time.

Get this: People who feel disconnected from their future selves even use different parts of their brains when thinking about that person compared to those who feel more connected! In one study, scientists found that certain areas of the brain were activated differently when these individuals thought about their present selves versus their future selves. Instead of perceiving their future selves as the same person, their brains reacted as if they were imagining a stranger!

If you tend to procrastinate when it's time to get your writing work done, you may want to ask yourself how *you* see your future self. Does that person seem similar to you? Do you feel a sense of responsibility toward them? Or does your future self seem distant and difficult to imagine, like someone you don't even know?

If you struggle to picture yourself a few years, a month, or even a week down the road, you may have just uncovered the key to overcoming procrastination.

The solution is to find ways to visualize your future self more clearly. If you can see that person as the same as the one in the mirror today—sharing the same doubts, fears, insecurities, and challenges without any sudden, miraculous abilities—you'll be more likely to overcome your tendency to procrastinate.

How to Better Imagine Your Future Writing Self

Stop imagining that by tomorrow, your fears, fatigue, and self-doubt will disappear. They most likely will not. In fact, if you procrastinate, they may only get worse. Your future self won't magically become a highly productive writer unless you start developing those skills today.

CREATE A COLLAGE.

Create a collage that represents where you want to be five years from now. Place a picture of yourself in the center, surrounded by images that reflect your aspirations—your book covers, book signings, public speaking events, and anything else that symbolizes your goals. Compile everything onto a single page, either printed or designed digitally for use as wallpaper. Display the finished product somewhere it will serve as a daily reminder of the steps you need to take today to be where you want to be tomorrow.

WRITE A LETTER TO YOUR FUTURE SELF.

Sit down and write a letter to the person you will be about two months from now. Ask a friend or loved one to send it to you in about eight weeks, or use an app like "Future Me" (futureme.org) to email it to yourself.

In your letter, reflect on the creative goals you hope to accomplish, the fears you want to overcome, and what you appreciate about yourself as a writer. When you receive it, open it and let it inspire you. Most likely, it will help you connect more deeply with your future self.

TRY A VISUALIZATION EXERCISE.

If you're a fan of meditation and visualization, try this: sit down in a comfortable place and take yourself on a journey to visit your future self. Start by envisioning yourself one year from now. Imagine you have a time machine that takes you there. Open the door, shake hands with your future self, and describe what you see.

What is that person doing? How do they look? What are they happy about? Are they pleased with their progress or disappointed? What advice do they have for you, their past self?

When you finish, write down your observations if you like.

The more often you engage in this and similar activities to strengthen the connection between who you are today and who you will become, the more responsible you will feel for that "other" person, and the less likely you will be to procrastinate.

Could You Relate?

We've just explored the three most common reasons writers procrastinate on their creative work, but we've only just scratched the surface. In the next chapter, I'll introduce the idea that there are different types of procrastinators and share some of the research behind this concept.

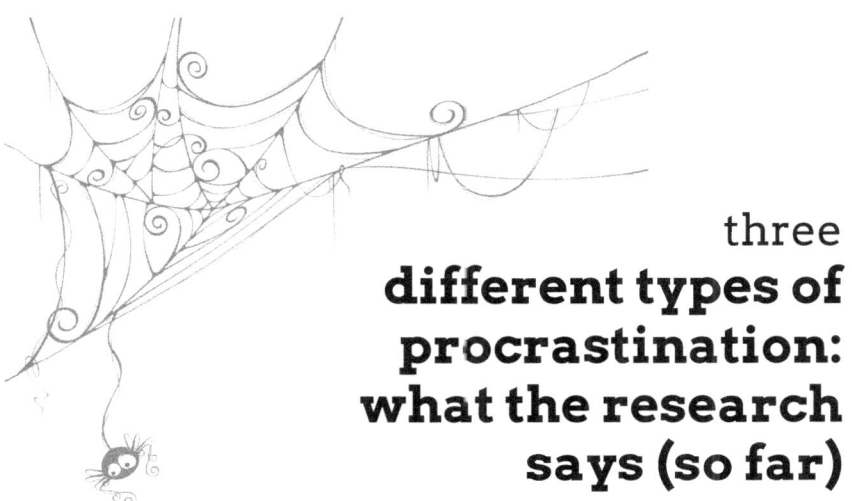

three
different types of procrastination: what the research says (so far)

WHAT KIND of procrastinator are you?

That may be the question on your mind right now. You might even be tempted to skip ahead to Chapter 4 to find out! You're welcome to do that, but if you're curious about where these types originated, this chapter is for you.

The short answer is? Research, blended with my knowledge and experience.

First, let's start with the research.

The Research Behind the 13 Types of Procrastinators

Scientists, psychiatrists, and other researchers have been looking into this idea of different types of procrastination for quite some time. As mentioned in Chapter 1, procrastination was originally viewed as a failure to regulate one's emotions and impulses. Those who procrastinated, the theory went, simply lacked the willpower or motivation to do what they should in the moment.

Several studies found that people procrastinated because:

- they were inefficient at managing their time
- they enjoyed the short-term benefits of procrastination

- they had trouble motivating themselves internally
- they experienced difficulty overcoming the gap between their intention to do something and actually doing it

This theory about the struggle to self-regulate still holds true, and one or more of these factors may very well be fueling your procrastination today. What's different now is that we know this isn't the *only* possible cause. For some people, these particular issues have little to do with it, if anything at all.

That's why many creative individuals struggle to overcome procrastination using the standard recommendations, because their problem isn't rooted in a lack of self-regulation.

Fortunately, over the past couple of decades, scientists have been delving deeper into the issue. In the process, they've uncovered some fascinating new findings.

The 5-Factor Model of Personality

Several studies have explored the relationship between procrastination and personality differences, as defined by the five-factor model. This established theory describes the broad traits believed to serve as the building blocks of personality. As you consider each of the five factors, ask yourself whether you might score high or low in each.

1. Extroversion
Those who score high in this trait are sociable, talkative, excitable, assertive, and expressive. They enjoy being the center of attention and meeting new people, find it easy to make new friends, and may speak before thinking. Those who score low in this trait are more reserved, find social events draining, need solitude to "recharge," dislike small talk and being the center of attention, and carefully think things through before speaking.

2. Agreeableness
Those high in this trait tend to be more cooperative, show interest in people, feel empathy and concern for those around them, and enjoy

helping. Those low in this trait are more competitive, have little interest in others' problems, may insult or belittle people, and might manipulate them to get what they want.

3. Openness
Those who test high in this trait tend to be more adventurous, imaginative, open to new experiences, and eager to learn. Those low in this trait are more traditional, struggle with abstract thinking, dislike change, and may resist new ideas.

4. Conscientiousness
Those high in this trait are thoughtful, organized, mindful of details and deadlines, exercise good impulse control, and enjoy having a set schedule. Those low in this trait are less structured and organized, often make messes or neglect responsibilities, and may procrastinate on important tasks, sometimes missing deadlines.

5. Neuroticism
Those who test high in neuroticism may be emotionally unstable or moody, experience chronic anxiety and/or depression, become easily upset, worry frequently, and struggle to recover from difficult circumstances. Those who test low in this trait are more emotionally stable, handle stress well, rarely feel sad or depressed, and find it easier to relax.

What the Research Says About Procrastination and Personality

In 2001, researchers asked university students to complete the Revised NEO Personality Inventory—which measures the five major domains of personality listed above—and found that procrastination was linked to both a low score in conscientiousness and a high score in neuroticism.

Those capable of self-discipline were the least likely to procrastinate —a connection that seems obvious—while impulsiveness and vulnerability were seen as strong predictors of procrastination. These results make sense, as conscientious students who are typically calm and resilient would be less likely to procrastinate.

However, the scientists also found that fear of failure, task aversion (avoiding a task for a specific reason), and difficulty making decisions were also associated with procrastination. Additionally, they found that some of these traits were identifiable in children as young as 7 to 11 years old.

In a more recent 2022 study, researchers revisited the five-factor model in relation to procrastination, but the results differed slightly. This time, the scientists introduced another aspect of procrastination into the mix: active vs. passive procrastination.

ACTIVE VS. PASSIVE PROCRASTINATION

Here's where we start to delve more deeply into the different facets of procrastination. It can get a little overwhelming, so I'll do my best to keep it simple for you.

Let's start with active versus passive procrastination. When you actively procrastinate, you do so on purpose to create a positive outcome. This is the student who deliberately delays doing his homework until right before it's due because he believes he concentrates better when he's under pressure.

You'll see some of these types of procrastinators showing up in this book. The problem is that regularly relying on this behavior may backfire, producing negative rather than positive outcomes. Nevertheless, it stems from a deliberate choice to procrastinate.

Passive procrastination, on the other hand, occurs when a person doesn't intend to delay tasks but does so due to an inability to take action. This type of procrastination is always associated with negative outcomes such as stress and anxiety.

This is the student who plans to do his homework during study period but can't get started because he fears he won't do it right. It's also the writer who wants to create a short story for a contest but fails to complete it in time because she feels too overwhelmed by the project.

Another key difference is that active procrastinators thrive on deadlines—they enjoy the thrill of working last minute—whereas passive procrastinators feel anxious, overwhelmed, and often guilty when they don't get the project done.

Both of these types have been identified in studies. There is some debate about whether active procrastinators truly benefit from their behaviors, but according to researchers in a 2005 study:

"The present results showed that although active procrastinators procrastinate to the same degree as passive procrastinators, they are more similar to nonprocrastinators than to passive procrastinators in terms of purposive use of time, control of time, self-efficacy belief, coping styles, and outcomes including academic performance."

In other words, the researchers were suggesting that active procrastinators, even though they were procrastinating, were more like those who didn't procrastinate in terms of their ultimate outcomes. In a more recent 2019 study, researchers again noted:

"Active procrastination can be an adaptive and productive coping style. It is associated with dependable temperament, well-developed character, and high emotional intelligence and predicts meeting personal goals."

In essence, the research seemed to be saying that if you purposely procrastinate because you thrive on last-minute work—and then you actually get your tasks done—you may resemble nonprocrastinators in your ability to manage responsibilities and stay on schedule.

Some research, however, contradicts these findings, suggesting that "last-minute" procrastinators experience high stress levels and are more vulnerable to burnout.

Bottom line: If you intend to do something but then you don't do it because you're *unable* to for whatever reason—anxiety, overwhelm, impulsiveness, etc.—the consequences are likely to be more detrimental.

The Science Doesn't Always Agree

Now we return to the 2022 study I mentioned earlier, in which researchers examined the five-factor model in relation to active and passive procrastination. They compared their findings to those of other similar studies and found some inconsistencies.

For instance, extroverted individuals were *more* likely to passively procrastinate because they wanted to go out and have fun with their friends rather than do their homework. This contradicted earlier studies suggesting that extroverts were *less* likely to procrastinate.

Similarly, conscientious students were *more* likely to passively procrastinate because they felt under pressure to meet the deadline and that pressure derailed their efforts. This finding differed from previous studies where conscientious people were *less* likely to procrastinate.

The researchers found no relationship between openness and passive procrastination, but this contrasted with some other studies that reported both positive and negative correlations between the two.

Agreeable individuals, on the whole, were less likely to procrastinate, whether actively or passively. Neurotic individuals, however, were generally more prone to putting things off. These results aligned with findings from other studies.

Procrastination is Complicated!

As we review these and other results, we can begin to see why procrastination is such a complex beast to tame. The reasons we procrastinate depend on numerous factors—our personalities, the situation, the specific task, its purpose, how we view that task, and more.

This is why getting to know yourself and recognizing when and why you procrastinate is crucial for your success as a writer.

One of the most important things to consider is how frequently you procrastinate, in general. Is it a mild habit for you, or more severe?

You can think of a scale like the following. Most of us aren't on the extreme right or left, but somewhere in the middle:

Mild 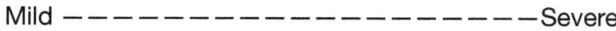 Severe

In the quiz coming up, you'll be able to judge how much procrastination may be interfering in your life based on your scores. This will give you some indication of its severity.

Mild to Severe Procrastination

Researchers have looked into this idea of severity, too. In one study, they analyzed data from over 700 people seeking treatment for their procrastination. Participants completed assessments measuring their procrastination tendencies, depression, anxiety, and quality of life.

After examining the data, the researchers identified five possible subgroups, or clusters, of procrastinators:

1. **Mild Procrastinators:** About one-quarter (24.9 percent) of the respondents fit into this group.
2. **Average Procrastinators:** Over one-quarter (27.89 percent) of the individuals.
3. **Well-Adjusted Procrastinators:** Only 13.94 percent of the individuals.
4. **Severe Procrastinators:** About one-fifth of the individuals (21.69 percent) fit here, which coincides with estimates that about one-fifth of the population struggles with serious procrastination issues.
5. **Primarily Depressed Procrastinators:** Only 11.55 percent of the individuals qualified for this group.

There are other studies like this in which researchers categorized procrastinators based on how frequently they procrastinated and how it impacted their quality of life. For example, one team analyzed survey responses from 990 German university students and identified six distinct clusters:

1. Pathological (10 percent)
2. Habitual
3. Average
4. Occasional
5. Unconcerned
6. Fast performers

The pathological group, specifically, differed from the others in a few ways. They were older and more likely to have failed to fulfill their study obligations. They were also more depressed.

So severity is something to consider. But so, too, is how procrastination affects different areas of your life.

Categories of Procrastination

You may remember this from Chapter 1, where we talked about procrastinating on a certain type of task versus procrastinating on almost everything. Now, we're going to take a closer look at how procrastination can show up in different ways.

Consider these three categories of procrastination, which help measure it's severity:

1. **Category 1:** Acute procrastination on one task
2. **Category 2:** Situational or "domain-specific" procrastination
3. **Category 3:** Chronic procrastination on all tasks

Category 1: Acute Procrastination
Acute procrastination is a short-term behavior that generally affects only one particular type of task. You may regularly procrastinate on doing your taxes, for example, or updating your website. This type of procrastination comes up only occasionally when you're facing that specific task.

Category 2: Situational or "Domain-Specific" Procrastination
Situational procrastination—also known as "domain-specific" procrastination—is a longer-term pattern tied to a particular domain, like your writing. You might stay on top of everything else, but when it comes to pursuing your writing dreams, you keep putting them off. Here are some examples:

- A student may struggle with the domain of "school" in general, but perform well at a part-time job.

- An adult may struggle in the domain of "work," struggling to complete tasks on the job, but never miss a beat when it comes to managing the household and looking after the kids.
- Even "bedtime" can be a domain. Perhaps you regularly delay going to bed, constantly struggling to maintain a consistent sleep schedule. (I'm raising my hand on this one!)
- People may procrastinate in other areas, such as finances (delaying bill paying), home maintenance (putting off house or lawn care), or relationships (failing to respond to calls or texts from friends and relatives).

Moving forward, we'll be zeroing in on your "writing" domain. You may find, however, that you can apply what you learn to other areas of your life, as well.

Chronic Procrastination
Chronic procrastination is more pervasive, becoming a person's default way of approaching most tasks and projects. It spans almost all domains and is the most destructive form of procrastination.

Determining *Your* Type of Procrastination

I hope you're starting to see how procrastination can be divided into various types, levels, and effects, and how understanding where you fit within these types may help you break the habit.

I wanted to share some of the research for a couple of reasons. First, to show that I didn't just pull these types out of thin air—there is significant research behind the concept. I've simply applied it in a way that is easy to understand and that translates into practical solutions.

Second, I wanted you to see that procrastination isn't just a matter of failing to meet your obligations. Multiple factors are likely at play. Becoming more aware of them can help you be more compassionate with yourself as you move forward. If you can do that, you'll be more likely to succeed in getting the writing done that you want to do without beating yourself up in the process.

Finally, it's important to know that we don't have all the answers yet —there's still much research to be done. The good news is that scientists are more invested than ever in understanding how procrastination maintains its grip on us. As their work continues, I imagine we'll learn more in the years ahead.

Meanwhile, we can't twiddle our thumbs and wait for the scientists to tell us what to do. We must take action based on what we know so far to make progress toward our writing goals and improve our lives, overall.

With that in mind, it's on to the quiz!

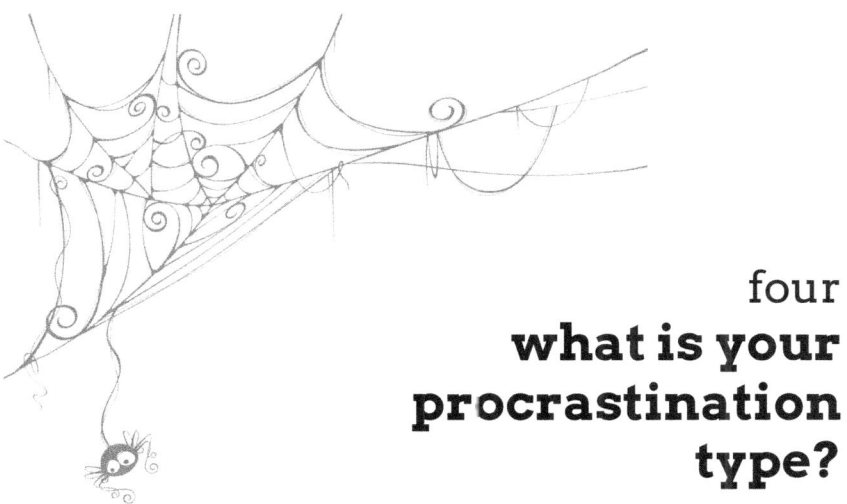

four
what is your procrastination type?

HERE WE ARE! It's time to get personal about your procrastination. The following quiz will help you identify the specific types that may be holding you back in your writing life right now. By the time you're done, you'll have a clearer understanding of why you tend to delay creative work and fresh insight into what's really going on in your mind when you put things off.

This will likely to take some time, so wait until you can set aside 15– 20 minutes. Meanwhile, keep in mind that while this quiz provides valuable insights into your procrastination tendencies, it isn't the ultimate authority on the subject. Though many writers have found it to be highly accurate, you should also rely on your own self-awareness to determine whether the results resonate with you.

If you prefer a more flexible approach, you can skip the quiz altogether and simply read the book to see which types speak to you along the way. Should you find yourself struggling with the quiz for any reason, this more intuitive method might be a better fit.

Finally, keep in mind that your results will likely reflect the type of procrastination you struggle with, but they may not point to just one specific type. Some writers find that they fit strongly into a single category, while others scored above the threshold in two or more types. At the end of the quiz, you'll identify your top three types, but depending on your scores, you can determine how much weight to give each one.

We'll discuss your results further in Chapter Five. For now, resist the urge to skip ahead. To get the most accurate and helpful outcome, don't read any more of this book until you've completed the quiz below.

Off you go!

Quiz

Welcome to the writer's procrastination quiz. For each statement, rate how much it applies to you on a scale of 1 to 5.

1. Never
2. Rarely
3. Sometimes
4. Often
5. Always

Keep in mind that you should respond as honestly as possible, **based on who you are now right now**—not who you'd like to be or wish you were. In other words, don't answer as your "ideal self," but as your true self. Try to be as objective as possible, viewing yourself from the outside based on what you typically "do," rather than what you *wish* you'd do or think you *should* do.

At the same time, **resist the urge to overthink your answers, as that can skew your results.** Move through the questions steadily, answering without too much delay. If you're unsure, simply go with your best guess.

The quiz should take you no more than about 15 minutes.

1. _____I feel anxious and uncomfortable when starting new tasks.
2. _____I enjoy thinking about new projects more than actually working on them.
3. _____I like to make my work as good as possible before finishing it.

4. ____When faced with a task or deadline, I feel an urge to rebel against it, even if I know it's important.

5. ____I easily get distracted by other things when I'm working.

6. ____When I don't finish things as quickly as I'd like, I tend to feel bad about myself.

7. ____I find it challenging to organize my tasks and priorities.

8. ____I frequently feel too tired to work on my tasks—even if they're important.

9. ____I often doubt my ability to do tasks well, making me hesitate to work on them.

10. ____I spend a lot of time analyzing the pros and cons of starting a task before actually beginning.

11. ____I regularly take on too many commitments because I'm excited about new opportunities or feel obligated to do them.

12. ____I like to challenge rules and instructions, preferring to find my own way rather than following guidelines.

13. ____I feel more energized and motivated when the deadline is approaching.

14. ____It's common for me to get drawn into fun activities when I should be working.

15. ____When it's time to work on a writing-related task, I frequently get stuck thinking about "what if" scenarios that prevent me from actually writing or doing the work.

16. ____I find it hard to stay focused on one thing at a time.

17. ____I love brainstorming new ideas but don't always follow through with them.

18. ____When I have a deadline, I tend to feel overwhelmed and stressed.

19. ____I often feel like I don't have enough energy to get going on a writing task.

20. ____I find it hard to create and stick to a plan for my projects.

21. ____I tend to procrastinate on tasks simply because I don't like being told what to do.

22. ____I feel bad about myself for procrastinating.
23. ____I'm likely to leave projects until the last minute to create a sense of urgency.
24. ____I keep tweaking my work to make it perfect, which delays finishing it.
25. ____The main reason I procrastinate on my writing projects is because I prefer to do fun things.
26. ____I procrastinate because I think if I finish a project, I'll have to face criticism or judgment.
27. ____I sometimes feel overwhelmed by all the commitments I've made.
28. ____It's common for me to worry about making mistakes when working on a writing project.
29. ____Sometimes, I catch myself feeling badly about how I should have worked on my project much earlier or gotten more done by now.
30. ____I struggle with managing my energy levels throughout the day.
31. ____I frequently lose track of my important tasks or deadlines.
32. ____I spend too much time analyzing options before making a decision.
33. ____I delay completing projects because I want to prove that I can succeed on my own terms.
34. ____I often feel other people's work is better than mine, no matter how hard I try.
35. ____I usually get busy with a task only when the deadline is near or when I run out of more enjoyable things to do.
36. ____I tend to feel my work is never good enough.
37. ____I rarely work on something until I have a sudden burst of inspiration.
38. ____I regularly underestimate the time required to complete a task.
39. ____I get a lot done, but often, the tasks I complete are not as important to me as those I don't finish.

40. _____It usually takes me several attempts to get started working on a project.
41. _____Usually, my guilt about not working on tasks sooner is what finally inspires me to action.
42. _____I overcomplicate simple tasks by thinking too much about them.
43. _____When I imagine working on a project, I often delay because I worry I'll mess it up.
44. _____When someone imposes a deadline or expectation on me, I sometimes intentionally push back or delay to assert my independence.
45. _____I rarely get serious about working on a task until I'm in a panic about it.
46. _____I may start working on a task, but if something more fun comes up, I'll go do that instead.
47. _____I usually find that it takes me longer to complete a project than I thought it would because I get distracted along the way.
48. _____I struggle to keep my workspace and projects organized.
49. _____I often feel like I need a nap or a break before I can work on my project.
50. _____I frequently feel overwhelmed by my schedule, making it hard to prioritize and work on important projects.
51. _____I usually wait to start a task until the last possible moment.
52. _____I delay starting projects because I want everything to be just right.
53. _____If I do complete a task, my thoughts are already focused on my next big idea.
54. _____I tend to think about what could go wrong instead of taking action.
55. _____Finishing a task isn't exciting to me—it's usually just something I have to get done.
56. _____When faced with a boring task, I typically handle it by multitasking with other activities.

57. ____After completing a task, I usually feel relieved, but I also feel shame or regret for procrastinating.

58. ____I often put off tasks because I feel physically or mentally drained.

59. ____I sometimes resist tasks or responsibilities, even if they align with my personal goals, because they come with external pressure.

60. ____I like working on lists, charts, and graphs to think through a project, which often stops me from getting anything done on the project itself.

61. ____I rarely start working on my most important projects —my "dream" writing projects—until I've cleared other urgent tasks off my calendar.

62. ____I often seek reassurance from others before I feel comfortable moving forward with my task.

63. ____I struggle to turn my creative ideas into actionable steps, so they often stay in the "idea" stage.

64. ____I have high standards and aim for perfection in all my tasks.

65. ____When I finish a task, I'm actually surprised I did it on time.

66. ____I struggle with organizing new projects and often feel unsure of where to begin.

67. ____After I start a project, I often find it hard to concentrate because I'm feeling tired or sluggish.

68. ____It's common for me to delay working on writing tasks —even if they're important to me—because I have too many other commitments.

69. ____When I'm working on a project, I'll abandon it if another great idea occurs to me.

70. ____I worry excessively about failing or not living up to expectations.

71. ____I put off starting tasks to avoid feeling controlled or constrained by external demands or expectations.

72. ____When planning a project, usually what I focus on most is how I'll reward myself when it's done.

73. _____I try to focus when working on a project, but I get easily sidetracked.
74. _____I often beat myself up for not being more productive.
75. _____Sometimes, after I start working on a task, a thought occurs to me, and 30 minutes later, I'm still thinking about or examining that thought in some way.
76. _____I frequently put off tasks that make me feel anxious or uncomfortable.
77. _____I spend a lot of time on minor details to ensure everything is perfect.
78. _____When faced with multiple tasks, I prioritize the ones with the nearest deadline.
79. _____I often intend to work on a project and find an hour later that I've spent the time organizing my thoughts and/or workspace.
80. _____I frequently second-guess my decisions, causing delays in my work.
81. _____I often say, "I'll do it later," because I'd rather enjoy myself now.
82. _____It's common for me to delay starting a project because I'm just not feeling up to it energy-wise.
83. _____I frequently find myself saying, "I'll get to it when I have time," but then that time never seems to come because I have so much to do.
84. _____I'm likely to hold off on submitting a project because I'm worried it's not perfect yet.
85. _____I often feel like an imposter as a writer.
86. _____I frequently check my phone and social media when I'm supposed to be focused on a task.
87. _____When I procrastinate, I feel like I'm letting myself and/or others down.
88. _____I often delay working on a project because I'm overanalyzing the steps involved.
89. _____I usually don't start work on a project until I finally get everything organized.

90. ____I'm more likely to finish a task when I'm under time pressure to do it (when the deadline is looming).
91. ____I prefer getting lost in daydreams about future projects instead of working on current tasks.

Answer Totals:
Add up your scores for the following groups of questions.

Type 1: 1___ 18___ 28___ 45___ 54___ 70___ 80___
TOTAL: ___

Type 2: 9___ 26___ 34___ 43___ 62___ 76___ 85___
TOTAL: ___

Type 3: 2___ 17___ 37___ 53___ 63___ 69___ 91___
TOTAL: ___

Type 4: 14___ 25___ 35___ 46___ 55___ 72___ 81___
TOTAL: ___

Type 5: 3___ 24___ 36___ 52___ 64___ 77___ 84___
TOTAL: ___

Type 6: 13___ 23___ 38___ 51___ 65___ 78___ 90___
TOTAL: ___

Type 7: 5___ 16___ 40___ 47___ 56___ 73___ 86___
TOTAL: ___

Type 8: 11___ 27___ 39___ 50___ 61___ 68___ 83___
TOTAL: ___

Type 9: 6___ 22___ 29___ 41___ 57___ 74___ 87___
TOTAL: ___

Type 10: 7___ 20___ 31___ 48___ 66___ 79___ 89___
TOTAL: ___

Type 11: 10___ 15___ 32___ 42___ 60___ 75__ 88___
TOTAL: ___

Type 12: 8___ 19___ 30___ 49___ 58___ 67___ 82___
TOTAL: ___

Type 13: 4___ 12___ 21___ 33___ 44___ 59___ 71___
TOTAL: ___

IN WHICH ROW WAS YOUR TOTAL THE HIGHEST? IDENTIFY your top three in order. If you had two or more with the same totals, record all numbers in which you had the second-highest number and then all numbers in which you had the third-highest number.

For example, a simple test result might look like this:

1. Score: 31—Type: 11
2. Score: 27—Type: 9
3. Score: 17—Type: 5

Your top three types would be:

1. Type 11
2. Type 9
3. Type 5

If your results had some numbers with the same totals, your result might look like this:

1. Score: 31—Types: 11 and 13
2. Score: 27—Types: 9, 10, and 12
3. Score: 17—Type: 5

Your top three types would be:

1. Type 11
2. Type 13
3. Types 9, 10, and 12

You can see above that we took your top score and applied that to your top two types. They aren't in any particular order—both types are equally strong for you. Your third type is one or perhaps all three of those you had in second place with a score of 27. As you read through the types, you can determine which of those three is likely the strongest. If they are equally strong, explore all three to see what solutions may help you.

How Much Does Procrastination Affect You? Pay Attention to Any Score of 20 or Higher

Most writers procrastinate to some degree, but the intensity varies from person to person. Some will find that only their top two types are at play on a consistent basis. Others will discover that the problem weaves its way into their writing world more pervasively.

In my research with authors and the 13 types, I've found one key takeaway: If you have a score of 20 or higher in any type, pay attention to it. Read the chapter for *all* of those types, not just your top two or three.

Your highest-scoring types are likely to affect you the most, but I've seen authors score over 20 in multiple types. Then, when they describe their struggles with procrastination, I can hear how it manifests in different ways, often reflecting characteristics from several types.

In other words, don't limit yourself. If three or more types have a score of 20 or higher, assume that all of them are influencing your writing on some level. In Chapter 18, we'll discuss your "procrastination blend"—how your various types interact to undermine your efforts.

If only your top one or two types had scores of 20 or higher, you're likely affected primarily by those types and not as much by others that had scores of less than 20 (though some writers still reported scores of 19 as being significant).

Another thing to consider: If *all* of your scores are 19 or below, you're probably a "mild" procrastinator, with the issue surfacing only occasionally in your writing life. A score of 25 or higher in any type may indicate a more moderate or severe form of procrastination—you can assess that based on your own experience.

Again, this shows that we are all *very* different in how we experience procrastination. We differ in:

- **How much we're affected:** Some of us have trouble only occasionally, others more often, and still others struggle with it a lot.
- **How many types:** Some of us battle with only one or two types of procrastination, while others may be affected by three, four, or more.

My goal with this book is to help you understand exactly how procrastination affects you in your own unique way. Then, I hope to guide you in making small changes that will enable you to reach your goals without procrastination holding you back.

Procrastination Types

Find all thirteen procrastination types, along with their abbreviated descriptions, below. This will give you a first glimpse into what might be happening with your particular type(s) of procrastination. When you're ready, turn to the corresponding chapters for more details, insights, and potential solutions. Each type has its own dedicated chapter.

Type 1: The Worrier
The Worrier becomes trapped in a cycle of anxiety and overthinking, making it difficult for them to start or finish tasks. Their mind races with fears and doubts, often leaving them feeling overwhelmed by deadlines and expectations. This inner turmoil prevents them from fully tapping into their creative potential.

Type 2: The Avoider
The Avoider shies away from tasks due to a deep-seated fear of failure and criticism. Rather than tackling their responsibilities, they seek distractions and comfort, often leaving important projects unfinished. Procrastination becomes a way to shield themselves from potential disappointment.

Type 3: The Dreamer
The Dreamer is brimming with creative ideas and visions but struggles to turn them into reality. Their imagination runs wild, often causing them to get lost in thoughts rather than taking action. This lack of focus leads to many unfinished projects as they jump from one idea to the next without committing.

Type 4: The Fun Seeker
The Fun Seeker prioritizes pleasure and excitement over responsibilities, which frequently leads to procrastination on important tasks. They thrive on spontaneity and entertainment, making it difficult to stay focused on writing. Their carefree attitude often results in last-minute scrambling to complete tasks.

Type 5: The Perfectionist
The Perfectionist is driven by an intense desire for excellence, which can paralyze them when it comes to completing their writing tasks. They worry their work won't meet their high standards, leading to endless revisions and delays. This relentless pursuit of perfection often leaves them feeling frustrated and stuck.

Type 6: The Crisis-Maker
The Crisis-Maker thrives on the adrenaline of working under pressure, frequently putting off tasks until the final hour. While they believe they work best in the heat of the moment, this approach often leads to stress and chaos as deadlines loom. Their creative process is a whirlwind, but the results can be haphazard.

Type 7: The Distracted

The Distracted individual finds it challenging to focus due to a constant barrage of interruptions and temptations. Social media, entertainment, and other distractions can easily pull them away from their work. As a result, they struggle to make meaningful progress on their projects.

Type 8: The Overdoer

The Overdoer fills their schedule with numerous tasks and commitments, leaving little room for creative work. They thrive on staying active but often feel overwhelmed by their responsibilities, making it difficult to prioritize their writing. This constant busyness can lead to procrastination on important projects.

Type 9: The Guilty

The Guilty type often feels weighed down by regret and self-criticism over their procrastination. They struggle with feelings of inadequacy and guilt for not being productive, often leading to a cycle of avoidance. Their desire to meet high expectations can make it difficult for them to take action.

Type 10: The Disorganized

The Disorganized type often has a chaotic workspace and lacks structure in their creative process. This disarray makes it difficult for them to focus or find what they need, leading to procrastination. Their creativity is vibrant, but it frequently gets lost in the clutter.

Type 11: The Overthinker

The Overthinker gets caught up in a loop of excessive analysis, preventing them from taking action. They mull over every detail, worrying about making the wrong choice. This tendency often leads to delays and a lack of productivity.

Type 12: The Tired

The Tired type often struggles with fatigue, making it difficult to find the motivation and energy for their creative projects. They may long to engage with their writing but wrestle with brain fog, exhaustion, or insomnia, making it hard to bring their full attention to the page when it's time.

Type 13: The Defier
The Defier thrives on rebellion and challenges conventional expectations, which can lead to procrastination. They have a strong desire for creative freedom, but their resistance to structure can leave projects incomplete or cause their stories to lack forward momentum. Their journey involves striking a balance between independence and productivity.

Make Sure Your Types Fit

Now that you know your types, do they make sense to you? If not, feel free to wait a couple of days and then take the test again. Feeling tired or getting distracted during the test can skew your results. Once you feel confident that your types align, turn to the corresponding chapters to learn more more about each one and start forming solutions.

five
the worrier

BASIC FEAR: *If I do this, I'm afraid it will go wrong.*
BASIC DESIRE: *I want to feel completely secure before I do anything.*
SUPEREGO MESSAGE: *You are okay only if you make no mistakes.*

HEY THERE, worrywart! You're an expert at the "what-ifs," which is great for plotting your stories, but not so great for your overall productivity. You dream of publishing your work for eager readers, but what if you fail? What if you can't find a publisher? What if you get tangled up in all the steps of self-publishing?

In general, you prefer to stick with those areas where you already have experience—that's your comfort zone, where you know what to expect. But in the writing world, we're constantly challenged to learn new things and explore new ways to share our work, and that scares you. It's unfamiliar ground, so the what-ifs spring up like weeds in your mind every time you think about it.

Change? "No thank you," you say, which means you're likely to keep doing things the way you always have, even if that approach isn't working for you anymore. Just the thought of doing something different stresses you out, so you avoid it at all costs.

If you asked your friends, they probably wouldn't notice this "worrying" thing about you because you keep your anxieties to yourself. But when you finally decide you need to shake things up, you tend to spend an inordinate amount of time thinking about your next step—researching it, planning it out, and preparing for it—because you don't want to be caught off-guard or have anything go wrong. Then, when it's time to take action, you freeze in indecision, letting your worries get in the way.

Ultimately, your hesitation leads to procrastination. If you don't find a way to move past your worrisome tendencies, there's a good chance you'll be in the same place three years from now.

Key Characteristics of The Worrier

As a Worrier, you may find that one or more of these habits and characteristics sound familiar:

- **Worry:** A tendency to worry about most things involving writing and your writing career. These worries frequently stop you from moving forward.
- **Anxiety:** You may feel anxious when you have to make a decision about something.
- **Overplanning:** Instead of taking action, you spend a lot of time researching, preparing, analyzing, and planning, putting off the real work of actually *doing* what's needed.
- **Resistant to change:** You're not into the "new" and would rather stick with the tried and true. When you sense that change is needed, you resist—and procrastinate.
- **Fear the unfamiliar:** Anything new or unknown seems risky to you. You'd rather avoid it.
- **Depend on others:** Because you worry, you like to turn to others for advice, reassurance, nurturance, and help. Without this support, you shy away from challenges.

- **Fail to commit:** Sometimes, you think about new projects that you'd like to try, but then you never commit, so it doesn't happen.

Strengths of the Worrier

As a Worrier, you have the ability of foresight. You can look ahead on any project and anticipate what might go wrong. You tend to plan in advance for these contingencies and have strategies in place to address problems if the worst happens. As a result, you are often well-prepared and avoid mistakes that others might overlook.

You may also tend to carefully consider every aspect of your work. Because of this, you are likely to produce high-quality results—once you overcome your anxiety and finish. You are driven by a deep care for your writing and strive to ensure that what you create is valuable and meaningful.

Challenges for the Worrier

Constantly thinking about what can go wrong prevents you from starting or making progress on your tasks. This is the main reason you procrastinate—your worries get in the way.

Typically, these worries are tied to external outcomes rather than internal doubts. You don't question your ability to write your story, for example, but you may worry about receiving negative reviews or not recovering the investment you made in producing your book.

You might also be concerned about disappointing others, which only heightens your anxiety. This can lead to overthinking or imagining worst-case scenarios, making it even harder to overcome procrastination and accomplish your goals.

The Worrier's Limiting Beliefs

- **If I make a mistake, everything will fall apart.** You believe that even one little misstep will lead to disastrous results. This creates a lot of pressure to be perfect and prevents you from starting.

- **I have to anticipate every possible problem before I can proceed.** You feel like you have to see and prepare for every possible challenge or obstacle that may arise. This causes you to overthink everything and delay taking action.
- **Mistakes and failures mean I've let everyone down.** You are most concerned with the results of your work and fear that if you make mistakes or something goes wrong, others will judge you or be disappointed in you.

Coping Techniques for the Worrier Procrastinator

1. **Set Micro Goals:** Since big projects can feel overwhelming and increase your anxiety, break down all your writing and writing-related tasks into smaller, more manageable pieces. For example, instead of aiming to write 1,000 words a day, set a goal of 250. Instead of writing for 30 minutes, try 10. Each time you accomplish a small goal, you'll reduce your anxiety and feel less overwhelmed.

2. **Limit Research and Planning:** As a Worrier, you tend to overplan, devoting all your time to research and analysis. It's one of the ways you procrastinate. To avoid falling into that trap, set clear time limits. For example, allow yourself two weeks for planning—no more. After that, you must take action on at least a few of your first micro-goals. Another approach is to keep track of the time you spend planning. Keep a log for a few weeks or months to see how much of your valuable personal resources go into this preparation phase. Then, decide when you'll stop planning and start working—and stick to it.

3. **"Chunk" Your Tasks:** To help alleviate anxiety about tackling a writing task, try the chunking technique. Set a timer for 25 minutes and work without interruption, setting your worries and cares aside for that limited time. When the timer goes off, you can take a break of at least five minutes or

longer if needed. Proceed one "chunk" at a time and see if you can bypass your worry and anxiety with each session.

4. **Be Compassionate with Yourself:** When worry and anxiety come calling, be kind to yourself. Accept that you may make mistakes, and treat yourself as you would a good friend pursuing their goal. Take yourself out now and then for a nice dinner, an art show, or a movie, and give yourself credit for the progress you've made.

5. **Create a "Worry Journal":** When fears circle in your mind, write them down in your journal. Give yourself a chance to question each one—is it real, or are your worries just running away with you? If it's real, decide how you will handle it if it comes up. (You're a good planner—this is where you can use that strength to your advantage.) If it's an imagined worry, write down why it's unlikely to happen. Journaling regularly can help clear your mind and make you feel more confident in handling future challenges.

6. **Set Clear Deadlines, but Include Buffer Zones:** We all need deadlines to stay on track, but Worrier procrastinators need them even more to stay accountable to their commitments. That said, it's important to include some buffer time to handle any anxiety that may come up, without adding extra pressure as the deadline approaches. For example, you might set a goal to complete your novel by December 1st, but allow a three-week buffer so that finishing by December 31st still counts as meeting your deadline. This approach keeps you on track while reducing pressure, so long as you treat December 1st as your primary deadline and stick to your plan.

7. **Visualize Success:** Meditation helps calm the mind and reduce anxiety. Practicing it regularly can improve your ability to visualize reaching your goals and experiencing the satisfaction that comes with them. There are plenty of excellent guided meditations on YouTube—start with one of those, and spend no more than 10 minutes a day on it.

After two weeks of daily practice, see if you notice a difference.

8. **Designate a "Worry-Free" Writing Zone:** Take a look at your writing nook. Does it feel comfortable and secure? If not, consider changing it up. Maybe you could add some cushions, a cozy blanket, a heated cup holder, and some other thoughtful touches to make it easier for you to work there without suffering from so much worry.

9. **Seek Positive Feedback:** This is where your writing group or accountability partner can help. Send them a piece of your work and ask for their positive feedback only—no negative feedback allowed at this stage! Positive reinforcement can help counter the worry that your work isn't good enough.

10. **Ask for Help When Needed:** Worrier procrastinators often thrive when working with a coach or mentor. You like that sense of security that comes with knowing someone has your back. Regular meetings with a coach provide not only positive feedback but also confirmation that you're on the right track and taking the necessary steps to minimize mistakes.

Who the Worrier Can Become: The Master Planner

When you move past procrastination to pursue your best self, you can become The Master Planner. You channel your caution and attention to detail into thoughtful, purposeful action plans that guide you toward your goals.

THE WORRIER'S BEST SELF

- **Calmly Strategic:** Instead of overthinking things or constantly fearing mistakes, you learn to use your natural foresight to plan and organize effectively. You anticipate challenges and obstacles without letting them hold you back, making you both well-prepared and proactive.

- **Thoughtfully Cautious:** You develop a "healthy" cautiousness, proceeding step-by-step in a careful way without allowing your caution to paralyze you. You think ahead and stay alert to signs of issues, while trusting yourself to respond appropriately.
- **Resilient:** As an evolved Master Planner, you know that mistakes are to be expected and that failure is part of the process. Instead of seeing every misstep as catastrophic, you recognize the value in learning and growing, and become a writer who can adapt and improve as you go.

In this best version, your ability to think ahead, care deeply about your craft, and stay disciplined helps you break the curse of procrastination and become more productive.

Action Plan for the Worrier Procrastinator

Worry and anxiety haven't helped you so far—they are unreliable companions on the road to writing success. It's time to shift your mindset to one that allows you to use your worries to create an actionable plan.

It begins when you commit to trusting yourself. Every step of the writing journey comes with uncertainty. You have to learn to move forward even when you're afraid something will go wrong. As a Worrier, your mind may race with what-ifs and worse-case scenarios, but when you realize that your need for safety is keeping you stuck, you'll begin to see why courage is essential.

Below, you'll find a sample action plan designed to help you to finish your novel. If you have a different project in mind—such as creating a new website, starting a blog or YouTube channel, or growing your newsletter audience—you can adapt the plan to fit your goal. The steps will likely be similar, as they're tailored to your specific type.

STEP 1: COMMIT TO THE PROJECT

Challenge to Overcome: *I want to do it, but I'm afraid I'll mess it up.*

As noted above, this is a critical first step, so mark it with some sort of ceremony. You could write out the commitment, sign it, and frame it. Or you might invite some friends over and tell them about it. This will not only help hold you accountable, but it might also provide some of the support you need. However you choose to do it, mark the occasion to make it real for you.

STEP 2: BREAK THE PROJECT INTO SMALLER PIECES

Challenge to Overcome: *It's all too much!*

One of your biggest challenges may be feeling overwhelmed by a project and fearing that it's "too much" to handle. To overcome this, break down large projects into smaller, manageable steps. You can organize these steps by word counts, chapters, sections, or even allotted time. For example, you might decide you'll spend 20 minutes a night on the novel for five nights a week, finish one chapter per week, or write 5,000 words a week. Write each of these steps down somewhere so you can keep track of them. As a potential Master Planner, you might also find it help to use charts for organizing this step.

Next, divide each step into even smaller chunks. If you want to write a chapter a week, for example, break that down to one scene a night, perhaps. If your average chapter is 4,000 words, write one thousand words four times a week.

When you start to feel anxious or worried, journal about your feelings. Remind yourself that each small step counts and that making mistakes is perfectly okay.

STEP 3: SET REALISTIC WRITING SESSIONS

Challenge to Overcome: *I'm not sure this chapter is going very well . . .*

Remember that you tend to overthink each step and anticipate every problem. At this point, it's important to remind yourself *not* to think about the novel as a whole. That will trigger your anxiety.

Instead, focus *only* on the task in front of you. If your original plan —to write 1,000 words today—feels overwhelming, reduce it by half and write only 500 words. It's okay if you have to extend the deadline. The most important goal is not completing the project perfectly; it's overcoming procrastination so that you can continue to make regular progress on it.

STEP 4: BANISH THE INNER CRITIC
Challenge to Overcome: *This is bad. I know it's bad.*

All writers need to silence their inner critic early on to finish their drafts. Worrier writers have an inner critic on steroids. Expect this strict, critical part of your brain to search for every little thing it can criticize. That means you have to learn how to shut it up. Listen for its complaints, then tell it you've heard enough and now, it needs to leave you alone. You're not interested in what it has to say until after you've finished the book.

STEP 5: GET AN ACCOUNTABILITY PARTNER
Challenge to Overcome: *My negative thoughts are spinning out of control.*

As a Worrier, you need support. This may come from a good friend, partner, local writing group, or even an online community. Share your commitment to finishing your novel with someone you trust, then ask them to help hold you accountable. When you start to catastrophize about everything that could go wrong, reach out to this person to gain a more balanced perspective.

You might also consider forming your own group centered around your goal. You could start a "write your novel" group, for instance, where members commit to getting their books written by the end of the year. Meet regularly to check each other's progress, share challenges, and offer mutual encouragement.

STEP 6: DEVELOP A "WHAT-IF?" CHECK

Challenge to Overcome: *This could go wrong, and this, and this!*

As a Worrier, you are very good at imagining all the what-if scenarios. What if your story has plot holes? What if the main character isn't likable? When these what-ifs start to plague you, write them down in your journal as they come to mind, then set aside a time each week to address them. For example, perhaps on Saturday morning, you gather all your what-ifs at the table. You read each one and ask yourself, "Is this a real issue right now, or is it just my worry talking?"

If it's a real issue, use your planning skills to devise a way to manage it if it does come up. If it's just your worry talking, remind yourself that worry will try to stop you, and refuse to be stopped this time.

STEP 7: FOLLOW THROUGH ON YOUR PLAN

Challenge to Overcome: *It wasn't going well, so I gave up on it.*

The danger is that you may give up on your novel (or other project) when your worries lead you to think about everything that could go wrong rather than what is going right. Remind yourself of your commitment, address each "what-if?", and at least once a month, take the time to list everything that is going well with your novel. Recall those writing sessions that left you feeling like you were flying among the clouds. Write down the parts of the story you feel good about—the dialogue, setting, or plot. Also, list the support you're receiving from friends and colleagues.

Give yourself every reason to keep going, despite whatever worries you may have! That's the way to avoid procrastination and complete your project.

The Most Important Thing for Worriers to Remember

If I were to pick one thing that you must remember as a Worrier procrastinator, it's this: *It's okay to feel anxious—taking action despite anxiety is what leads to progress.*

Write this down and hang it up somewhere in your writing nook to encourage yourself to keep moving no matter how worried or anxious you may feel.

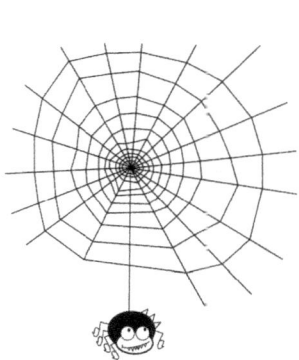

Exercise: Master Plan Your Next Project

OKAY, MASTER PLANNER, IT'S TIME TO MAP OUT YOUR PLAN for your next project. Use this fill-in-the-blank section to get you started.

1. The project I really want to complete next is
   _____.
2. This is important to me because
   _____.
3. I will make a commitment to this project by
   _____ (creating and signing a contract, holding a "commitment" party with family or friends, marking my completion date on my calendar, etc.).
4. When I complete this project, I'm going to feel
   _____ (descriptive word for how you'll feel!).
5. I'm going to sit down and break up this project into micro-steps on _____ (date).
6. I'm going to break down those micro-steps into even smaller steps on _____ (date).

7. I will add deadlines to each of those micro-micro steps (!) on _____ (date), building in a buffer of at least 4 weeks for my ultimate completion date.
8. I will reach out to my _____ (friend, partner, writing group, online writing group) and let them know about my goal, asking for their support in completing it.
9. I plan to meditate at least three times a week at _____ (time of day) to help clear my mind and calm my anxiety.
10. I've purchased a new journal in which I plan to write down any worries or anxieties that come up so I can deal with them without succumbing to procrastination!

six
the avoider

BASIC FEAR: *If I show them this, they'll know I'm not as good as they think I am.*
BASIC DESIRE: *I want to feel completely safe and accepted while expressing my creativity.*
SUPEREGO MESSAGE: *You're okay only if you're really good.*

WHERE DID SHE GO? Wasn't she going to write? Ah, we're talking about the Avoider type of procrastinator. You are the one who avoids doing things that make you feel bad. You may have great ideas for stories but then struggle to get started because the blank page feels intimidating or the thought of failure haunts you. You may often abandon your stories halfway through because your self-doubt overcomes your motivation. When it's time to write, publish, or go on a podcast to market your book, you shy away from it because those negative emotions come up and you'd rather not feel those.

You may also struggle with imposter syndrome, which is similar to self-doubt, though it's typically associated with having some success and not feeling worthy of it. Maybe your first book sold really well, but you think it was a freak accident, and you're afraid your next one won't sell as well, so what's the point of trying? That would just make you feel bad.

To protect yourself from difficult feelings, you sidestep writing tasks, convincing yourself that you will get to them "later" or that you need more time to prepare. As a result, your projects remain unfinished, and the pressure of looming tasks creates a cycle of avoidance and guilt. If you were to ask your friends, they might comment on how talented you are and how much they love your writing, yet they don't understand why you don't do more to get it out into the world.

Whether it's fear of failure, rejection, or even success, you procrastinate on writing because of the emotional weight it carries. Ultimately, you keep your creativity on hold and your dreams out of reach—not because you lack ideas or talent, but because you dread the potential negative outcomes of putting your work out into the world.

Key Characteristics of The Avoider

As an Avoider, you may find that one or more of these habits and characteristics sound familiar:

- **Paralyzed by fear:** Due to fear of criticism, failure, or rejection, you put off your writing tasks.
- **Self-doubting:** You frequently struggle with self-doubt and imposter syndrome, second-guessing your abilities.
- **Concerned about other's opinions:** You often worry about what others will think of your work, and would rather have them think you lack effort than ability.
- **Uses excuses:** You're good at coming up with excuses for why the writing work isn't done, not only to others, but also to yourself.
- **Reluctance to start:** You hesitate to start on a new writing-related task until you feel "ready," which is often never.
- **Devoted to unimportant tasks:** You're more than happy to work on tasks that aren't important or lack the emotional weight that writing carries for you. You are even good at

creating things to do so you can feel productive when you're avoiding what's important to you.

- **Emotionally vulnerable:** Writing is often personal and emotionally revealing, and that scares you sometimes, so you steer clear, even though it matters to you.
- **Reluctance to share:** When you complete a piece of writing that you're proud of, you may put off sharing it for fear of criticism.

Strengths of the Avoider

One of your biggest strengths as an Avoider is your acute awareness of others' feelings and perspectives. You are a sensitive person who easily picks up cues about what others are feeling or thinking in the moment. When you tap into this sensitivity in your writing, you can create emotionally resonant characters that readers will love.

Another way that you excel is through your constant striving for improvement. Your tendency to doubt yourself can be positive if it motivates you to regularly seek new ways to improve, grow, and refine your craft as a writer. It may also keep you humble enough to successfully collaborate with a mentor or editor who can help you progress.

Challenges for the Avoider

Your challenges center around your fear of others' opinions. You procrastinate because you're afraid that if you complete your work and people judge it negatively, you'll feel bad. Unfortunately, this keeps you stuck in a vicious cycle, because it's only by showing your work to others and receiving feedback that you can improve.

You may also have difficulty making decisions. You constantly second-guess yourself and doubt your abilities, making you unlikely to trust your ideas or gut feelings about what to do next. Additionally, you may struggle to set up a regular writing routine because you find it difficult to stay consistent. You schedule a time to write, but your tendency to avoid the task disrupts your ability to establish a productive habit.

The Avoider's Limiting Beliefs

- **I'm not good enough.** This core belief leads you to doubt your writing abilities, convincing yourself that your work will never be good enough to avoid criticism.
- **If I show my work, I'll be judged harshly.** You rarely think of people liking your work. Instead, your dominant belief is that they will criticize it or put it down, which prevents you from taking any risks.
- **It's safer to stay in my comfort zone.** Putting your work or yourself "out there" feels risky and unsafe to you. Inside, you believe that procrastinating on your writing keeps you safe, though in truth, it only limits your growth.

Coping Techniques for the Avoider Procrastinator

1. **Create a "No-Judgment" Zone:** Designate a space where you can write without fear of being judged. It doesn't matter where it is, only that you know you can write there peacefully, without anyone ever seeing your work if you don't want them to. Put safeguards in place if needed, such as passwords on your computer or locks on your files.
2. **Visualize Sharing:** Try a form of meditation called "visualization," in which you visualize sharing your work with someone and the positive feedback they may give you. Choose a quiet place free from distractions and imagine a supportive friend, family member, or fellow writer who supports you. Hear that person's encouragement and warmth. Imagine positive reactions like a smile, interest, and questions that encourage you to share more. Feel the joy and relief of sharing your work.
3. **Share Your Writing:** Start out small with one person you trust. Share a short piece of writing, and then ask them to tell you what they liked about it (positive comments only to begin with). When the session is over,

write down every nice comment the person had to say. You may also start your own "sharing circle," which might consist of a small number of writers who share their work without criticism. As a next step, begin to share your writing on a blog, on Medium or Substack, or on another type of platform where you can regularly get feedback. If you are very sensitive to negative comments, it may be best to save this step for later, but eventually, it's a great way to build more confidence in sharing your work. Some platforms like Wattpad and Subreddit allow you to share your writing anonymously, which may provide a good stepping stone.

4. **Create a "Comfort-Zone Expansion Plan":** Develop a plan that will help you step outside your comfort zone in small, manageable increments. Steps might include sharing your work, as outlined in #3, then perhaps joining a writing group, signing up for a workshop or class, organizing a small informal reading with friends, or hiring a mentor or coach. Give yourself time to adjust to each step before moving forward. Gradually, you'll build the courage needed to face any criticism that may come your way.

5. **Start a "Strengths Journal":** Choose a journal that you will use exclusively for recording things about yourself that highlight your strengths. Begin by noting things you think you're good at. (For example, "I'm a good writer" or "I'm good at dialogue.") Next, ask those closest to you what they consider your strengths to be, and write those down as well. Regularly add entries to your strengths journal, and revisit it whenever you need a boost of confidence.

6. **Police Your Self-Talk:** Avoiders are usually not very nice to themselves. They are always putting themselves down and denying their positive qualities. Give your inner critic a name, then identify it every time it comes up. If the voice says, "This story is crap," recognize that it's "Bob" talking, and tell him to sit down and be quiet—you didn't ask for his opinion. Simply becoming aware of how often this voice

speaks to you can help you redirect your thoughts toward a more positive tone.

7. **Visualize Success:** Meditation is good for anyone, but Avoider procrastinators should definitely make time in their schedules for it. It helps quiet your mind and reduces the self-doubt and anxiety that tend to take over when it's time to write or publish. Simply search for guided meditations on YouTube—you can find several free ones that are around 10–15 minutes long. After two weeks of daily meditation, see if you don't notice a difference.

8. **Embrace Fail-Forward Challenges:** To face your fear of failure, set up a series of playful, low-stakes challenges that actually encourage it. For example, commit to posting a draft or unedited piece of your work on social media or your blog, emphasizing that it's simply meant to be shared without worrying about perfection. Alternatively, pound out a piece of writing in ten minutes, bring it to your writing group, and see what they have to say. Then reveal *after the fact* that you created it in just ten minutes. You may be surprised by their reactions!

9. **Create a "Bravery Jar":** Set up a physical jar in your writing nook where you can drop in small notes describing any acts of bravery related to your writing or marketing efforts. Did you send a query letter to an editor or agent? Add that to the jar. Did you share a blog post or short story? That's another note. Each time you face a fear and take action, write it down and add it to the jar.

10. **Go on a Writing Adventure:** Set aside a day or weekend to write in a new, inspiring location. This might be a local park or café, or you could head out to a bed-and-breakfast or lakeside cabin for the weekend. Bring some specific writing prompts or challenges that encourage you to write in a different style or genre than usual, and consider leaving comfort items like your laptop behind. The point is to shake up your usual writing routine a bit to make the process feel lighter and more spontaneous.

Who the Avoider Can Become: The Brave

When you push past procrastination to pursue your best self, you can become The Brave. You use your sensitivity, humility, and desire for growth to continue learning and expanding your skills as a writer.

THE AVOIDER'S BEST SELF

- **Fearless Creator:** Instead of shaking in your boots at the idea of writing something emotional or sharing your work, you feel the fear and do it anyway, continually putting yourself out there and risking failure to make your writing dreams come true.
- **Resilient Learner:** You view setbacks not as stopping points but as changes in direction on your way to success. You understand every rejection and criticism brings you one step closer to mastering your craft and honing your voice.
- **Supportive Community Member:** Understanding how frightening the writing process can be, you become the one who engages with fellow writers and offers encouragement and support to build meaningful connections.

In this best version, you seek out challenges as opportunities for growth, experiment with various writing styles, allow your creativity to flourish, and embrace a fulfilling writing life despite your feelings of fear, self-doubt, or imposter syndrome.

Action Plan for the Avoider Procrastinator

Your fear of failure and your emotional vulnerability are holding you back. It's time to summon your courage and face your fears if you want to make your writing dreams come true.

It begins when you commit to being brave. Every part of the writing journey takes courage. Every writer must find the courage within themselves to do the things that frighten them. As an Avoider, you may struggle even more due to your emotional vulnerabilities. But when you realize that you're allowing your fear to stop you from becoming who you were meant to be, you'll understand why courage is so necessary.

Below you'll find a sample action plan to help you finish your novel. If you have a different project in mind—such as creating a new website, starting a blog or YouTube channel, or growing your newsletter audience—you can adapt the plan to fit your goal. The steps will likely be similar, as they're tailored to your specific type.

STEP 1: ACKNOWLEDGE YOUR FEELINGS.

Challenge to Overcome: *Instead of facing my feelings, I will simply procrastinate.*

If you're procrastinating on your writing, it's because you have some difficult feelings associated with it. Maybe the story you're working on is bringing up things that you'd rather not feel or remember. Or perhaps the idea of finishing and sharing your story has you tied up in knots.

Procrastination has been giving you an easy way out, but it's time to change that. Start by setting aside 10 minutes a day to journal about your feelings surrounding writing or the writing project you've been procrastinating on. Write about your self-doubt, fears, and any negative emotions that come up when you think about this project. Then challenge those feelings by asking yourself questions like, "Do I know that this will happen?" or "Is this really true?" Use your journal as a way to disarm your fears and build your courage.

STEP 2: CREATE A SAFE WRITING ENVIRONMENT

Challenge to Overcome: *I can't face these feelings!*

Create a safe space where you can experience your negative feelings and still know that you'll be okay. Choose a writing nook that feels comfortable, then surround yourself with items that inspire you. Put up pictures of those writers you admire and of people you know are rooting for you. Remind yourself that you are safe in this space and that any negative feelings will pass.

STEP 3: USE POSITIVE AFFIRMATION

Challenge to Overcome: *I must listen to my inner critic because he (or she) is right.*

It's time to overrule your inner critic. Practice telling "him" to leave you alone and replace his snarky comments with positive affirmations. It helps if you write out a list of these affirmations before you get started. Some examples include:

- I am a capable writer, and I'm getting better every day.
- My stories are worth telling.
- Some people may not like my stories, but others will.
- I'm a creative and imaginative person.
- I can feel myself getting braver every day.
- I am overcoming self-doubt and can feel my courage growing.

STEP 4: USE VISUALIZATION TO REHEARSE SUCCESS

Challenge to Overcome: *If I start, I'll fail or prove I'm not good enough.*

You often procrastinate because you fear failure and criticism. Visualization can help you shift your focus from potential negative outcomes to more positive, empowering ones. Spend 5–10 minutes each day visualizing yourself completing the writing task you're working on. Picture the process: sitting down to write, seeing the words fill the page, and feeling the satisfaction of finishing.

STEP 5: MAKE A DEAL WITH A SUPPORTIVE PARTNER

Challenge to Overcome: *I'm afraid they won't like my work.*

To combat your fear that others will criticize your writing, it's important to have a close friend or family member to help you set mini-deadlines for your writing. Every other week or once a month, share your work with them. You may also do this with another writer who is trying to overcome Avoider tendencies. The two of you can keep each other going until you reach "the end."

Step 6: Create a "Good Enough" Draft
Challenge to Overcome: *It's no good!*

Most writers worry that their writing is no good. As an Avoider, this worry may be even harder for you to overcome. Commit yourself to producing a "good enough" draft (or a "good enough" website, newsletter, or whatever it is). Remind yourself that this is *not* the draft you will submit to publishers or publish yourself. It's simply a draft to tell yourself the story. You can worry about the rest later.

When self-doubt creeps in, remind yourself that it's okay—all you're aiming for here is "good enough." Prioritize finishing the manuscript (or any other task) over making it perfect.

Step 7: Celebrate Your Accomplishment
Challenge to Overcome: *It wasn't that big a deal.*

Your tendency is to shortchange yourself. You may finish a novel and say, "It wasn't that big a deal," or "It was just a novel. Nothing important." Far from it! If you hang in there and defeat procrastination long enough to finish your novel, you absolutely must make a big deal of it—at least to yourself—because it *is* a big deal.

We teach our brains how to behave in the future by how we respond to our actions in the present. If you say "no big deal" when you complete your novel, your brain will absorb that message. Then, the next time you want to write a novel, it will say, "Why bother? It's no big deal." And procrastination will worm its way back into your writing life. Don't let that happen. Do something you really enjoy to celebrate your accomplishment.

The Most Important Thing for Avoiders to Remember

If I were to pick one thing that you must remember as an Avoider procrastinator, it's this: *Your worth as a writer is not defined by others' opinions.* We all hope for readers who enjoy what we write, but you can't get there by constantly second-guessing yourself.

Summon the courage to write, share your work, improve, share it again, and keep going until you begin to feel more confident in what you're doing. Only by embracing a courageous mindset can you break free from avoidance and honor your creativity without the burden of self-doubt and criticism.

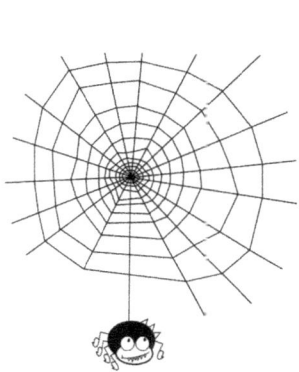

Exercise: Rewire Your Inner Critic

ONE OF YOUR BIGGEST OBSTACLES IS OVERCOMING THE tendency to criticize yourself. You want to encourage a more positive, cheerleading inner voice. Start writing down every negative comment you hear your inner voice say, and then turn it around into a positive one.

Let's say your story is rejected by a publisher or agent. Normally, you might say, "I just got rejected." Rejection brings up all sorts of negative feelings. You might feel like you're not good enough, like you don't belong, or that your work is unwanted.

But you can rephrase this negative self-talk. Instead of calling it a rejection, call it a *redirect*: "I just got redirected." This has an entirely different meaning. The rejection is no longer about the quality of your writing or whether you have writing talent—it's all about *where you submitted the piece*. Moreover, it *directs* you to submit it somewhere else. Feels better, doesn't it?

Here's another example: Instead of calling a one-star review a "negative review," how about calling it a "not-for-me" review? A negative review places all the emotion onto the work itself. You feel like a pincushion where every unflattering word is a personal stab from a small, sharp object. You experience pain and remorse, and you may begin to question your writing ability and talent.

A *not-for-me* review, on the other hand, puts the review back into the reader's court. The book simply was not for him (or her). Rather than suggesting something is wrong with your book, it implies only that the book and reader didn't match up.

See how this works?

Now it's your turn. Write down at least five statements that your inner critic typically says to you, and reframe each into a statement that points you in a more positive direction. You might set it up something like this:

Critic's Statement	Your Counter-Statement
This story isn't going well.	This story is almost halfway done—I'm making great progress.

seven

the dreamer

BASIC FEAR: *My writing will never live up to the vision I've imagined.*
BASIC DESIRE: *I want my work to be as amazing on the page as it is in my head.*
SUPEREGO MESSAGE: *You must create something extraordinary, or it's not worth doing at all.*

YOU HAVE BEAUTIFUL, inspiring dreams of where you'd like to go as a writer. New ideas are like chocolate to you—you can't resist them—and you're constantly coming up with more. Imaginative and whimsical, you love spending time in your made-up world. You may have several stories started, but you struggle with finishing them. You can clearly envision your project completed, but when it comes to actually sitting down and doing the work, it feels far less exciting, so you procrastinate.

Deep down, you may believe that you are special in some way and that fate will surely intervene to make your dreams become reality. The thought of having to work on the details is frustrating, even downright distasteful.

When you finally accept that you must tackle the nitty-gritty to bring your sparkly vision to life—and you actually schedule time to sit down and work—you quickly find yourself distracted by new ideas. You're vulnerable to "shiny object syndrome," meaning you're easily pulled off course by new and exciting opportunities. You'll be working on one story when, suddenly, another idea will pop into your head, tempting you to pursue that one instead.

Many creative people know what it's like to get caught up in a cycle of chasing new ideas. We love novelty, and there's nothing more enticing than something we haven't tried yet. The Dreamer, however, has a Ph.D. in generating new ideas but never acting on them.

You may be tired of friends asking you when you're going to finish that book you've talked about for so long. Or maybe they've stopped asking altogether, knowing you love to dream up new ideas but rarely follow through.

For the Dreamer, the gap between vision and action is wide, often leading to a vicious cycle of endless brainstorming, daydreaming, fantasizing, getting excited, and starting, but never finishing.

Key Characteristics of The Dreamer

As a Dreamer, you may find that one or more of these habits and characteristics sound familiar:

- **Endless ideas, little action:** You're full of creative energy and always have new story ideas, but it's hard for you to translate those ideas into words on the page.
- **Grand visions:** In your mind, you are a highly successful writer. You imagine your writing projects as masterpieces, picturing elaborate scenes and perfect endings. It is often these lofty imaginings that make it hard for you to do the real work of writing, as you fear it will not live up to your vision.
- **Vulnerable to shiny object syndrome:** You're easily distracted by new ideas and often abandon current projects for the excitement of starting something fresh. This leads to mountains of unfinished first drafts.

- **Lack of routine:** You resist structured writing routines, preferring to write only when inspired. That can lead to long gaps between writing sessions and is a big reason your projects remain unfinished.
- **Abhor the details:** As someone who loves to imagine the big picture, you abhor the details. The idea of slaving away day-to-day on a story fills you with frustration. You don't want to have to deal with all that little stuff. You just want that shiny new story to arrive.
- **Goal-setter with no plan:** Setting goals is not a problem for you. You just don't have a plan for how to reach those goals, so they remain ethereal ideas in your mind.
- **Difficulty with time management:** Time tends to fly by when you're envisioning a grand future for yourself. Dreamers can get stuck between imagining greatness and taking the first step toward it.

Strengths of the Dreamer

Your biggest strength is your creative vision. You are a big-picture thinker, capable of visualizing a future that aligns perfectly with your dreams. With a vivid imagination and a knack for generating unique ideas and rich storylines, you can think outside the box, make connections others might overlook, and craft fresh, original writing.

You're also deeply motivated by inspiration. When duly motivated, you can infuse your work with great passion and meaning, sometimes becoming almost obsessed with an idea The key is to harness this inspiration and channel it into a writing practice that carries you beyond the point when you might otherwise abandon a project in favor of yet another shiny new idea.

Challenges for the Dreamer

You want your ideas to take shape in the real world, but your biggest fear is that once you create the project, it won't live up to your vision of it. When you imagine sitting down to write the next chapter of your book, your Dreamer side recoils. You get lost in the endless possibilities of what the story *could* become, but struggle to face what it *is* today. Revising drafts or tackling difficult plot points feels tedious or uninspiring, so you allow yourself to procrastinate instead.

You might also be a perfectionist, though in a different way than the Perfectionist procrastinator. Your drive isn't about making the story flawless in terms of grammar or structure; rather, you have a strong desire for it to fully capture your creative vision. Since it's rare for any project to completely live up to such an ideal, this pursuit leaves you feeling stuck and never quite satisfied, pulling you further into procrastination.

The Dreamer's Limiting Beliefs

- **My ideas are too big for me to handle.** You often believe that the scale of your imagination is beyond your ability to bring your ideas to life. This can lead to overwhelm, a fear of failure, and ultimately, procrastination.
- **I'm not ready yet.** Because you feel you have to produce the most amazing, outstanding work ever, you often feel like you're not "ready" to start. Instead of realizing that the best work often takes multiple drafts, you believe you must be in the right frame of mind to create it the first time out. You wait for inspiration, delaying the project.
- **I'll have time later to get it right.** You imagine a future in which you'll be perfectly suited to create the work you envision and believe you will always have more time to complete your projects. This belief keeps you in the realm of ideas rather than making regular progress week to week.

Coping Techniques for the Dreamer Procrastinator

1. **Create a System for Prioritizing Certain Ideas:** You have plenty of ideas, but you're not sure which one to focus on. You need a system to help you decide. One approach is

to take each story idea (or website idea or marketing idea) and create a quick outline of how you would bring it to life. Often, shiny new ideas lose their appeal when you take this step, which can help narrow your choices. You can also think about spending at least a year with this idea and see how that grabs you. Does it excite or drain you? Rank your ideas based on your level of enthusiasm and emotional connection, then choose the top one or two to pursue.

2. **Commit to Finishing Your Story (or Related Writing Project):** You cannot get better or reach your goals with a file full of unfinished projects. One finished project—even if it doesn't live up to your vision—is much more meaningful than fifty great ideas. So, once you choose a project, commit to finishing it *no matter what!* Even if you think it's horrible —even if it gets hard to work on—do it anyway.

3. **Spin Your Dreams Into an Actionable Plan:** It's time to bring your dreams down to earth by creating an actionable plan. Start by choosing a project. Then, decide when you will work on it each week, how you will break it down into manageable chunks, and set deadlines for completing each step.

4. **Limit Daydreaming Time:** Become more aware of when you're daydreaming or brainstorming new ideas. Recognize that this tendency, while creative, may be holding you back. When it happens, take note and limit yourself to no more than five minutes. Write down your ideas, then return to the task at hand. Discipline yourself to resist the urge to chase down every new, shiny idea.

5. **Use Visual Mapping Techniques:** Dreamers thrive with vision boards, maps, sketches, and collages that link big ideas to the necessary details. There are many different methods you can use. Here's an example for you. Take out a piece of paper and write down the main idea of your project (e.g., your novel's premise) in the center. Enclose it in a circle. Next, draw lines extending outward to represent key elements of your story, such as character arcs, plot points,

settings, or themes. Add details and connections with smaller branches, including character motivations, specific scenes, and major story points. Make planning your story enjoyable so you can begin to see that it's not just the idea you love—it's the process, too.

6. **Inspire Yourself Daily:** You must be willing to write even when you're not inspired, or find ways to inspire yourself regularly. Dreamers do better with the latter, so think about little things you can do that will inspire you to write. Read a page from an author you admire, listen to music that enhances your scene, meditate for ten minutes, or head to an art museum to write there.

7. **Practice Focusing on One Thing:** Spend twenty minutes a day focused on the one story idea (or writing project idea) that you chose to pursue. If you feel overwhelmed or worried that your work will not live up to your expectations, remember that this isn't about that. It's about training your brain to focus on one thing. Get in the habit of doing this for short daily periods, and gradually, you'll get better at it.

8. **Story Cubes for Daily Inspiration:** Purchase a set of Story Cubes or make some of your own. These are dice-like cubes that have different images, words, or symbols on their faces. You simply roll the dice, then create a narrative based on the results, or incorporate what you see on the dice into your story. This can give you a new way to inspire yourself to get to work, as you're challenging yourself to bring these story elements to the next scene you have to write.

9. **Create a Group of Dreamer Writing Friends:** Consider joining or even creating a Dreamer's writing group with the goal of encouraging and inspiring one another to get the work done. Try to meet a couple times a month to check on one another's progress. Get creative about making your gatherings fun while creating results. Pledge to walk away with an outline of your book, for example, or with an action plan to self-publish your book.

10. **Get an Assistant:** If you're still struggling to make your writing projects a reality and can afford it, consider hiring an assistant to help you. This person could take over some of the details of the writing life to free you up to pursue your big ideas. You're not looking for someone to do your writing work for you. But perhaps they can design your website, create a book marketing plan, take care of your social media channels, or manage other aspects of the writing journey that you don't like to deal with.

Who the Dreamer Can Become: The Inspired Creator

When you leave procrastination behind to pursue your best self, you become the Inspired Creator. You harness your imaginative powers and visionary ideas and transform them into tangible works of art, stories, or other projects that resonate with others.

THE DREAMER'S BEST SELF

- **Focused Visionary:** You no longer stop with your visions but know how to choose those ideas you want to pursue, then hone in on the details needed to make your projects a reality. You have systems in place that help you break your vision into actionable steps, and get help where needed to complete all those steps.
- **Expert Inspirer:** You know how important inspiration is to your work. You research and learn about inspiration, always trying new ways to keep yourself going on a project so that you are able to complete it.
- **Compassionate Encourager:** Understanding that no story or writing project is ever perfect and that many fall short of your lofty goals, you have become more compassionate toward yourself. You see the writing journey as one of constantly trying to get closer to your vision. But you no

longer fear falling short as you accept your innate human imperfection.

In this best version, the Dreamer still loves brainstorming ideas, but has become much more adept at choosing the best ideas and bringing them to fruition.

Action Plan for the Dreamer Procrastinator

Your fear of not living up to your lofty visions—and your distaste for the details—is holding you back. It's time to get your hands dirty if you want to make your writing dreams come true.

It begins when you commit to actually *creating*. Anyone can dream, but as a real writer, you must get into the habit of taking an idea and following it through.

When you realize you're allowing your lofty visions to stop you from becoming who you were meant to be, you can understand why action is so necessary.

Below is a sample action plan for the Dreamer procrastination type to finish a novel. If you have a different project in mind—such as creating a new website, starting a blog or YouTube channel, or growing your newsletter audience—you can adapt the plan to fit your goal. The steps will likely be similar, as they're tailored to your specific type.

STEP 1: CHOOSE YOUR PROJECT.

Challenge to Overcome: *I like all my ideas, but I don't know which one to pursue, so I procrastinate.*

You often procrastinate to avoid facing the fact that some of your ideas may not be as good as you thought they were. They seem shiny and promising at first, but when you try to wrestle them into a real story, they can quickly become messy and flawed.

Put all your ideas in a file or on index cards in front of you. Expand on each one with one a sentence, then two, then more. Move from one to the other, gradually expanding each. Eventually, you'll find that some ideas keep growing while others fade.

Keep going until you're left with two or three ideas that hold your interest. See which one stands out, then move on to the next step.

STEP 2: OUTLINE YOUR NOVEL.

Challenge to Overcome: *The details are no fun.*

Use one of the coping techniques listed above (such as getting together with writing friends) to make this stage of the writing process inspiring.

Instead of simply writing the outline on a paper, try using sticky notes on the wall or a whiteboard to map it out. (See the exercise below.) Have snacks available and play music in the background to make the activity more engaging.

If you're a pantser rather than a plotter and prefer not to outline, use this step to get to know your characters, research your timeline or setting, or explore your theme more deeply. Incorporate photos, videos, and even Tarot cards to make this part of the planning process more inspiring.

STEP 3: CREATE A WRITING ROUTINE.

Challenge to Overcome: *Discipline is drudgery.*

Use everything you can think of—movies, books, music, movement, new locales, friends, and more—to spark your creativity. Maybe on Monday, you write while listening to music that inspires a scene. On Tuesday, you meet with other writers at the library to write.

Wednesday, you head to your favorite café to enjoy a coffee and snack while working on your piece. On Thursday, you take a break from writing to create a visual representation of your next chapter, perhaps using Canva or a poster board. And on Friday, you write by hand in your favorite notebook.

STEP 4: FOCUS ON FINISHING

Challenge to Overcome: *When a project gets hard or too detailed, I give up on it.*

Change your focus from "this has to be extraordinary" to "this has to be done!" Only by writing your story all the way from beginning to end will you learn how to write one. And in truth, you'll have to do that over and over again before you get good at it.

Remind yourself that dreams don't make you a writer—writing does. Once you've chosen your project, finish it no matter what. Even if it's "bad" (and remember, we all think our stories are bad until we finish them and fix them), you'll be much further along if you do.

STEP 5: VISUALIZE SMALL SUCCESSES

Challenge to Overcome: *I am successful only if the project is extraordinary.*

To get you through the hard parts, visualize success, but be careful. As a Dreamer, your tendency will be to envision only the highest level of success—things like bestseller status and boatloads of money from sales. Bring your definitions of success down to earth.

Create a vision board that shows you typing "The End" on your story. Include a photo of your favorite restaurant where you and a partner or writing friend will go to celebrate when you finish your book. Envision success, but let small successes to be good enough for now.

STEP 6: GET HELP

Challenge to Overcome: *If I can't just daydream this into being, it's not worth doing.*

Dreamers can benefit from seeking help when needed. Consider hiring an assistant to handle routine tasks you dislike, such as posting to social media or updating your website. Work with a coach or editor to keep you on track when you feel like giving up.

Believe in yourself enough to invest in your growth. This step could be the difference between achieving your writing goals or merely dreaming about them.

STEP 7: KEEP A "DREAMS" VS. "DONE" JOURNAL

Challenge to Overcome: *I believe that dreaming is doing.*

As a Dreamer-type procrastinator, you struggle with getting things done because dreaming about them actually *feels* like doing them. You need to realize that there is a clear difference between the two and then practice regularly showing yourself that difference. One way to do that is to keep a "dreams vs. done" journal.

Divide each page of the journal into two columns, one labeled "dreams" and one labeled "done." Begin by writing down your writing dreams. Start with at least five on the first page.

At the end of the day, write down what you have completed when it comes to writing. Maybe you wrote 500 words, outlined your novel, or created a self-publishing plan.

Try to update this journal at least once a week—more often is better, as it will remind you to focus on finishing things. Even small completed tasks are accomplishments!

The Most Important Thing for Dreamers to Remember

If I were to pick one thing that you must remember as a Dreamer procrastinator, it's this: *Dreams get you nowhere without action.* As long as your book is only an idea in your head, it does not exist—not in the real world. You have to put in the work to *make* it exist.

Once you do that, you will be addicted, because there's nothing like holding your own book in your hands, having a professional-looking website, or launching your first self-published book onto the market.

In the end, doing is a lot more fun than dreaming. You just have to convince yourself of that!

Exercise: Storyboard Adventure

LET'S MAKE THE DETAILS OF WRITING A STORY MORE motivating. Try this exercise.

- **Gather supplies:** Get a large piece of paper or a whiteboard, sticky notes, markers, and any other colorful materials you enjoy.
- **Visualize your ideas:** Start by brainstorming all the ideas you have for your novel or writing project. Write each idea on a separate sticky note.
- **Create a storyboard:** Arrange the sticky notes on the paper or board to create a visual storyboard. Group related ideas together, and start to sketch out a loose flow of how your story might progress.
- **Add fun details:** Incorporate drawings, doodles, or symbols that represent different elements of your story. This not only makes it visually appealing but also encourages you to engage with the material in a more playful way.
- **Set mini-goals:** Once your storyboard is complete, choose one section or idea to focus on each week. Break it down into smaller, manageable tasks that feel less daunting.
- **Celebrate progress:** As you complete each task, reward yourself with something enjoyable, whether it's a favorite snack, a fun outing, or an hour watching your favorite show.

eight
the fun seeker

BASIC FEAR: *Writing will always become boring eventually.*
BASIC DESIRE: *I need writing to be exciting or I can't stick with it.*
SUPEREGO MESSAGE: *You should always enjoy what you're doing—if it's not fun, it's not worth your time.*

ARE WE HAVING FUN YET? This is the question that is always on your mind. As long as writing feels like a good time, you will stick with your daily practice. But the instant it gets difficult or starts to challenge you, that part of your brain that measures "fun" will turn on the alarm. Suddenly, you'll get the urge to head out to the park or meet with friends. You'll fall victim to distraction and spend hours on a video game that you planned to play for only 10 minutes before getting back to writing.

You have a huge fear of missing out. When you sit down to write, your brain thinks of all the other fun things you *could* be doing that you're not doing because you're writing. You don't see your behavior as all that unusual. Everyone likes to have fun, and we all tend to ditch our responsibilities now and then for a little playtime. The problems arise when your inner self really wants to write and knows that you're avoiding the hard work it's going to take. Then your "fun" time is tainted by your feelings of guilt, anxiety, and self-recrimination.

You thrive on excitement and spontaneity, so you may love writing certain action scenes or climactic moments, but struggle with the scenes in between. You have a natural curiosity and active imagination. But if you see writing as a commitment, you may feel that it's restricting your freedom somehow, which will lead you to procrastinate.

The main problem for you is viewing your writing as a chore, drudgery, or something you "have" to do. As long as it remains that, your dreams will stay out of reach.

Key Characteristics of the Fun Seeker

As a Fun Seeker, you may find that one or more of these habits and characteristics sound familiar:

- **Driven by excitement:** You love the thrill of new ideas and are easily energized at the beginning of a project. But once the novelty fades and the real work begins, you have trouble sticking with it.
- **Spontaneous and impulsive:** You love writing when the inspiration strikes rather than following a schedule. You can dash out a great amount of writing in a short time, but your overall productivity may suffer.
- **Dislikes boredom:** Anytime something feels boring, you're on to the next thing. You rarely give something a chance to "become" more interesting as you go.
- **Easily distracted:** You can be vulnerable to shiny object syndrome, becoming easily distracted by new, exciting ideas, making it difficult to see any of your stories through to completion.
- **Playful with the process:** You enjoy making writing fun and work well when you use tools or methods that insert more playfulness into the process.

- **Highly creative and imaginative:** You are bursting with creative ideas and naturally love experimenting with new genres or writing techniques.
- **Difficulty with long-term focus:** You thrive on short bursts of energy, but struggle with the long-term marathon often required for book writing.

Strengths of the Fun Seeker

Your biggest strength is your natural enthusiasm and energy for life. Your passion for creativity and adventure drives you to embrace spontaneity, explore new ideas, and dive headfirst into projects that excite you. When your work aligns with your interests and desire for stimulation, you can produce with remarkable energy.

You're also highly adaptable, able to shift and change with ease. Your open-minded approach allows you to pivot quickly and explore different creative avenues without becoming overly attached to one way of doing things. You enjoy bringing a lighthearted tone into your work, which can make your stories fun and engaging for readers. When collaborating with others, you often serve as a motivator, making projects enjoyable and inspiring those around you to stay energized and excited.

Challenges for the Fun Seeker

Your biggest challenge is your tendency to lose focus and motivation when a task starts to feel mundane, boring, or tedious. Since writing is often a long, detail-oriented process that requires sustained effort over time, you quickly become distracted and start seeking something more enjoyable. You resist structured schedules and deadlines, feeling stifled by anything you see as too rigid. Unfortunately, this lack of routine can make building momentum on a story difficult, leading to a pattern of starting strong but then fizzling out before making real progress.

Anything that drains the joy from the writing process becomes a threat. Tasks like editing, proofreading, submitting, and marketing may feel dull and joyless. Instead of confronting the discomfort, you tend to abandon unfinished projects to pursue your next fun activity.

The Fun Seeker's Limiting Beliefs

- **If it's not fun, it's not worth doing.** You believe that if a task feels boring or difficult, it must not be the right thing for you to do. You think creativity should always be enjoyable, but you struggle to see the value in pushing through the less exciting parts of the writing process.
- **I'll lose my freedom if I commit to a structured routine.** You see routines and structure as limiting. They are like shackles on your fun-seeking soul, so you worry that setting deadlines or following a daily writing routine will crush your spontaneity and creative spark.
- **I'll never finish anything because I get bored too easily.** You fear you will never finish anything because you think the excitement will always fade before you do. Over time, this can make you incapable of making your writing dreams come true.

Coping Techniques for the Fun Seeker Procrastinator

1. **Gamify the Writing Process:** Your best way to outwit procrastination is to make your writing fun, no matter what stage you are in. Try turning it into a game, complete with challenges and goals with rewards for each. For example, you could give yourself points for completing each chapter and treat yourself when you hit a certain milestone. Use your creative imagination to make the game as complex as possible so you tap into your brain's desire for adventure. You could go so far as to create your own board game to get you from idea to finished novel!
2. **Write in Short Bursts:** You already excel at short, creative bursts of writing, so use this to your advantage. Break your writing sessions into short spurts of 15–30 minutes. Set a timer and go. Knowing that you have to write for only a

limited time can help avoid boredom and increase productivity while leaving room for play afterward.

3. **Add a Challenge for Each Writing Session:** Make your short-burst writing routine even more fun by setting a challenge at the beginning. Today, see if you can finish the scene before your 15 minutes is up. Or see if you can write your way out of a sticky plot point before the timer goes off. Get used to regularly challenging and rewarding yourself so every step along the way feels like part of a game-like process.

4. **Create a Flexible Writing Schedule:** Create an overall flexible writing schedule that allows for spontaneity and breaks. Let's say you want to finish your novel by the end of the year. Set a goal of completing two chapters a month. If you complete your chapters by the third week of the month, take the last week off. Or set a goal of finishing at least one book by the end of the year, but have two you're working on. Allow yourself to switch back and forth, pursuing the one that feels most fun to you during each writing session.

5. **Incorporate Play Into Brainstorming:** Use playful techniques like mind-mapping, writing prompts, Tarot cards, and story blocks to explore new ideas. If you're unsure how your characters should interact in chapter six, experiment with different approaches until you find one that excites you. Engaging in this type of creative play can help relieve any pressure you feel as you go from one chapter to the next, keeping the process enjoyable and preventing procrastination.

6. **Collaborate with Other Writers:** Collaborate with other writers to supercharge your productivity. Use the board game you created, or set up simple milestones and compete with the others to see who completes each one first. Or, consider working with another writer on your story. When you get bored with it, send it over to your partner, and vice-versa. If you find the right person, this may be the key to getting your books finished.

7. **Mix Writing with Other Activities You Love:** When writing starts to feel like a chore, bring in other activities you enjoy. Play music that engages you while you write your scene. Head out to your favorite park or café to write. If you're artistic, sketch out pictures of your characters as you brainstorm dialogue for a certain scene. Another idea is to increase the challenge in your writing session. Try writing your scene in rhyme. Or make each sentence start with the same letter. You can always change the writing later. The point is to do something that will make it easier for you to see the process as fun.

8. **Work On More than One Project at Once:** We mentioned this above, but you can use it as a main coping technique to help you avoid procrastination. When one project starts to feel boring, switch to the other, and vice versa. This can help keep you engaged and moving forward. It's often best if the two projects are significantly different— one fiction and one nonfiction, perhaps. Or one romance and one thriller. There is a risk that, eventually, both projects will seem boring to you, and you'll be tempted to start a third. Stick with only two, as otherwise you'll never complete anything. If both start to feel tedious, go to your other coping techniques to spark fun in at least one of them so you can get going again.

9. **Raise the Stakes of Your Story:** Consider that your writing project has become boring because you've lost interest in the story itself. What can you do to make it more interesting? Here's a tip: Focus on your antagonist. Often, a story starts to feel boring or lackluster because there isn't enough danger. The stakes aren't high enough. Focus more on the bad guy. Put your characters through a more perilous journey that is more exciting.

10. **Use Fun Writing Apps**: If you find your excitement waning, try using an app. Here are some available at the time of this writing that may help— **Habitica:** This gaming app treats your life like a game. There are in-game rewards and

punishments that motivate you. There is also a strong social network that may inspire you. You can set up your own goals, so feel free to include your writing goals. **Write or Die:** This one ups the stakes, as it will start deleting your work if you're not able to match the writing pace you set for yourself! It does include a way to get rewards, but it also has consequences and stimulation modes that can be particularly motivating. **Call of Writing:** This app helps you get past writer's block and encourages you to get more writing done faster.

Who the Fun Seeker Can Become: The Joyful Creator

When you are your best self, you become the Joyful Creator. You bring all your love of fun and enjoyment to your writing, embracing spontaneity and innovation while maintaining a balance between playfulness and focus.

The Fun Seeker's Best Self

- **Playful Yet Productive:** While keeping your playful spirit, you can also meet deadlines and complete products. You enjoy the process for the most part, but know how to motivate yourself to achieve your goals.
- **Fearless Experimenter:** You are unafraid to take risks and try unconventional approaches to writing and the writing business. You are the one coming up with new ideas that others may emulate later. You embrace the unknown and are willing to step outside your comfort zone, which allows you to grow as an artist.
- **Magnetic Storyteller:** With your infectious joy and natural enthusiasm, you become a storyteller who captivates with your adventurous tales. You can blend fun into any plot, giving readers an experience that leaves them coming back for more.

In this best version, you no longer fear boredom but understand you have the power to infuse any activity with interesting, challenging, and engaging aspects.

Action Plan for the Fun Seeker Procrastinator

Your fear of boredom is holding you back. If you want to make your writing dreams come true, it's time to take matters into your own hands.

It starts with taking responsibility for making your writing process more enjoyable. If the task ahead feels tedious, don't procrastinate—take action to change that. Use your imagination to create game-like scenarios that draw you back to your project again and again until you finally type "The End."

Below, I've outlined a sample action plan for the Fun Seeker procrastination type to finish a novel. If you have a different project in mind—such as creating a new website, starting a blog or YouTube channel, or growing your newsletter audience—you can adapt the plan to fit your goal. The steps will likely be similar, as they're tailored to your specific type.

Step 1: Set a Fun Goal

Challenge to Overcome: *Finishing a novel is going to get boring eventually.*

You usually procrastinate to avoid boredom, which means the goal of "finishing a novel" may not work for you.

Instead, rethink this goal and make it more fun. Start by simply rephrasing it. Rather than saying, "Finish your novel," you could say, "I'm going to create a wild adventure!" or "I'm going to build my dream world."

Here's another idea: what if, instead of just "finishing your novel," your goal was to "host a monthly story party?" You could aim to complete certain sections of your story by each month's meeting, and invite friends over to read and celebrate with you.

If they're up to it, you could even have them to play a part in the story.

STEP 2: CREATE A FUN WRITING ENVIRONMENT.

Challenge to Overcome: *Writing means just sitting and typing —boring.*

The basics of writing are admittedly not very exciting. Design a writing space that sparks joy and creativity.

Use colors that excite you. Include fun decorations, comfortable seating, and snacks you enjoy. Bring in a mini refrigerator. Go all out to make this area a place you want to return to again and again.

Just be sure to minimize distractions—no televisions or social media. Instead, focus on things that will stimulate your imagination and make going on your fictional (or nonfictional) adventure fun.

STEP 3: DEVELOP A PLAYFUL WRITING ROUTINE.

Challenge to Overcome: *I'm obligated to sit down and write (sigh).*

Most writing routines lack imagination. You need a routine, but that doesn't mean it has to be dull.

Maybe you start each session by reading something fun for five minutes or freewriting about a whimsical topic. Choose a funny picture each day to write about before shifting into your story.

Create themes for each day of the week—Monday, you focus on your hero, while Friday belongs to your antagonist. Make playlists to match each theme and use them on the appropriate days while you're writing. Set aside at least one day a week to write with friends at the library or a café.

Treat your writing time like a creative laboratory. Try out different rituals, environments, and mini-games to see what gets the words flowing. And why not make Friday the day you enjoy your favorite treat while writing? Even small incentives can help rewire your brain to look forward to the page.

STEP 4: GAMIFY THE PROCESS

Challenge to Overcome: *I'll never get this finished.*

Writing a novel is a long process, and it can feel tiring and uninspiring once you reach the middle of the story. To help prevent procrastination, use the coping technique above—gamify the process.

Give yourself points for each goal you achieve, track them on a chart, and set up rewards, as well as punishments or consequences, to keep yourself motivated. Better yet, involve other writers and turn it into a friendly competition.

STEP 5: USE FUN REWARDS

Challenge to Overcome: *I won't be motivated enough to finish.*

When you gamify the process, it helps to have rewards baked in that are sure to motivate you. Think about options like fun outings or purchases, time off, or a day at the spa, if these sound tempting.

But these may not work for you.

If not, get creative. Treat yourself to a themed movie night at home with family and friends. Organize a mini treasure hunt with clues leading to a treat. Sign up for a fun workshop or class unrelated to writing, or indulge in a subscription box that tempts you.

STEP 6: PRACTICE GUIDED MEDITATION

Challenge to Overcome: *Everything has to be an exciting adventure.*

Your mind is always seeking excitement and stimulation, which can make quiet, reflective moments a challenge. You can work around this by finding ways to make your writing tasks more fun, but it also helps to get more comfortable with a quieter mind.

Meditation is the best way to do this. If you're groaning already (!), give it a chance. Start with a fun guided meditation that lasts only 5–10 minutes. Every time you practice quieting your mind, you give yourself the gift of improving your ability to focus.

STEP 7: CREATE A FUN COUNTDOWN

Challenge to Overcome: *This is getting too hard!*

Often the most difficult part of the novel-writing process is pressing through to the end. Create a fun countdown.

Set a date for when you want to finish and mark that date. Then, work your way back, creating milestones along the way that you want to reach. These may include a finished outline, completed chapters, or book sections that bring the story closer to its conclusion.

Next, design a colorful calendar or chart where each completed task earns you a fun sticker or some kind of fun mark or reward. Finally, include a visual of the great celebration you'll have when you reach the final page.

The Most Important Thing for Fun Seekers to Remember

If I were to pick one thing for you to remember as a Fun Seeker procrastinator, it's this: *Boredom isn't something to fear or avoid but something to transform with your own creativity.*

In other words, it's up to *you* to make your writing process fun! In the past, you may have believed that boredom was out of your control—if a task seemed boring, there was nothing you could do but avoid it.

But now you know that isn't true. You can use your imagination to turn even a dull task into something fun.

Of course, some writing-related tasks will always be more naturally enjoyable than others. But with your innate fun-seeking nature, you can make even the more tedious ones "fun enough" to at least get them done.

When you do, be sure you share your ideas with other writers. Even non-Fun Seekers like to find new ways to spice up their writing routines!

Exercise: The Joyful Reimagining Challenge

IT'S TIME TO FLEX YOUR FUN-MAKING SKILLS. THE OBJECTIVE is to transform a boring writing task into an enjoyable one.

1. **Identify the task:** Choose a specific writing task that feels tedious, such as editing a chapter, outlining a plot, or drafting a character description.
2. **Set the scene:** Create a fun atmosphere. Play upbeat music, light a candle, head out to a café, or invite a friend over.
3. **Gamify the process:** Turn the task into a game.
4. **Editing challenge:** Set a timer for 20 minutes and see how much you can edit in that time. Write down the total word count or paragraphs, then try again. Treat yourself when you perform best.
5. **Character bingo:** Create a bingo card with different character traits or plot elements. As you write or edit, mark off the squares for each element you incorporate.
6. **Add a creative twist.** Infuse your personality into the task. If you're editing, make a game of finding the funniest typos or writing an alternate version of a sentence in a different style (like a superhero movie or fantasy epic).
7. **Reflect on the experience.** Did you enjoy the project more? If so, why? If not, why not? Write down what worked and what didn't, then brainstorm ideas for how you might transform other tedious tasks in the future.

nine
the perfectionist

BASIC FEAR: *If I share my work, I will be exposed as inade-quate, flawed, and worthless.*
BASIC DESIRE: *I want to create something so perfect that no one can find fault with it and everyone will recognize my talent.*
SUPEREGO MESSAGE: *You must produce flawless work or you will never be worthy of success.*

PERFECTIONISTS LIKE THINGS TO be flawless, tend to be overly critical—particularly of their own work—and rarely celebrate accomplishments, always believing they could have done better. As a Perfectionist procrastinator, you may have some or all of these characteristics, with one key addition: your perfectionism leads to procrastination.

The biggest reason is your fear of falling short of perfection. You worry that if your writing doesn't meet your exacting standards, it will be rejected by editors and agents or criticized by readers. This fear of judgment can be so overwhelming that you never finish your projects, convinced they will never be "good enough" to share.

You also tend to fixate on tiny details. You may obsess over a single sentence for hours, losing valuable time could have been spent finishing your chapter. You might believe you're being productive, but in reality, you're stalling your progress. Perfectionists, as a rule, take longer than anyone else to complete their projects, if they ever finish them at all. You can revise endlessly, but this, too, is a form of procrastination, keeping you from ever declaring a piece finished. Unfortunately, this not only prevents you from reaching your writing goals but also robs you of the mistakes all writers need to make in order to grow and improve.

The pursuit of perfection may also lead to burnout. All the nitpicking leaves little room for fun, creativity, or enjoyment in the writing process. Your relentless focus on eliminating every potential flaw drains your energy, making the work feel exhausting rather than fulfilling. Ultimately, you struggle to relinquish control, feeling the need to manage every aspect of the process down to the finest detail. This leaves little room for spontaneity, experimentation, or the messy creative process that original work often requires.

For you, procrastination is a form of protection—a way to maintain the illusion of flawlessness and avoid criticism or humiliation. Your friends may admire your high standards and praise your work ethic, but they don't realize how much it's holding you back. By not allowing yourself to explore the full range of your artistry without fear, you deny yourself the freedom to grow and create without constraint.

Key Characteristics of the Perfectionist

As a Perfectionist, you may find that one or more of these habits and characteristics sound familiar:

- **High standards:** You set impossibly high expectations for your writing, trying to make every story, paragraph, and sentence perfect. This usually delays your progress.
- **Fear of failure:** You're terrified of making mistakes, having your work criticized, or watching a project fail. You do everything you can to avoid that, which means you may rarely, if ever, share your work or publish your writing, or simply face a big internal battle every time you do so.

- **Over-focus on details:** You tend to fixate on small things, such as a missing comma or a sub-par sentence. You'll spend too much time on these while avoiding or ignoring the overall project.
- **Endless revising:** You're on draft 54 and still no closer to choosing a publication date. Just when you think you may be ready, your fear takes hold and you decide to do "one more draft" instead.
- **Analysis paralysis:** To avoid making mistakes, you may get caught up in overthinking each step in the writing or publishing process. This stops you from making critical decisions that could move your career forward.
- **Procrastination as a defense:** You indulge in procrastination to protect yourself from failure and criticism.
- **Difficulty letting go:** You struggle to publish or share your work as you feel it is never "good enough." This can keep you stuck for years on one project, ultimately reducing your chances of building a successful writing career.
- **All-or-nothing thinking:** Nothing short of perfect satisfies you. If you have ten five-star reviews but one four-star, that's not good enough.

Strengths of the Perfectionists

Your biggest strength is your strong drive for excellence. You consistently push yourself to improve, refine your skills, and surpass your previous achievements. As long as you don't let this tendency slow you down, you're capable of producing high-quality results that are widely admired. You have a keen eye for detail, often noticing things others might overlook. Many Perfectionists excel as editors for this very reason.

You may also have a strong sense of organization and structure or a clear vision of how you want your story to unfold. You might be meticulous in outlining and planning, which can be especially beneficial for long works, such as fantasy and science fiction novels, as it ensures that every aspect of your world remains logical and consistent throughout a story or series.

Challenges for the Perfectionist

Your biggest challenge is your fear of failure. This may lead you to procrastinate, as those super-high expectations create too much pressure. Even after you finish the story, your drive for excellence can result in an endless cycle of revisions, where no draft ever feels satisfactory. The constant pressure you put on yourself can lead to burnout, and your hesitation to share your writing may also lead to isolation, which, in turn, can lead to depression. You might wrestle with time management, too, as the time you spend on small details may cause you to miss deadlines.

You may find it difficult to make decisions, delaying paying for a conference until it's too late because you fear the investment may not be worth it and will leave you feeling like you chose "incorrectly." To overcome these challenges, you have to learn to accept yourself as a flawed human being whose creative works are valuable, even if they're not perfect.

The Perfectionist's Limiting Beliefs

- **If it's not perfect, it's not worth doing.** You believe that any work that is less than perfect is a failure. This leads to endless revisions and an inability to finish your projects.
- **I can't afford to make mistakes.** You feel that every mistake is disastrous for your career as a writer. This may lead you to avoid getting feedback on your writing, which can stall your progress and keep you stuck.
- **My worth as a person is tied to the quality of my writing.** It might be hard to separate yourself from your work, which can lead to anxiety, self-doubt, and more procrastination.

Coping Techniques for the Perfectionist Procrastinator

1. **Set Progress-Focused Goals:** Your best way to outwit procrastination is to focus on progress over perfection. Instead of having "the perfect novel finished" as your goal, focus instead on having "a finished novel." Celebrate milestones such as finishing a chapter or reaching 20,000 words. To avoid letting perfectionism slow you down, set a goal of "good enough to go to the editor" rather than "perfect." Give yourself a limited number of additional drafts before sending it off.

2. **Practice Writing Imperfectly:** Schedule regular "write badly" sessions. Set a timer for 10-30 minutes and use that time to simply write for the joy of writing. Let the grammar problems, tense issues, inconsistent characterization, and any other "flaws" go. The goal is to see how much writing you can get done when it's imperfect. You may be surprised at the quality of the results!

3. **Limit Revisions to a Set Number:** To get out of the endless-revision cycle, limit the number of revisions you will allow yourself for each story. Three is a nice number—no more than three revisions or drafts. If that feels uncomfortable, set a number that works for you, but remember: your goal is to finish this project, not make it perfect, so set your limit wisely.

4. **Set Deadlines for Completion:** If you don't set deadlines, you'll be tempted to delay finishing or publishing out of fear that the work won't be "ready." Set firm deadlines to help avoid this destructive tendency. Go beyond just a completion date—set deadlines for multiple steps along the way, such as when Chapter 10 will be finished and when you'll send the project to an editor. Then, stick to your deadlines. Don't allow yourself to reschedule them simply out of fear.

5. **Use a Priority Filter:** Learn to view every project through a priority filter. Identify which projects or aspects don't need to be perfect, freeing yourself to focus on what truly enhances your work. This approach can also improve time management, especially as you become better at recognizing when certain projects are "good enough" to be considered finished.

6. **Develop Self-Compassion:** Perfectionists often treat themselves far more harshly than they do others. Try extending the same kindness to yourself that you would to a friend. Recognize that mistakes and imperfections are part of the writing process. Celebrate your efforts more often, and be more forgiving of your shortcomings.

7. **Seek Feedback Earlier in the Process:** Perfectionists typically spend too much time trying to perfect a piece before seeking feedback. To break this habit and to practice confronting your fear of failure, gather the courage to share drafts of your work earlier in the process. Choose a trusted friend, writing group, or writing coach who will treat your work with respect. Then send it off deliberately before you think it's perfect. The feedback will help you improve faster and ease the pressure to get everything absolutely right.

8. **Embrace Incremental Improvement:** Ask yourself: How smart it is it to expect myself to get this story perfect the first time out? You wouldn't expect that of anyone else, yet you probably expect it of yourself. Instead, focus on gradual progress. Recognize that you'll need to write many stories to improve as a writer or even come close to the high standards you've set. Understand that each draft—and even each published book—is just one step along the way. View your writing journey as a long-term process, with each achievement bringing you closer to your overall goals.

9. **Create a "Good-Enough" Mantra:** You may believe that "perfect" is better than "done," but the opposite is often true: Done is better than perfect. Remind yourself of this, especially when working on lower-priority tasks or projects.

It's particularly helpful when you catch yourself stuck in endless revisions or obsessing over minor details.

10. **Create an Anti-Perfection Ritual:** To further impress upon your mind that perfection is not a good goal, try developing a playful ritual that symbolizes letting go. Maybe you scribble wildly on a piece of paper before you start writing. Or you begin a paragraph with a ridiculously absurd sentence. Or you rearrange a few things in your writing nook to look silly or messy. The point is to physically and mentally signal to yourself that you are *not* going for perfection during this writing session.

Who the Perfectionist Can Become: The Master Craftsperson

When you're at your best self, you become The Master Craftsperson. You bring your desire for quality along with your attention to detail to bear on your work but focus equally on progress and completion so you can move ahead in your writing career, step by step.

THE PERFECTIONIST'S BEST SELF

- **Quality Producer:** You create high-quality writing projects that shine as a result of your special care. Because of your commitment to improvement and your attention to detail, your stories are true works of art.
- **Compassionate Creator:** You are compassionate with yourself, realizing that mistakes are part of the process. You no longer expect everything to be perfect and are kinder to yourself than before, treating yourself with more gentleness.
- **Resilient Learner:** You no longer fear feedback but use it to help yourself improve and learn. You have a mindset that prioritizes growth over perfection.

In this best version, you work hard to produce quality products, but no longer let your fear of failure stop you.

Action Plan for the Perfectionist Procrastinator

Your desire for perfection is holding you back. It's time to banish the inner critic if you want to make your writing dreams come true.

It begins when you give up on the idea of being perfect—for good. You make peace with the fact that no writing project will ever be perfect, and realize that you *must* be brave enough to accept "good enough." Furthermore, you must learn to value yourself and your creative offerings regardless of what anyone else may say.

Below, I have a sample action plan for the Perfectionist procrastination type to finish a novel. If you have a different project in mind—such as creating a new website, starting a blog or YouTube channel, or growing your newsletter audience—you can adapt the plan to fit your goal. The steps will likely be similar, as they're tailored to your specific type.

STEP 1: DEFINE "GOOD ENOUGH" STANDARDS

Challenge to Overcome: *I must set impossibly high standards for every project.*

You feel the pressure of your high standards every time you think about writing, which is often the reason why you procrastinate. Start your novel journey by setting "good enough" standards. In most cases, simply "finishing" the book is good enough! If this is your first novel, let that be your standard.

If you've written novels before, you might include "finishing" along with one additional goal to help this book surpass your last one. Maybe your dialogue will be tighter, your settings more immersive, or your characters better developed. Whatever standards you choose, keep them low! If they seem "too low" to you, then you're doing it right.

STEP 2: ESTABLISH A "SHUT-UP" TIMER

Challenge to Overcome: *I have to fix every flaw as I go.*

Your tendency to want to fix everything as you write is like driving while pressing the gas and brake pedals at the same time—it slows you down and increases the risk that you'll never finish. To counteract this tendency, set a timer for 25 minutes and make yourself write *without* fixing anything. Tell your inner critic to take a nap. Once the timer goes off, it's your choice—you can keep writing if it's going well, or take a break and reflect on what you did. Do your best to resist criticizing your work until you get to your second draft.

STEP 3: CREATE A "MISTAKE" JOURNAL.

Challenge to Overcome: *I absolutely cannot make a mistake.*

Purchase or choose a new journal to record your so-called "mistakes" as you work on your novel. This can help you resist the urge to fix the story as you go, giving you a place to note your concerns. You can always come back and address them later if you want, but don't be surprised if recording your mistakes this way helps you realize that they aren't as big a deal as you think.

STEP 4: SET MINI DEADLINES

Challenge to Overcome: *I must revise and revise until it's perfect.*

To help foster the "progress" over "perfection" mindset we discussed, set several mini-deadlines to guide yourself from beginning to end on this novel or any other writing project. A final deadline is important, but setting deadlines for completing each chapter may be even more important. If you're unsure how your chapters will unfold, that's okay. Commit to finishing one every week or every other week, depending on what works for your schedule.

STEP 5: CREATE A REWARD SYSTEM FOR PROGRESS

Challenge to Overcome: *Perfection must always come first.*

Deadlines help, but you probably need more to overcome your desire to perfect every sentence. Try celebrating your smaller achievements more often. Take a weekend to figure out what rewards truly motivate you. Every time you complete a rough draft of a chapter, give yourself one of those rewards—and stick to it! Don't neglect yourself. Repeating this process teaches your brain that progress, even without perfection, is valuable.

STEP 6: TRY "BACKWARDS" WRITING

Challenge to Overcome: *Everything must be done sequentially and perfectly.*

As a Perfectionist, you may trap yourself in a cage of your own making. You think everything must be perfect, and you must go step by step from beginning to end. This might work, but in some cases, it can squash the creative process. Try breaking out of that cage by jumping around in your story (if that appeals to you at all!). Instead of starting at the beginning, write your climactic ending instead, or pick any place in the middle and have fun with it.

The idea is to bypass the pressure of proceeding perfectly so that your writing feels more like playing, giving you the freedom to create without so many self-imposed restraints.

STEP 7: HOST A "GUILTY PLEASURE" WRITING RETREAT

Challenge to Overcome: *Writing is a chore.*

Infuse more fun into your writing process by organizing a day-long or weekend retreat with a playful theme, such as "guilty pleasures." You can do this alone or invite some other perfectionist-oriented writers to join you, either in person or virtually.

During your retreat, write while indulging in your favorite snacks or music. Clear your to-do list of all other responsibilities, leaving only writing and writing-related tasks. If possible, escape to a cabin or another scenic location that inspires you. The goal is to step away from your usual high standards and create an environment where you can express yourself freely without judgment.

The Most Important Thing for Perfectionists to Remember

If I were to pick one thing that you must remember as a Perfectionist procrastinator, it's this: *Progress, not perfection, is the key to unlocking your creativity and completing your work.*

In the past, you may have believed that perfection was what mattered. You absolutely must divorce yourself from that belief, as it keeps you from making your writing dreams come true.

You will make mistakes. You will have failures. I hope you find the courage to face them head-on so you can become the masterful craftsperson you were born to be.

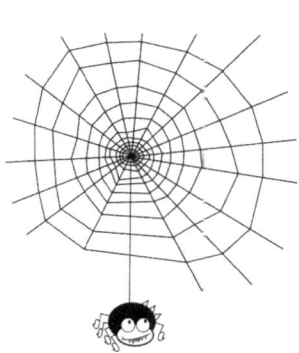

Exercise: The Flawed Character Workshop

IT'S TIME TO FLEX YOUR "IMPERFECT CREATING" MUSCLES. Try this exercise.

- **Choose a flaw:** Give yourself five minutes to brainstorm a list of five potential character flaws. Examples may include greed, narcissism, excessive criticsm, jealousy, or laziness. Once you have your list, review it and select one to explore further.

- **Create a character profile:** Spend 10–15 minutes developing a character who embodies this flaw. Include their name, age, and background, as well as how this flaw impacts their life and relationships. Explain how the flaw might prevent them from achieving what they want most.
- **Write a scene:** Once your character profile is complete, set a timer for 20 minutes and write a scene that highlights your character's flaw in action. Perhaps the flaw leads to conflict with someone the character deeply cares about or results in a humorous situation. Feel free to exaggerate the flaw for comedic or dramatic effect. Have fun with it!
- **Reflect on the flaw's impact:** When you're finished writing, reflect on how the flaw made your character more interesting and relatable. What strengths might emerge from this "weakness?"
- **Share your work:** Share your character and scene with a fellow writer or friend you know will be supportive. Ask them what they think of the character's flaw and how it impacted the scene.
- **Record your conclusions:** Jot down three things you learned about embracing imperfections—in your characters, writing, and yourself. Can you see that they can be valuable assets in storytelling and perhaps in life in general?

ten

the crisis-maker

BASIC FEAR: *If I don't feel pressure, I'll never get it done.*
BASIC DESIRE: *I need the adrenaline rush to feel truly motivated and alive.*
SUPEREGO MESSAGE: *You can only perform your best work when the pressure is on and time is running out.*

"I HAVE A LOT OF TIME!" the Crisis-Maker says. "I don't have to do it yet."

Your friends encourage you to do the project *now*. They know you like to wait until the last minute and then rush about in a frenzy. They worry the stress isn't good for you, but you have a secret—you thrive on it. Or at least, you think you do. That pressure of an impending deadline is what spurs you into action. Besides, when you wait until the last minute, your work is usually great! So what's the problem?

This pattern is likely to cause issues in your writing life—if not now, eventually. For one, writing a longer work in one short burst of activity is nearly impossible. You may be able to pound out a short story or even a novella in one fell swoop, but if your writing dreams include publishing books, this method isn't likely to work as well. Rushed writing can also result in work that lacks depth, polish, complex plots, well-developed characters, and more.

Burnout is another potential issue. It's hard for anyone to sustain a long-term creative output with a zig-zag pattern of inactivity followed by stressful and hurried production. As you get older, it will become even harder as your body and mind struggle to manage sudden changes in schedule and energy-output.

Another issue is a lack of consistency. If you work intensely on your story for a few days and then leave it for weeks, it becomes difficult to keep track of what's going on. Inconsistency also robs you of the cumulative benefits of a regular writing routine, which helps improve your skills over time.

Time management may be a struggle, as well. You'll likely underestimate the time it takes to complete a project, and in your last-minute rush, neglect crucial steps like editing and proofreading—resulting in stories that are riddled with errors. For you, adrenaline is the fuel, and you don't know how to get the work done without it.

Key Characteristics of the Crisis-Maker

As a Crisis-Maker, you may find that one or more of these habits and characteristics sound familiar:

- **Thrives under pressure:** You think you do your best work when the stakes are high and the deadline is fast approaching. You feel a rush of adrenaline in these moments that fuels your creativity and focus.
- **Last-minute worker:** You often delay working on projects until the very last moment. You may put off tasks for days or even weeks, waiting for the intense urgency to kick in.
- **Procrastination justification:** You justify your tendency to procrastinate by saying you work best when the deadline is looming. You think that procrastination helps you think more clearly or perform at a higher level.
- **Inconsistent productivity:** You experience bursts of frantic productivity followed by long stretches of inactivity.

Without an immediate deadline, you often struggle to stay motivated and engaged with your writing.

- **A skewed view of time:** You underestimate how much time it will take to get a project done while overestimating how much time you have to do it. You assume you can accomplish a huge task in a short amount of time, which leads to rushed or incomplete work.
- **High stress tolerance (you think):** You usually handle high levels of stress well, and may even accept it as a normal part of your creative process. This can come back to bite you later, however, in the form of health troubles like fatigue, back pain, increased vulnerability to infections, and other stress-related issues.
- **Prone to burnout:** Relying on last-minute energy surges can lead to physical and emotional exhaustion. You may feel drained and burned out after your frenzied writing sessions. This, in turn, can lead to long delays before you get back to writing again.

Strengths of the Crisis-Maker

Your biggest strength is your ability to thrive under pressure. When the deadline is looming and time is ticking away, you can summon an impressive burst of energy, focus, and creativity. You have a knack for managing the chaos of last-minute work. You are good at thinking on your feet and improvising when things don't go as planned. This adaptability makes you a resourceful problem-solver, especially in unpredictable situations.

You are also good at finding clarity and drive in the midst of pressure. You can prioritize under stress, and can act decisively in critical moments. If a crisis is at hand, you are just the person to help manage it!

Challenges for the Crisis-Maker

Your biggest challenge is your reliance on pressure to get things done. You excel in last-minute sprints, but this habit often leads to unnecessary stress and anxiety—not only for you, but those around you. The initial adrenaline rush seems exciting, but once it's passed, it's likely to leave you feeling drained and prone to burnout. That's when you'll probably notice your mistakes or realize that you could have done better work had you given yourself more time.

Your other big challenge is inconsistency. This is particularly important in the world of writing, where consistent effort is needed to create quality novels and other books, as well as to improve your skills over the years. Ultimately, you risk sabotaging your success by not giving yourself enough time to reflect, revise, and improve your work.

The Crisis-Maker's Limiting Beliefs

- **I work best under pressure.** You have convinced yourself that you need the adrenaline rush of an impending deadline to be productive. You also believe that your work will not have the same intensity or quality without it.
- **I can always catch up later.** This belief gives you an excuse to procrastinate. You think you can afford to delay because you can rush it all together when the deadline comes.
- **Planning kills creativity.** You may feel that setting up a regular writing schedule or working steadily will stifle your creative flow. You prefer the spontaneous bursts of inspiration you associate with working under a time crunch.

Coping Techniques for the Crisis-Maker Procrastinator

1. **Practice "Urgency-Free" Writing Sprints:** You have to show yourself that you *can* produce quality creative work without being under the intense pressure of an immediate deadline. To do that, challenge yourself to do focused writing sprints. Set a timer for 30 minutes and write as much as you can on something that is *not* due anytime soon. If you can, compare the result to writing you've done while

under pressure. Ask yourself: Do I see a big difference between these pieces—the one written under pressure and the one that wasn't?

2. **Create an Honest "Worst-Case Scenario" Plan:** When you feel the urge to procrastinate on your writing, take five minutes to write down the worst-case outcome of rushing the task. If it's just a one-page story, it might not be a big deal. But if you're working on a novel, it could have serious consequences for your writing career. Maybe you don't finish the book at all—or maybe you do, but because you rushed it, you receive several negative reviews. How would that affect you? Once you're done, see if you don't feel motivated to do at least a little work on the project today.

3. **Create an Emergency "Fire-Drill" Writing Schedule:** Since you thrive on the adrenaline rush, try to build it into your regular writing routine. Randomly set alarms throughout your week that signal an impromptu five-to-fifteen-minute writing session. Treat these sessions like emergencies where you must write without distractions for short, intense bursts. See how many words you can get down!

4. **Host a "Deadline Party":** Invite some of your fellow writers over (or gather online) to work on your projects under the same deadline pressure. Bring music and snacks, and give yourselves a short amount of time (30–45 minutes) to get your next chapter (or another project) done. When the timer goes off, share how much you accomplished with each other. This can help make writing fun while still generating a sense of urgency.

5. **Use Pressure Points from Your Personal Life:** You can create a sense of urgency by tying your writing to other pressure points in your life. For example, if you have a family reunion coming up in a week, challenge yourself to finish two chapters before then. Not only will this add the pressure you need, but it will also give you a wonderful sense of accomplishment before the event arrives.

6. **Create a Writing Soundtrack:** Music has a way of tapping into our nervous system. To get your adrenaline pumping during a writing session, turn on some pulse-pounding tunes. Better yet, create a playlist to use whenever you need an extra boost to get to work. Start playing it before you even sit down to write, and let it put you in a creative mood.

7. **Identify Your Other Motivators:** Right now, you may believe that adrenaline is your only motivator, but no one is driven by just one thing. What has motivated you to work hard in the past? Was it the thought of winning an award, influencing others, or making someone's life better? You might also consider what your boss could say to push you to work harder—or what your partner might say. The more you think about it, the more ways you'll discover to motivate yourself to get your writing done.

8. **Give the Writing Five Minutes:** You believe your writing will not be fun or exciting unless you wait until the last minute. But have you challenged that belief? Try giving your writing a chance to impress you. Set a timer and write for five minutes. Does the writing draw you in? Does the process get you excited as you go? Often that is the way writing works. It doesn't sound exciting when we think about it, but once we start doing it, our love of writing takes over and we get lost in the flow.

9. **Emergency Task List:** One of the things you struggle with is the tendency to think you have more time than you actually do to complete a project. To rid yourself of this delusion, create an "emergency task list" of all the writing tasks that need to be completed around a single piece. Let's say you want to publish a novel a year from now. Usually, you would procrastinate until a few weeks before your deadline and then rush to get it done. To stop yourself from doing that, create a list of all the tasks that you'll need to complete in that year. Don't forget to include multiple drafts (to catch plot problems and smooth out the prose),

developmental editing, copy editing, proofreading, cover design, launch plan, and more. Creating a realistic list of everything that needs to be done can make it more likely that you'll feel the urgency to get started now.

10. **Journal About Your Crises:** Journaling about your past crises and their outcomes can be helpful. Each time you face a crisis, write down what it was like, noting both the good and bad results. This practice may help you challenge your belief that treating every task as a crisis is beneficial. After reflecting on the experience, jot down ideas for what you could have done to prevent it, and how that might have made the process easier for you.

Who the Crisis-Maker Can Become: The Dynamic Achiever

When you're at your best self, you become the Dynamic Achiever. You harness your energy of urgency without succumbing to the chaos of last-minute scrambles. You embody a proactive mindset, turning potential crises into opportunities for creativity and productivity.

THE CRISIS-MAKER'S BEST SELF

- **Proactive Planner:** You set your own emergencies, anticipate problems that may arise, and push yourself to complete your projects by your own deadlines.
- **Stress-Resistant Innovator:** You remain adept at managing crises and keep your head during stressful situations. You are calm under pressure and view obstacles as opportunities for creative problem-solving.
- **Bursting Producer:** You engage in regular short bursts of writing that feel exciting. By scheduling multiple short bursts per week, you manage to finish lengthy works while staying true to your own creativity.

In this best version, you commit to continuous improvement, broadening your understanding of what drives you and tapping into a variety of strategies to stay on task.

Action Plan for the Crisis-Maker Procrastinator

Your reliance on last-minute emergency deadlines is holding you back. It's time to find other methods of motivation if you want to make your writing dreams come true.

It begins when you give up on the idea of allowing only *outside pressures* to spur you to work. You understand that to reach your writing goals, you must be internally motivated and come up with your own deadlines. Further, you must learn to value the work you do when the pressure is off, convincing yourself that your creative talent is not limited to adrenaline-fueled binges.

Below, I have a sample action plan for the Crisis-Maker procrastination type to finish a novel. If you have a different project in mind—such as creating a new website, starting a blog or YouTube channel, or growing your newsletter audience—you can adapt the plan to fit your goal. The steps will likely be similar, as they're tailored to your specific type.

STEP 1: REVERSE ENGINEER YOUR DEADLINES
Challenge to Overcome: *I'll wait until the last minute.*

You've decided to write a novel and have given yourself a year to do it. What would you normally do? Wait around until a few weeks before the deadline and then rush to write a novel in three weeks or so?

Instead, reverse-engineer your final deadline along with all the smaller deadlines leading up to it. You can base these on word count, or, if you've outlined your novel, on chapters. Treat each mini-deadline as if it were the final one—this is crucial. Otherwise, you might ignore them and wait until the last minute. If necessary, make every mini-deadline feel like a crisis, but be sure to meet each one to stay on track and increase your chances of finishing this book!

STEP 2: IMPLEMENT A "CRISIS-BUDDY" SYSTEM

Challenge to Overcome: *I usually isolate during writing sessions.*

It's easy to put off your work when you're the only one who knows about it. Consider partnering up with another writer. Set up regular bi-weekly check-ins where you share your progress and goals for the next check-in. Knowing someone else is in the same boat can increase the pressure to get things done while creating a sense of camaraderie in the face of deadlines.

STEP 3: WRITE IN SHORT BURSTS

Challenge to Overcome: *I must feel under pressure when writing.*

You can simulate the feeling of being under pressure by setting a timer for your writing session. It's usually best to to give yourself a little *less* time than you think you need to complete your chapter or meet your set word count. That will help push you to write a little faster, creating that sense of urgency you like.

You can write an entire novel using only short bursts of writing. You just have to make sure that you engage in these short writing sessions regularly. Make sure you have a goal to reach for each session. Without a goal, you won't feel any pressure.

STEP 4: USE YOUR OTHER MOTIVATORS

Challenge to Overcome: *I am only motivated by pressure, stress, and adrenaline.*

If you want to finish your novel—which is typically a long-term, marathon-like project (not a short sprint)—it's critical to identify and use your other motivators. Keep in mind that you can use both positive and negative motivators. A positive motivator, for example, is your inner desire to finish this novel because it's important to you. A negative motivator is how disappointed you will feel in yourself if you *don't* finish the novel.

Here's another example: You might want to write a book because you know it will bring meaning to your life. A related negative motivator could be imagining yourself at 85 years old, holding out your hands and realizing there's no book in them.

It can help to figure out what's really behind this desire to write your book. Write down each of your reasons—the positive motivators—then write the related negative motivators for each. Use these to push yourself to stick to your writing routine.

STEP 5: UP THE STAKES FOR YOURSELF

Challenge to Overcome: *It doesn't matter if I meet my own deadlines; they don't cause crises.*

You know that if you don't meet the deadlines you set for yourself, very little will actually change. Treat them with a laissez-faire attitude and your life—and your novel—will likely stay right where they are now. Think about that—ten years from now, your book could still be unfinished.

Create some bigger stakes for yourself. Let's say you fail to finish chapter three by your deadline. Try using a tool like *Beeminder* (available online at the time of this writing at beeminder.com). Set your goals and give the program your credit card. If you don't meet your goals, your payment method will be charged! You'll lose money if you don't get the work done.

You can also do this with a friend or family member. It doesn't have to be about losing money. Maybe you make a deal with your partner that if you miss your deadline, you'll have to handle all the household chores for a week. Use whatever works for you, but raise the stakes enough to keep yourself motivated.

STEP 6: NEGATIVE REINFORCEMENT ALARM

Challenge to Overcome: *Nothing will happen if I procrastinate.*

Building on step five, this step also uses negative reinforcement to encourage you to get your writing done. Create an alarm on your cell phone to go off every hour that you haven't written. When it goes off, you have to do something unpleasant (like a chore or 10 push-ups). The idea is to create an uncomfortable association with inactivity, pushing you to write to avoid the negative consequences.

STEP 7: REWARD YOUR PROGRESS

Challenge to Overcome: *A regular writing routine is unexciting.*

Right now, you probably see writing as a chore without the pressure of an urgent deadline. You need to change that viewpoint.

Start by creating rewards for yourself for meeting your mini-deadlines. Whenever you sit down to write and you reach your goal (a certain word count or amount finished), reward yourself. *Every time.* Give yourself a treat, allow yourself to procrastinate on something else (like doing the dishes or fixing the broken door), grant yourself an extra 30 minutes of leisure time, or whatever you can think of.

The key is to *make yourself happy.* You want to gradually associate regular, routine writing with pure enjoyment.

The Most Important Thing for Crisis-Makers to Remember

If I were to pick one thing that you must remember as a Crisis-Maker procrastinator, it's this: *Last-minute work will never make you a great writer.*

In the past, you may have believed that urgent action was what mattered. You absolutely must let go of that belief as all it's doing is holding you back.

I hope you will find other ways to motivate yourself so you will write regularly and consistently. That's the key to finding your voice, improving your stories, and reaching greater heights.

Exercise: The Non-Crisis Writing Sprint

IT'S TIME TO TEACH YOURSELF THAT YOU CAN WRITE effectively without the pressure of an urgent deadline, proving that your creativity and productivity don't depend on a crisis.

- **Set an intentional non-crisis deadline:** Choose a project or section of a project you've been putting off (like a chapter, short story, or blog post). Give yourself a firm, non-urgent deadline a reasonable distance away, like seven days from today.
- **Create daily writing sessions:** Break your project into three to five writing sessions (depending on the project's size). Each session should have a specific word count or section goal to complete in a set time frame (like 500 words or a complete scene in 30 minutes or less). Schedule these sessions on your calendar, spreading them out over the week.
- **Simulate pressure with a timer:** Set a countdown timer for each session. Give yourself less time than you think you will need. The trick is to simulate the focus you feel during last-minute crunches.
- **Track your progress:** Keep a log of your daily progress to show yourself how you're doing. Record how much you write in each session on a calendar or in a journal. Add how it felt to write without the looming panic of a hard deadline.

- **Reward yourself for early completion:** If you finish the project or task before the seven-day deadline, reward yourself!
- **Reflect on the experience:** After you've finished the exercise, ask yourself these questions: Did I feel productive without a looming deadline? Was my writing better or worse —or the same—than it is during a last-minute rush? How were my stress levels during this week compared to a crisis week?

eleven
the distracted

BASIC FEAR: *If I have to sit still and focus without anything exciting going on, I'll lose my energy and motivation.*
BASIC DESIRE: *I need to be constantly stimulated and interested to stay motivated.*
SUPEREGO MESSAGE: *If you don't keep switching to something new and exciting, you'll miss out.*

YOU'RE WORKING AWAY on your writing, and then—*ding!*—you get a notification on your phone. It takes you only five minutes to respond, but when you try to go back to your story, you find you've lost your train of thought.

Every writer is vulnerable to distraction, but as a Distracted procrastinator, you may feel constantly pulled in multiple directions, to the point that your distraction interferes with your ability to reach your writing goals.

You may sit down to write and then remember you forgot to return a call. Rather than setting that task aside until your writing is finished, you will likely succumb to the distraction. Or maybe you're writing away when you realize you need to research part of your setting. You get on the internet, and before you know it, your writing time is gone, and all you have to show for it is a bunch of open tabs on your browser.

It doesn't help that there's so much vying for our attention these days. Since you probably have a cell phone with you regularly, it can become a constant battle to keep your focus on your work when there's always something else fun or interesting to look at. One of your main challenges is the allure of instant gratification. Whereas writing requires a lot of focused work before you see rewards, social media can provide an immediate hit of good feelings, making it more attractive in the moment.

You may also struggle with time management. You might set up a 30-minute writing session, but if you get distracted during that time, you're unlikely to reach the goal you set for yourself. This can leave you feeling behind and overwhelmed.

For you, the tendency for your mind to wander is your Achilles' heel. The challenge is to learn to focus your scattered energy and avoid distractions long enough to finish your work.

Key Characteristics of the Distracted

As a Distracted, you may find that one or more of these habits and characteristics sound familiar:

- **Difficulty maintaining focus:** You have trouble maintaining focus on anything for a very long time. Your attention is often pulled in various directions, whether by external distractions (like social media or things happening around you) or internal distractions (like daydreams or anxieties).
- **Easily swayed by new ideas:** You are often vulnerable to "shiny object syndrome," wanting to chase after exciting new ideas rather than stick with one through to completion.
- **Chronic multi-tasker:** You tend to juggle many things at once. You believe you can handle it all, but this usually slows you down and makes you less productive on things that matter, like your writing.

- **Prone to overwhelm:** Since you have so many new, exciting ideas, you may feel overwhelmed and unsure about which one to pursue. If you try to do more than one, you may spread yourself too thin, leading to fatigue and low motivation.
- **Reliance on external stimulation:** You may rely heavily on external stimulation to maintain engagement and focus. You may feel bored or restless when the writing process becomes too routine, leading you to succumb to distracted procrastination.
- **Fleeting motivation:** Your motivation tends to come in surges, often sparked by shiny new ideas or sudden bursts of inspiration. It may fade quickly, however, when the work gets challenging.
- **Trouble prioritizing:** With so many things in your life vying for your attention, you may find it difficult to set priorities. Your lack of clarity can lead you to procrastinate or hop from one idea to the next without fully committing to any one thing.

Strengths of the Distracted

Your biggest strength is your ability to generate diverse ideas. Because you're constantly exposed to new stimuli—whether by perusing the internet, talking to others, or exploring various interests—you often have a lot of concepts and perspectives at your fingertips. This can be particularly beneficial in writing, where originality and a fresh view-point can set a piece apart.

You may also be highly adaptable. Your frequent shifts in focus help you become comfortable with change and uncertainty, allowing you to adjust your narrative or writing style to suit various themes or audiences. Your quest for novelty may also lead you to connect with a rich tapestry of influences, which can inspire your writing in unexpected ways.

Challenges for the Distracted

Your biggest challenge is your inability to concentrate for long periods. Being frequently distracted can lead to fragmented thinking, making it difficult for you to develop cohesive narratives or fully fleshed-out ideas. As you jump from one task to the other, you may also struggle to maintain momentum, running out of steam before you make any significant progress. As the unfinished projects pile up, you can feel frustrated and plagued by self-doubt.

When you're not actively engaged in something stimulating, you may feel restless or bored, leading you to seek distractions rather than face the discomfort of sitting down to write. Avoiding focused tasks can also create a sense of dependency on distractions, making it even harder to learn how to be quiet, alone, and focused on a piece of writing.

The Distracted's Limiting Beliefs

- **I have to multitask to be productive.** You often believe that juggling multiple tasks will lead to greater productivity. This can cause you to split your attention across too many activities, resulting in lower-quality work on any task, like your writing.
- **I can't focus on one thing without external stimulation.** This belief makes you think that you *have* to have external stimulation—music, social media, or other forms of entertainment—to be able to write. You may struggle to work in quiet environments or on projects requiring sustained attention.
- **Any distraction is worth my time.** This belief leads you to abandon your writing at the slightest distraction, even if it isn't important.

Coping Techniques for the Distracted Procrastinator

1. **Create a Distraction-Free Writing Nook:** Wherever you normally write, make that a "distraction-free" zone. Keep your phone out of the room. Simply turning it off is not enough, because your brain will still be thinking about it. Put it in another room on silent (or turned off) so it doesn't interrupt you. Turn off your access to the internet, too, so you don't start browsing, and have a pair of noise-canceling headphones ready to use.

2. **Schedule Distraction Swaps:** Allow yourself to indulge in distractions occasionally, but swap them for writing time. If you spend 15 minutes perusing YouTube videos, for example, commit to writing for at least 15 minutes afterward. Think: "distraction for writing." Be willing to trade one for the other on a regular basis. It may help you get your writing done!

3. **Allow Yourself to Experience "The Flow":** Ask yourself if you've ever experienced the "flow" state. This is when you get so lost in your writing that you lose track of time. That is the reward of focused concentration. If you have experienced that before, remind yourself of how good it feels! If you haven't experienced it or if it's been a while, try these methods for getting there: **Use music.** Put on some instrumental music, close your eyes, breathe deeply, and sink into your story. **Use your body.** Try to *feel* the way your point-of-view character feels, right down to her skin. *Be* your character. **Meditate.** Use a guided meditation for 5-10 minutes before you start writing. **Work out . . . hard.** If you've ever experienced the "runner's high," you know what it's like to work out hard and then feel that blissful euphoria. Get yourself good and wiped out, then before you flop down on the couch, write for 20 minutes!

4. **Use Audio Affirmations:** When you're feeling inspired, record some positive affirmations for yourself as a writer. You can speak them into your cell phone or record them in

some other way so you have them handy. Some examples include: a) I want to stay focused on my writing. b) Today, I will easily get lost in my writing session. c) I will keep my attention on my writing until my time is up. Listen to these affirmations before your writing sessions. Let them remind you of your commitment to writing without distraction.

5. **Leave Landmarks:** If you must respond to something that pulls you away from your writing, leave yourself a landmark —a clue that will help you more quickly get back on track when you return. Try typing the last thought you had before the interruption, make a quick note of the problem you were trying to solve, or jot down the next step you planned to take. Leave breadcrumbs on the page to guide you back.

6. **Know What Can Wait:** Not every interruption is important, and not every notification needs to be attended to *right now.* Remind yourself of how important your writing is to you, then set your priorities. Allow yourself to be distracted only by emergencies or high-priority matters. Write those things down and try to keep the list under five. Remember, most things can wait until after your writing session.

7. **Practice Rituals that Clear Your Mind:** Distracted individuals typically have minds that race at 90 miles per hour. You're thinking about this and that, that and this, so that when you sit down to write, it's hard because your brain is still stewing over so many things. Create some "mind-clearing" rituals for yourself. Perhaps you meditate for 5–10 minutes before writing. Maybe you close your eyes and practice deep breathing for three minutes. Or you might jot down everything you're thinking about in a notebook. Try to be consistent with the rituals you choose —the more you practice them, the more you'll train your brain to relax and focus.

8. **Make a Soundtrack of Focus:** Music has a unique way of syncing up with the brain, helping you to focus on your

story and facilitating that meditative state that helps you create. Build a playlist filled with instrumental music or even nature sounds that help you stay on task. You can also use tools like Pandora to help create your playlists.

9. **Schedule Unplugged Writing Sessions:** Have at least one day a week when you completely unplug from technology—including computers, phones, and the internet. Use pen and paper instead, allowing for a more tactile and focused writing experience without the usual digital distractions. To help yourself relax even further into your story, take your notebook to a park, riverwalk, or café.

10. **Get Some Sensory Focus Tools:** Use sensory tools like fidget spinners, spinning tops, stress balls, or textured fabrics while writing. Keep them within easy reach in your writing nook to help provide a physical outlet for nervous energy and help maintain focus. These small tools can prevent distractions and improve concentration on your writing project. Even a soft scarf draped around your neck, a fuzzy blanket, or a scented lotion can keep you grounded.

Who the Distracted Can Become: The Focused Visionary

When you're at your best, you become the Focused Visionary. You harness your natural curiosity and creativity to maintain a clear vision of your goals while effectively managing distractions.

THE DISTRACTED'S BEST SELF

- **Distraction Manager:** You've learned how to manage your tendency to become distracted by making agreements with yourself on when distraction is allowed and when it's not. You are no longer yanked about by any distraction that comes up.

- **Curiosity-Driven Explorer:** You embrace your natural curiosity and use it to fuel your creativity. Instead of viewing distractions as obstacles, you use them to gather inspiration and new ideas, without letting them take you off task for too long.
- **Mindful Presence:** Since focus is often difficult for you, you've developed several techniques to help you improve. You may practice daily meditation or journaling to clear your mind before engaging in focused work. You have learned what methods work for you and you use them regularly.

In this best version, you commit to improving your ability to focus, without losing your natural tendency to be fascinated by a lot of different things.

Action Plan for the Distracted Procrastinator

Your vulnerability to distraction is holding you back. It's time to find new ways to resist distraction and bring this tendency under control.

It begins when you let go of the idea that you can indulge in distractions and still become the writer you want to be. To reach your writing goals, you must commit to giving more focused attention to your work. Additionally, you must learn to value longer periods of concentration, proving to yourself that you can tolerate the discomfort that distraction-free time may bring.

Below is a sample action plan for the Distracted procrastination type to finish a novel. If you have a different project in mind—such as creating a new website, starting a blog or YouTube channel, or growing your newsletter audience—you can adapt the plan to fit your goal. The steps will likely be similar, as they're tailored to your specific type.

STEP 1: CREATE A DISTRACTION-FREE WRITING ZONE
Challenge to Overcome: *If distractions come up, I'll lose my focus.*
Take some time to look over your writing nook and see if you notice

things that regularly distract you. If there's a TV, for example, move it to another room (or move your writing nock somewhere else.) If the room is open to the rest of your family and you can see their comings and goings, try to find a new place to write. Some writers even use closets so they can sequester themselves away! Take this step seriously—it matters a lot.

STEP 2: USE A DISTRACTION JOURNAL

Challenge to Overcome: *My racing thoughts make it difficult to concentrate.*

Keep a "distraction journal" near your writing desk. Before you start writing, use it to jot down any racing thoughts. If more of those thoughts come up while you're writing, quickly write them in your journal, then get back to your story. This technique helps clear your mind without completely breaking your focus.

STEP 3: CREATE A FLEXIBLE OUTLINE

Challenge to Overcome: *I get distracted by my ideas, and then I lose my place.*

Whether you like to outline or not, creating a very simple flexible outline can help you stay on task. Break your story down into main sections. The three-act structure is a good place to start (beginning, middle, end). Then break those sections down further into key scenes or plot points.

This can give you a basic framework for your novel, but that doesn't mean it has to be restrictive. The goal is to give yourself a roadmap so you can jump around and write different sections without getting lost.

STEP 4: LIMIT ONLINE TIME WITH SCHEDULED BREAKS

Challenge to Overcome: *I'm tempted to look at things online, and then I don't get my writing done.*

Keep your phone out of the room and your internet turned off while you're writing. You can use apps like Freedom and Cold Turkey to help.

If you're writing a part of your story and need the internet—perhaps for research—schedule specific times for that and limit those times. You can do the same with your social media. Allow yourself five minutes to check it before you start, then promise yourself you won't check it again until your writing session ends.

STEP 5: PLAY "DISTRACTION BINGO"

Challenge to Overcome: *Giving in to distractions is more fun than resisting them.*

Make your own bingo card filled with common distractions, like "check Facebook," "watch cat videos," or "do the dishes." Fill it up with the things that usually pull your focus away from writing.

At your next writing session, set a timer for 25 minutes and start writing. If you feel the urge to give in to a distraction before the timer goes off, don't succumb—write it down on a piece of paper (or on the back of your bingo card), then keep writing.

Every time you complete a writing session without giving in to a distraction, cross off the one you almost fell for. When you get five in a row or complete the entire card, reward yourself!

STEP 6: BUILD A PROGRESS JAR

Challenge to Overcome: *It feels as if I'll never get to the end.*

If you can see the progress you're making, it can help motivate you to resist distractions. Try this: take a glass jar and make it into a "progress" jar. Dress it up with decorations, and have it sitting right by your writing desk.

Every time you reach a goal—such as finishing a chapter, writing 500 words, or editing for a half-hour—put a colorful token, marble, paper clip, M&M, or whatever you like into the jar. As the jar fills up, you'll have a clear visual representation of your progress.

STEP 7: IDEA PARKING LOT SYSTEM

Challenge to Overcome: *If I have a new idea, I must act on it immediately.*

To stop yourself from allowing your new ideas to pull you away from the one you're working on, try this: implement a "parking lot" system. Begin by choosing your medium—a physical notebook, a digital document, or an app. Then, whenever you're writing and a new idea occurs to you, jot it down in your chosen medium.

Let's say you picked a notebook. You can break it up into sections if you like—new story ideas, new plot approaches to this book, new character ideas—whatever works.

Even if it's an idea for the story you're working on, it's best *not* to pursue it until your writing period is over, so write it down somewhere in your parking lot system. Do be brief. The idea is to capture the essence of the idea without letting it derail your story.

Finally, designate specific review periods where you will review your new ideas. Prioritize which ones are worth pursuing. If they have to do with the novel you're working on, determine how you will incorporate those ideas into the plot. Commit to reviewing your ideas only during your designated times. Don't let this interfere with your writing time.

The Most Important Thing for Distracteds to Remember

If I were to pick one thing that you must remember as a Distracted procrastinator, it's this: *Staying focused on one thing at a time can transform your creative chaos into meaningful progress.*

In the past, you may have believed you couldn't focus for very long. You absolutely must let go of that belief, as all it's doing is holding you back.

I hope you will find ways to encourage yourself to focus so you can write regularly and consistently. Even a little bit of focus, repeated often, can change everything.

Exercise: The Distracted Writer's Treasure Hunt

IT'S TIME TO TEACH YOURSELF THAT YOU CAN WRITE effectively without succumbing to distractions! Just follow the directions below.

1. **Set the scene:** Gather some colorful pens, sticky notes, and paper, along with a pair of dice and something to use as a marker, like a penny or a small action figure.

2. **Create a treasure map:** Draw a simple path on a piece of paper that leads to a "treasure" of your choosing. It could be a snack, a favorite drink, or another small treat of some sort. Mark the path with steps along the way.

3. **Writing prompts as landmarks:** Each step on the map represents a writing prompt or idea related to your novel. For example: *The Hidden Village:* Write a short paragraph describing a village that no one knows about in your story. *The Secret Weapon:* Create a unique object your protagonist uses to defeat the bad guy. *The Unexpected Ally:* Describe the character who unexpectedly helps your main character.

4. **Set a timer:** Set a timer for 20–30 minutes. Then roll one die and move your penny or action figure the appropriate number of steps. Read the writing prompt, then write until the timer goes off.

5. **Continue to travel:** Use your treasure map as a fun distraction whenever you feel the urge to check social media or something similar.
6. **Celebrate the treasure:** When you complete the journey and reach the treasure, reward yourself with your chosen treat. This helps reinforce the positive association between "fun" and "writing," and shows how enjoyable it can be to focus and ignore distractions.
7. **Play again!** If you like, change the writing prompts you used and play again!

twelve
the overdoer

BASIC FEAR: *If I don't keep everything under control and do it all myself, I'll fail or let everyone down.*
BASIC DESIRE: *I want to feel valued and accomplished by doing everything I can for everyone.*
SUPEREGO MESSAGE: *You are only worthy if you're constantly productive and taking care of everything.*

YOU HAVE no problem working hard—you're constantly on the go, getting it all done. Your friends would probably say you're one of the busiest people they know. So, how do you end up procrastinating?

At first, it doesn't make sense. You tackle new projects all the time and see them through to completion, except for in one area. For you, that area is writing. You procrastinate because you have too many other things to do. You're overwhelmed, really, trying to juggle it all. With a million priorities competing for your attention, writing feels like just another task on an already endless "to-do" list.

One of your biggest struggles is setting boundaries. You take on way too many responsibilities, whether you can handle them or not. When someone asks you to do something, the word "no" feels foreign. You know what your priorities are—writing is likely one of them—but you don't act accordingly.

You may dream of taking time off to relax, but when you manage it, you feel guilty. In truth, you lack real self-discipline. Surprising, isn't it? You feel like you're constantly disciplining yourself to stay on task, yet when it comes to your personal needs, you neglect them. You wear yourself out, ignore your health, and still push yourself to meet everyone else's expectations. The discipline you need to care for yourself and your writing dreams is missing.

Underneath it all, you may be struggling with low self-esteem. You equate being "busy" with being valuable. It bothers you that your dreams are withering away, but you don't want to disappoint others. And maybe, deep down, you fear that if you did make time for writing, it wouldn't be that good anyway. Then what? Better to stay busy doing all the little things that others value than to risk failure at something that truly matters to you.

Key Characteristics of the Overdoer

As an Overdoer, you may find that one or more of these habits and characteristics sound familiar:

- **Chronic helper:** You are always quick to lend a hand, which is admirable in one way, but not when it requires you to put your dreams, priorities, and needs on the back burner.
- **Difficulty saying "no":** Because you like to help and hate to disappoint people, you rarely if ever tell anyone "no." This leaves you frequently overscheduled and overwhelmed with all you have to do.
- **Compulsive doer:** You are often pulled in multiple directions, juggling personal, professional, and creative commitments, which prevents you from dedicating focused time to your writing.
- **Constant busyness as a badge:** You may not admit it, but you take pride in staying busy all the time. You find

validation in being consistently occupied. "Look how much I do!" you may secretly say to yourself. All this "doing" makes you feel worthwhile, even if your productivity has nothing to do with your writing.

- **Reluctance to delegate:** Your friends and family may have witnessed your exhaustion and suggested you delegate some of your tasks to others, but you have a hard time doing that. You feel like you need to do everything yourself to ensure it's done "right."
- **Difficulty prioritizing:** With so many competing tasks in your life, you may find it hard to decide which ones are most important. As a result, writing might end up at the bottom of the list.
- **Guilt-driven workload:** Even when you know you're overloaded, you still feel guilty if you're not constantly busy. You may see writing as "selfish" or "indulgent," making it easy for you to procrastinate so you can pursue other more "productive" or "practical" pursuits.

Strengths of the Overdoer

Your biggest strength is your powerful combination of energy, dedication, and perseverance in everything you do. You are known for getting things done, possess a strong work ethic, and are committed to excellence. You are probably highly organized and can create detailed plans that help you manage a variety of tasks well while keeping track of all the essential details.

You may also have a deep sense of responsibility. Your motivation comes from a genuine desire to help other people, making you a valued member of various groups. In summary, you are a powerhouse of "get-it-done" ability, but it's often at risk because of your tendency to overextend yourself.

Challenges for the Overdoer

Your biggest challenge lies in your inability to set boundaries and prioritize your goals. You feel obligated to meet others' needs and expectations, often to the detriment of your creative pursuits. You fill your schedule with tasks that may be valuable to others but leave little time for writing.

You may also struggle with a desire for perfection and control. If you think that no one else can do things as well as you can—or that they *won't* do those things for some reason—you will hesitate to delegate tasks or let others step in to take some things off your plate.

You may also suffer from burnout and guilt. When you manage to snatch a little time for writing, you may feel guilty for "indulging" in your own creative pursuits rather than doing something for someone else, which you may see as more "productive."

The Overdoer's Limiting Beliefs

- **If I'm not constantly busy, I'm not valuable or productive.** You will likely equate your self-worth with how much you can accomplish in a day. This may lead you to fill your time with countless tasks, regardless of their relevance to your personal goals.
- **My own projects aren't as important as what others need from me.** You may view your personal goals, including your writing goals, as "selfish" or less valid compared to the goals of others.
- **My writing can wait until everything else is taken care of.** You believe you can get everything else done and *then* tend to your own goals. But with your ever-growing to-do list, that rarely happens, leaving your creative projects perpetually on hold.

Coping Techniques for the Overdoer Procrastinator

1. **Commit to a Daily "Write-First" Ritual:** If you follow no other rule, this one will help you make great progress! It's time to put what *you* want *first* in your day. Get up thirty or even fifteen minutes earlier and write before doing anything else. Don't check your cell phone. Don't even get dressed if you don't have to. Get up, sit down, open up your computer or notebook, and write until your time's up.

2. **Conduct a Weekly Task-Thinning Ritual:** Once a week, sit down with your to-do list and pick at least three non-essential tasks to eliminate or delegate. The goal is to free up some time for both writing and self-care. You can make it fun by giving yourself "points" for each to-do item you get rid of, then giving yourself a reward when you reach 25 points, or whatever total you like.

3. **Make a Reverse To-Do List:** Each morning, in addition to listing what you *have* to do, make a list of what you'll choose *not* to do so you can have more time. Perhaps you will *not* do the dishes today because you've delegated them to someone else. Or maybe you will *not* mow the lawn, as you've hired someone to do it. Regularly doing this exercise can get you into the habit of cutting things out that you don't really *have* to do as often as you do them.

4. **Set Three Priorities:** Take a weekend morning or evening to set three priorities for the upcoming week—things that matter most to you. Make writing one of them. Next, set three priorities for the month. Again, include writing or a writing-related task. Finally, set three priorities for the year. A year from now, what do you want to have accomplished? Define those goals and commit to them.

5. **Practice Saying "No":** Usually, when we don't want to do something, we spend way too much time explaining why we can't, leaving room for debate. Instead, just say, "No." At most, "I'm sorry, no," or "I'm sorry, I can't," and leave it at that. If the other person pushes back, listen until they're

143

done, then repeat, "I'm sorry, I can't." Practice setting boundaries for yourself and honoring what you need!

6. **Accomplishment Reflection:** At least once a week, sit down and list everything you accomplished on the left side of a sheet of paper. Then, draw a line down the middle and, on the right, write "yes" or "no" in response to this question: *Will this matter 10 years from now?* It's okay if some tasks have a "no" next to them, but if every answer is "no," it's time to reassess your priorities. Make sure you're including tasks that truly matter, like writing your book!

7. **Value-Based Journaling:** Spend some time once a day for seven days, focusing on your core values and what brings meaning to your life. Use a journal to record what you hope to have accomplished by the time you turn 80 years old. Are your daily actions aligning with those desires? You can also reflect on how you're doing each day, in terms of making sure you spend time on your priorities as well as everyone else's.

8. **Celebrate Non-Busy Moments:** If you typically feel guilty when you get some time off, it's time to turn those feelings around. Make a conscious effort to celebrate those moments of stillness or relaxation as achievements! Try creating a "relaxation jar" where you drop in a coin, marble, sticky note, or M&M every time you manage to carve a little time out of your day to write or relax. Watch the jar to see if it's filling up like it should or if you need to schedule more downtime.

9. **Replace "But" with "And":** You may typically say something like, "I want to work on my book, but I told my friend I'd go to the meeting." Start changing the "but" to an "and" so you say, "I want to work on my book and I told my friend I'd go to the meeting." This gives you two issues you need to contend with rather than pitting the two against one another. Take it one step further by adding a "so" statement to resolve the problem. For example: "I want to work on my book and I told my friend I'd go to the

meeting." Then add something like, "So I'll go to the café after the meeting and write for 30 minutes there." This may help you with this immediate problem, while gradually allowing you to start matching your words with your actions.

10. **The Approval-Free Challenge:** Create a 30-day challenge where you intentionally engage in activities or make decisions that are entirely your own without seeking approval or input from others. One day, you might say "no" to someone who asks you to do something. Another day, you could make an important decision by putting yourself first, rather than asking others what they think. Try taking a day off for your own self-care, declining an invitation so you can work on your story, or picking up a non-productive hobby that makes you happy.

Who the Overdoer Can Become: The Balanced Creator

When you're at your best, you become the Balanced Creator. You embrace productivity and self-care, setting appropriate boundaries and prioritizing your writing alongside other commitments.

THE OVERDOER'S BEST SELF

- **Focused Guardian:** You protect your time and energy by setting clear priorities and boundaries. You recognize the value of distinguishing between what truly matters and what doesn't, allowing you to balance responsibilities with personal goals.
- **Compassionate Cheerleader:** You embrace self-acceptance and practice compassion toward yourself. You recognize that your self-worth is not tied solely to your output or productivity, allowing you to engage in creative activities without being afraid of being judged or criticized.

- **Purposeful Achiever:** You use your ability to get things done in a healthier manner that aligns with your personal values and well-being. You focus your energy on activities that bring you joy, meaning, and fulfillment.

In this best version, you use your strengths to help others and yourself, getting the little things done and the big things, too.

Action Plan for the Overdoer Procrastinator

Your attachment to busyness is holding you back. It's time to get in touch with your self-worth as a human being so you can allow yourself to devote your energy to those projects that matter most to you.

It begins when you give up on the idea that you can do it all—everything everyone else needs you to do and your creative work, too. You understand that to reach your writing goals, you have to make room for your passion projects in your schedule. Further, you must learn to value downtime, daydreaming time, and "selfish" time to seek out inspiration that sparks your creativity.

Below, I have a sample action plan for the Overdoer procrastination type to complete a novel. If you have a different project in mind—such as creating a new website, starting a blog or YouTube channel, or growing your newsletter audience—you can adapt the plan to fit your goal. The steps will likely be similar, as they're tailored to your specific type.

STEP 1: ESTABLISH A CLEAR VISION

Challenge to Overcome: *It's difficult to choose a direction because I'm overwhelmed by all the tasks on my list.*

Your bulging to-do list leaves you with little time to figure out what this novel will be. So give yourself a weekend to think about it. If you have several ideas, write them all down and determine which one you want to pursue for the next year or so.

Next, craft a detailed outline of the novel, if you like. If you don't like to outline, try creating a vision board. Either way, having some sort of path laid out for yourself will help you to make progress even when you only have short periods in which to write.

STEP 2: SET REALISTIC DAILY GOALS

Challenge to Overcome: *I have too much to do!*

Break your writing schedule down into achievable daily goals. You tend to bite off more than you can chew, so it's best to set smaller goals than you think you should. Maybe you write 500 words on some days, but only 250 on others. You could finish a scene or a chapter per day.

Give yourself bigger goals on some days and smaller ones on others so you can be flexible with your schedule. The main thing is to get some writing done on most days—defeat procrastination!

STEP 3: CREATE A DEDICATED WRITING SPACE

Challenge to Overcome: *Too many commitments keep my thoughts racing.*

Take some time to ensure your writing space helps you get away from it all. You need a place free of distractions and reminders of your endless to-do list.

If you don't have an extra room to dedicate to this purpose, try to section off an area somehow. (You can use drapes, foldable room dividers, or other pieces of furniture.) Then, fill it with things that inspire you, like books, art, and motivational quotes.

STEP 4: DECIDE HOW YOU'RE GOING TO ASK FOR HELP

Challenge to Overcome: *I have to do everything myself, so I have no time to write.*

Decide now how you will scratch some things off your to-do list by asking for help. Can your family members assist with home chores and other activities, at least on some days? Are there tasks at work you can offload so you can get home on time? Can someone else take over one of your community responsibilities for a few weeks? Might you hire a babysitter to watch the kids two afternoons a week so you can write?

Step 5: Go On Inspiration Dates

Challenge to Overcome: *When I finally do sit down to write, I'm exhausted.*

You may have trouble writing when it's time because you're so tired from everything else you've been doing. Try to schedule at least two "inspiration" dates per month. Give yourself at least an hour to do something that inspires you.

Maybe you go to a concert or museum, take a walk by a river or lake, enjoy a long drive in the country, or get lost in a library or bookstore. Choose an activity that helps you feel more relaxed, but that also taps into your creative side so the next time you sit down to write, your muse is ready to go.

Step 6: Prioritize Your Tasks

Challenge to Overcome: *Everything is urgent and important.*

In your writing life as well as in life in general, you can get bogged down with everything that needs to be done. You can't do everything at once, so use the Eisenhower Matrix to help determine what needs to be done *now*.

This productivity tool is named after former President Dwight D. Eisenhower, because he once quoted Dr. J. Roscoe Miller's proclamation: "I have two kinds of problems: the urgent and the important. The urgent are not important, and the important are never urgent." (Dr. James Roscoe Miller was the twelfth president of Northwestern University, serving from 1949 to 1970.)

To use this tool, draw two intersecting lines on a piece of paper to create four equal quadrants. The X-axis (horizontal) represents urgency, and the Y-axis (vertical) represents importance.

That means the top left quadrant will show you tasks that are both urgent and important (do them now), while the top right houses important but not urgent tasks (schedule a time to do them). At the bottom left you have tasks that are not important but urgent (can you delegate them?), and on the bottom right are those that are neither urgent nor important (delete or eliminate these if you can).

Fill in your quadrants with everything on your to-do list, including the tasks necessary to reach your writing goals. When you're done, you should have a clearer idea of what you need to do next, and what can be set aside for now.

STEP 7: INCORPORATE ACCOUNTABILITY

Challenge to Overcome: *I have to spend my time on what others need.*

You may struggle to stay committed to your writing goals because you feel that others always want you to do be doing things that benefit them. It's time to find a writing buddy—either locally or online—who can help you get your writing done. Schedule regular check-ins where you can share your progress and challenges with this person. Having someone else check in can also help you balance your priorities with those of others in your life.

The Most Important Thing for Overdoers to Remember

If I were to pick one thing that you must remember as an Overdoer procrastinator, it's this: *Your worth is not tied to how much you accomplish for others.*

In the past, you may have believed that only what you did for others "counted"—that your own creative endeavors weren't worth much. You absolutely must divorce yourself from that belief, as all does is hold you back.

True fulfillment comes not from endless doing, but from directing your energy toward what genuinely matters. I hope you will focus on fewer, more purposeful tasks—like finishing your novel—which will give you the space you need to truly thrive and find joy in your accomplishments.

Exercise: The "Essentials Only" Jar

It's time to practice prioritizing only the most meaningful tasks for a set period. The idea is to help yourself learn to let go of "doing it all."

What You'll Need:

- A small jar labeled "Essentials Only"
- Slips of paper or sticky notes
- A pen

Steps:

1. **Write down all your current tasks:** Spend 5–10 minutes listing everything you need to accomplish in the coming week. Include tasks like finishing the next chapter of your story, writing a character sketch, or outlining your novel, along with everyday responsibilities such as grocery shopping, paying bills, cleaning the house, and taking the kids to school.
2. **Select three essentials:** Choose three tasks from the list that are essential to making progress on your writing goals and living your life in general. Write each of these on

separate slips of paper or sticky notes and place them in the "Essentials" jar.

3. **Commit to a "one-week essentials" challenge:** For the next week, focus on completing the three chosen tasks and ignore, delay, or delegate any non-essential tasks.
4. **Celebrate your wins:** When you complete one of the "Essentials" tasks related to writing, take the slip out of the jar and celebrate with something fun like a coffee break or dinner out.
5. **Reflect on what's left:** At the end of the week, review the other uncompleted tasks from your initial list—those that were not essential. Did leaving them undone impact you as much as you expected?

thirteen
the guilty

BASIC FEAR: *I've already wasted too much time, and it's too late to make up for it.*
BASIC DESIRE: *I want to feel like I'm finally rectifying all my past mistakes and moving forward.*
SUPEREGO MESSAGE: *I should be doing more to make up for everything I've neglected—anything less is failing.*

OH, if only you could have done better!

You are a writer who constantly feels the heavy burden of procrastination. You don't just procrastinate—you carry the weight of your guilt for not getting your work done. Your thoughts are filled with regret and self-reproach for what you see as your failure. Yet, despite your recriminations, you struggle to break this difficult habit.

You have an internalized sense of responsibility to your work, as well as a healthy ambition to take your talent as far as you can. You'd think these characteristics would lead to success—and they could—except for the paralyzing cycle of procrastination that grips you.

Here's how it goes: You procrastinate on a project. Instead of forgiving yourself and starting fresh next time, you blame and criticize yourself. Rather than motivating you to get the work done, your guilt

153

only worsens the problem, making it even more likely that you'll delay writing again.

Deep down, you believe you've already wasted too much time and that it's too late to make up for lost ground. You're too hard on yourself and often feel inadequate. Even when you do sit down to write, you struggle to focus because you're preoccupied with thoughts of how you should have started sooner or done better in the past.

You may also frequently compare yourself to other writers. When you see them achieving milestones in their careers, it makes you feel even guiltier. This, in turn, can increase your procrastination, reinforcing the idea that you'll never be able to catch up, so why try?

To break out of this vicious cycle, you must forgive yourself for past shortcomings and find a way to make a fresh start. If you can develop a more forward-looking mindset instead of constantly dwelling on the past, you'll be more likely to make progress. Ultimately, you must learn to show yourself more compassion and focus on what you can do today to reclaim your creative confidence.

Key Characteristics of the Guilty

As a Guilty, you may find that one or more of these habits and characteristics sound familiar:

- **Overwhelming self-criticism:** You harshly judge yourself for not writing enough or missing deadlines. Your inner dialogue is filled with self-reproach, making it difficult to move forward because you think you've already failed.
- **Fixation on the past:** You tend to dwell on past mistakes, missed opportunities, and unfinished projects. You often replay scenarios in your mind where you should have been more productive, trapping yourself in a loop of regret.
- **Paralyzing sense of responsibility:** You have a strong sense of responsibility when it comes to your writing goals. You may feel like you're letting yourself or others down by not meeting your deadlines. This heightened pressure can paralyze you, making it harder to sit down and be creative.

- **Comparison to others:** If you see another writer accomplish something, that may bring up your feelings of guilt all over again, or make those feelings stronger. Seeing others succeed reminds you of where you're falling short, making it hard to focus solely on your own journey.
- **Perfectionism with a guilt twist:** Even when you do get some writing done, you tend to feel guilty for not meeting your high standards of productivity or output. If you write five pages, you'll tell yourself it's not enough—you should have written ten.
- **Emotional exhaustion:** The constant cycle of guilt and regret wears you down emotionally. You are likely to feel drained, and this lack of energy can be another factor encouraging future procrastination.
- **Fear of starting again:** You often dread sitting down to write, fearing the words will confirm your worst suspicions —that you've fallen too far behind or lost your touch. This is especially true when working on a long story, like a novel. If you return to it and realize you've forgotten something, it can make you even less likely to start again.

Strengths of the Guilty

Your biggest strength is your deep sense of responsibility and duty. When it comes to your writing, you care deeply about its quality and potential significance. You want to create something meaningful and impactful, and may see your work not just as a creative outlet but a reflection of your values and ideals.

You are also likely to have an introspective nature that encourages reflection. You often think about your progress and strive to correct your mistakes. This strength can make you skilled at editing and revising your work if you can get to that stage.

Challenges for the Guilty

You struggle with a paralyzing sense of unworthiness, feeling as though you can never do enough or be good enough. This can create a cycle of inaction, where instead of writing, you become consumed by negative thoughts about your past failures. The weight of this emotional burden can make it difficult for you to start a project, let alone see it through to the end.

Another challenge is overcompensation. You constantly try to make up for lost time or past mistakes by pushing yourself too hard. This can lead to burnout, as you may set unrealistic expectations for yourself. You also fear disappointing others, which may drive you to take on too much, making writing feel more like a punishment than a fun, creative outlet.

The Guilty's Limiting Beliefs

- **I don't deserve success because I haven't worked hard enough.** You don't feel you've "earned" the right to achieve your writing goals. Because you've procrastinated, you don't feel worthy of recognition.
- **My past mistakes define me, and I'll never get past them.** Your guilt over previous failures or unfinished projects may make you believe that you're trapped in the past. You see every setback as evidence that you'll continue to fall short.
- **I've disappointed others, and I can't make up for it.** You often feel a strong sense of responsibility to others, including readers, loved ones, and mentors. You may believe that by procrastinating, you've let them down and that no matter how much you achieve in the future, it won't erase their disappointment.

Coping Techniques for the Guilty Procrastinator

1. **Create a "Redemption List":** Instead of focusing on past mistakes and failures, start keeping a running list of your accomplishments. Consider getting a journal and using it each night to record your progress. Any time you complete a writing task—no matter how small—add it to your list. This helps remind you that you're actively making up for lost ground.

2. **Write a Forgiveness Letter:** To release your guilt, you need a ritual. It's not something you can just "think" about and be done with it. Start by writing a letter to yourself. Acknowledge your guilt, what makes you feel guilty, and how you think you've let yourself or others down. When you've exhausted your feelings, allow yourself to let go of that guilt. You may want to crumple up the letter and burn it, or attach it to a balloon and let it go.

3. **Set "Good Enough" Deadlines:** Instead of constantly punishing yourself for your "inadequacies," focus on steady progress by setting "good enough" deadlines. You don't have to have your entire novel done in 30 days. Instead, give yourself some slack. Three chapters in thirty days will be great if you make it happen!

4. **Turn Guilt Into Gratitude:** Whenever you start feeling guilty about procrastinating, intentionally shift your energy by creating a quick gratitude list. Grab a piece of paper and jot down five things you're grateful for that you've already achieved or learned. Even if you haven't written in a while, you can focus on the fact that you're still passionate about your project and that you have the opportunity to work on it when you're ready.

5. **Implement a "Guilt-Free" Zone:** Try to make your writing space a "guilt-free" zone. When you sit in your writing chair, you are not allowed to think about when you procrastinated before or about how much you haven't gotten done. When you're in that chair in your writing

nook, you only have to focus on the writing task before you, without judgment.

6. **Write in Short, Guilt-Free Bursts:** Rather than trying to meet your high standards of completing a whole project in one writing session (to make up for some past inadequacy), set a timer for just 10 or 15 minutes. While the clock is ticking, focus solely on the scene you're writing. Don't worry about quality or quantity. When the timer goes off, congratulate yourself for making progress and go on with your day.

7. **Visualize Finishing for Joy, Not Obligation:** You may procrastinate because you see your writing as a chore or obligation. You might feel that you owe it to yourself or someone else to get it done or that you *have* to get it done for some pressing reason. As a result, sitting down to write can feel like dragging yourself by the scruff of the neck to your chair. Counteract all this heavy sense of responsibility with something new—a sense of joy. You started writing because you enjoyed it, right? Let's get back to that feeling. Take five minutes before writing to imagine how happy you'll be when you finish your story. You might also put up sticky notes or pictures that help you reconnect with the joy of writing. Write messages like, "This is fun!" or "Can't wait to see what happens!" and tape them to the wall.

8. **Create a Fun Guilt Jar:** Right now, guilt is your go-to emotion when it comes to your writing, and it's fueling your procrastination habit. That means you need to become more aware of when you're feeling guilty, then stop and turn it around. One way to do this is by creating a "guilt jar." Set a big glass jar somewhere visible and gather a bunch of small, fun kids' toys, like the kind you'd find at a party store. Look for things like googly-eyed creatures, spinning tops, or toys that make funny noises. Every time you feel guilty or catch yourself thinking about how you've "failed again," drop one of those toys into the jar. The idea is that each moment of guilt contributes to a jar of laughter. Once

the jar is full, celebrate! Throw a party with your kids, friends, or anyone you like. Dump out the toys and share silly stories about them. You could even hide them and give out prizes to those who find the most. Turn your guilt into a source of fun.

9. **Pump Up the Self-Compassion and Forgiveness:** Guilt and self-criticism go together. You feel guilty for failing to live up to your intentions and criticize yourself for it, adding more negativity to the mix. The fix for this is self-compassion. Next time you're feeling guilty, counteract your negative self-talk with statements like these: *It's okay to feel this way. Let it go and try again.* Or, *I know you're struggling with this. It's okay. You're going to get it next time.* Here's something to consider: In a study of 119 university students, researchers found that those who practiced self-forgiveness after procrastinating on studying for their first exam were less likely to procrastinate on the next one. In other words, forgiving yourself for procrastinating can actually help break the cycle and reduce the chances of it happening again.

10. **Reframe Your Guilty Thoughts:** Anytime you think a guilty thought, take a moment to reframe it. Here are some examples: a) Change "I should have finished my chapter by now" to "I'm taking steps to write my chapter and I can make progress on it right now." b) Change "I haven't been writing as much as I should, and I feel so behind" to "I've taken breaks to recharge, and that's part of my creative process. I can start writing again today." c) Change "I let my guilt get the better of me again—I'm such a failure" to "I'm working to overcome my guilty feelings, but it takes time. Today, I can redirect my focus to being present with my writing."

Who the Guilty Can Become: The Unashamed Hustler

When you're at your best, you become the Unashamed Hustler. You take pride in your ability to work hard and commit fully to your responsibilities, while also cultivating a new sense of self-compassion and forgiveness.

THE GUILTY'S BEST SELF

- **Focused and Purposeful:** You are clear about your goals and driven by a sense of purpose. You channel your energy into productive writing sessions and prioritize progress so that even when you don't reach your goals, you're ready to get back into it again the next time.
- **Self-Compassionate:** You know that mistakes and setbacks are part of the creative process. You don't dwell on these but allow yourself to learn from your experiences so you can move forward.
- **Future-Oriented Achiever:** You resist focusing on the past and turn your thoughts to the present and future. You've learned to let go of the past so you can finally enjoy your writing time.

In this best version, you use your strengths to work hard without allowing guilt to get in the way.

Action Plan for the Guilty Procrastinator

Your attachment to guilt is holding you back. It's time to get in touch with your self-compassion so you can reconnect with the joy of writing.

It begins when you give up on the idea that you can make up for all your past mistakes. You understand that to reach your writing goals, you have to let go of the past and forgive yourself. Further, you must learn to value "good enough" so that you stop your painful cycle of procrastination and self-recrimination.

Below, I have a sample action plan for the Guilty procrastination type to finish a novel. If you have a different project in mind—such as creating a new website, starting a blog or YouTube channel, or growing your newsletter audience—you can adapt the plan to fit your goal. The steps will likely be similar, as they're tailored to your specific type.

STEP 1: NAME YOUR INNER CRITIC

Challenge to Overcome: *I'm weighed down by self-blame and negative inner dialogue.*

Give your inner critic—the one who always reminds you of your failures and makes you feel guilty—a name. Try something silly like "Grumpy Greg" or "Critical Cara." Every time you hear the voice bringing you down, visualize this silly character and tell her to lighten up or go away.

This can help reduce the critic's emotional power over you. It also creates some distance between you and this negative part of you.

STEP 2: CREATE A "FORGIVENESS RITUAL"

Challenge to Overcome: *I feel too guilty to move forward.*

Set up a fun ritual at the end of every writing session to release guilt. You could do a silly dance to symbolize shedding past mistakes.

Or write down any supposed past mistakes on a piece of paper, fold it into a paper airplane, and send it across the room. Use your imagination. The goal is to do something "active" that symbolizes forgiving yourself.

STEP 3: SET PLAYFUL CHALLENGES

Challenge to Overcome: *I feel like whatever I do is never enough.*

Create a writing challenge to finish your chapter or word count for the day, even if it's terrible. If you think it's going badly, lean into that and make it even worse.

Have fun with it—go crazy. Make the plot ridiculous, the characters unbearably dull, and the setting completely absurd. If you allow yourself to play with it, you'll loosen up your creative blocks and be better able to write as you want the next time.

STEP 4: REWARD THE HARD DAYS

Challenge to Overcome: *I don't deserve any rewards because of my past mistakes.*

On those days when you feel particularly stuck or tempted to procrastinate, promise yourself a reward if you simply sit down and write—anything. It doesn't matter what you write, only that you write. Make the reward something that excites you—a great meal, a long walk, a fun movie, or a favorite treat.

STEP 5: USE GUILT AS A FUEL (WHEN NEEDED)

Challenge to Overcome: *Guilt paralyzes me.*

Try to turn your guilt into motivation to write. Tell yourself something like, "I've felt guilty long enough. Let's put that energy into writing today." Guilt can be draining, but reframing it as fuel may give you with a burst of focus when needed.

STEP 6: WRITE UP A "GUILT-FREE DRAFT" AGREEMENT

Challenge to Overcome: *My guilt keeps me from getting over the rough patches.*

Writing a novel is like going on a long journey. There will be rough spots along the way. In the past, your guilt kept you from pushing through them. It's time to change that.

Make a formal agreement with yourself that your first draft doesn't have to make up for all your past mistakes or failures. All that matters is moving forward and getting it done.

Promise yourself that you will not allow guilt to stop you. Set a deadline for finishing the novel, and when you falter, re-read this agreement and start over again.

STEP 7: BREAK THE NOVEL INTO FRESH SECTIONS

Challenge to Overcome: *As guilt compounds day by day, I eventually give up.*

To stop guilt from piling up and weighing you down, break your novel into smaller, "fresh" sections or scenes. Treat each one as if it were a new beginning. Bring that energy to each new section. This helps you let go of past struggles and procrastination and approach each writing session with a clean slate.

The Most Important Thing for Guilty Procrastinators to Remember

If I were to pick one thing that you must remember as a Guilty procrastinator, it's this: *Every day is a fresh start, and past procrastination doesn't define your future progress.*

In the past, you may have believed that you had to make up for all your past failures before you could move forward. You absolutely must divorce yourself from that belief, as all it's doing is holding you back from making real progress today.

I hope is that you will show yourself more compassion and forgiveness, which will empower you to gradually limit procrastination's hold over you so you can experience the joy of finishing your project. Give it a try. You may find that self-compassion isn't as difficult as you think!

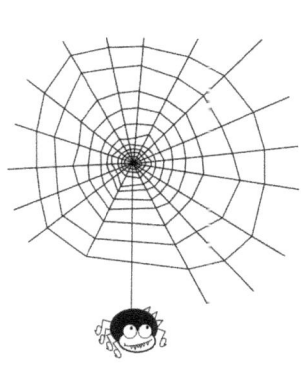

Exercise: The "Daily Win" Notebook

IT'S TIME TO FOCUS MORE ON YOUR WINS THAN YOUR LOSSES. This exercise can help.

WHAT YOU'LL NEED:

- A special notebook in which to record your "wins"
- Markers, stickers, or anything you like to decorate the notebook

STEPS:

1. **Set a daily writing goal:** Set a modest daily writing goal, such as writing 300 words or spending 20 minutes working on your novel.
2. **Create a "win" list:** Every time you reach your writing goal, record it in your "wins" notebook. Make it fun by using your markers and stickers, or if enjoy drawing, decorate the page to celebrate your accomplishment. Treat your time in this journal as a small reward for getting your writing done.
3. **Forgive and hustle:** At the end of each day, take a moment to review your wins list. Instead of thinking about what you didn't get done, look at what you *did* accomplish. Say out loud, "I forgive myself for past mistakes, and today, I'm proud of this win!"
4. **Keep adding to your wins:** As you fill up your wins notebook, regularly review all the progress you've made. Doing this often enough will help shift your focus from guilt to pride, and you'll want to keep the momentum going.

fourteen
the disorganized

BASIC FEAR: *No matter how hard I try, everything always feels like a chaotic mess, and I'll never be able to pull it all together.*
BASIC DESIRE: *I just want to feel like everything is in order and in control.*
SUPEREGO MESSAGE: *I can't succeed because I lack structure and organization.*

NOW, *where was that file? I was going to work on that story today. Let's see . . .*

As a Disorganized procrastinator, your main issue is your, ahem . . . disorganization. You may struggle with managing your writing space, writing tools, and files, or you may find it hard to manage your time, tasks, and ideas, losing track of what you were working on and what you need to do next.

Your problems with organization result in procrastination when you have to waste time preparing your workspace or files when you'd rather be writing. You may get caught up in "busy work" like cleaning your desk, putting your story files in order, or updating your idea list, to the detriment of your most important work: writing your stories all the way to "the end."

Your procrastination may also stem from your resistance to "dealing with the mess" waiting for you on your desk, your computer, or in your daily schedule in general. To fit writing into your busy life, you have to organize your time, and that may be what's stopping you.

Long stories, like novels, also need organization. Without some sort of system, you may forget important plot points or lose sight of your overall narrative structure. You may feel like you're always playing catch-up, which can cause you to procrastinate just to avoid dealing with it. Interestingly, procrastination and disorganization feed off each other. When you put off work on a project, your tasks pile up and become disorganized. When you're disorganized, it's easy to put off your work to organize things instead. The two together create a vicious cycle that builds a wall between you and your dreams.

Key Characteristics of the Disorganized

As a Disorganized, you may find that one or more of these habits and characteristics sound familiar:

- **Chaotic workflow:** You have trouble maintaining a clear structure in your writing process and/or writing space. Your ideas, notes, and drafts may be scattered across different platforms or spaces, making it difficult to locate critical information when needed.
- **Lack of time management:** You may struggle with completing your work if you lack a set schedule or writing routine. You might jump between writing projects without finishing any, or feel overwhelmed when your tasks pile up around you.
- **Avoidance:** Your disorganization becomes a source of stress for you. Rather than confronting it, you may avoid the problem entirely.
- **Difficulty prioritizing:** Without clear organization, you're likely to have trouble distinguishing between high-priority and low-priority tasks. Everything may seem equally urgent

or overwhelming, which can cause you to spend time on less important details while neglecting major writing goals.

- **Overcomplicated systems:** Ironically, because you know you're disorganized, you may create overly complex systems to try to get organized, yet later discover those systems are too hard to maintain. You might try new apps or software programs or invest in a variety of planners without a cohesive strategy, which could result in more chaos rather than less.
- **Impulsive task switching:** Because of your disorganization, you may frequently switch from one task to another, driven by sudden impulses rather than a structured plan. This makes it hard to build any sort of progress on one particular project and makes it nearly impossible to complete a novel.
- **Emotional clutter:** Clutter in your outer world can become clutter in your mental world. If you feel overwhelmed by your tasks and projects, you may also start to struggle with self-doubt and anxiety about your ability to make your writing dreams come true. This emotional overwhelm also leads to a cycle of avoidance and stress.

Strengths of the Disorganized

One of your biggest strengths is your ability to come up with innovative ideas and unconventional solutions. You tend to embrace chaos, which leads to an ability to think outside the box and perhaps even to come up with creative breakthroughs that more organized thinkers may have overlooked. This can inspire originality in your writing, resulting in imaginative stories with fresh perspectives.

You may also be an avid explorer that thrives on spontaneity. Without the need for a rigid plan, you may thrive in environments where structure is minimal and enjoy a more relaxed approach to your writing process that fosters a sense of playfulness.

Challenges for the Disorganized

One of your biggest challenges is your inability to maintain a structured approach to your writing projects. Without a clear plan or timeline, you may become overwhelmed by everything you need to do. This can lead to procrastination, because you just don't know where to start.

You also struggle with a tendency to shift between different tasks, preventing you from fully immersing yourself in a story. This constant switching interrupts your flow and leads to missed deadlines or incomplete work. Trying to prioritize tasks is also hard for you. Without clearly defined priorities, you may end up spending your precious time on tasks that don't really matter while neglecting the ones that would actually move your writing career forward.

Finally, disorganization can lead to a negative self-image, leaving you feeling like you're always behind and unable to keep up.

The Disorganized's Limiting Beliefs

- **I'm just not an organized person; it's not in my nature.** You have a fixed mindset about your abilities and may feel resigned to your disorganized habits, believing you can't change them.
- **Order will stifle my creativity.** You may believe that you can be creative only in a messy environment, so you resist any sort of improvements to your organization.
- **I have my own system of organization—I can find things when I need them.** You may fool yourself into believing you can find things when you need to, even though you just spent thirty minutes yesterday looking for your notes. Or you may think you can complete your story when you're ready, even though when you tried to work on it yesterday, you realized you'd forgotten what your antagonist was doing.

Coping Techniques for the Disorganized Procrastinator

1. **Use a Color-Coded System:** The best thing you can do for yourself is to create systems of organization that will work for you. Here's one to try: assign different colors to different types of writing tasks. Then, in your planner or digital task manager, use these colors to make it easier to locate what you need when it's time to write. Another idea is to use different colored sticky notes. Write down small, achievable goals on each one, then place them around your writing workspace. When you complete a task, remove the note and enjoy the space you've created!

2. **Practice Working "in the Mess":** If you start writing but then feel compelled to clean your desk or organize your files, try this: pause the cleaning impulse and write "in the mess" for five more minutes. If you get lost in the story, keep going! The idea is to practice moving forward on your project even in the midst of the disorganization so that it can no longer stop you. Your goal is not a clean desk but a finished story!

3. **Designate a Clutter-Free Zone:** Not everything in your life has to be perfectly organized and neat. You can make big improvements in your writing process by creating just one specific area where you can write without distractions—e.g., without clutter. Choose a corner of your desk or perhaps another area altogether where clutter is not allowed. Keep only the bare minimum here—a chair and computer. Then try to write there for 20 minutes at least three times a week.

4. **Prioritize Your Top Task:** Never mind trying to organize *all* your tasks. Just take a look at the next writing project you want to complete. Write down the next thing you must do on it, then make it one of your top priorities for the day or the coming week. This allows you to unload your worry about other tasks and projects. Focus on one project only and get that done. Let the rest go

5. **Create a Writing Template:** Templates can be lifesavers when it comes to staying organized. Develop a template for the different types of writing you do—perhaps a short story template, a blog template, or one for articles. Include sections for ideas, research notes, outlines, character profiles (if applicable), plot points, and other key details. Once you have your template, it will be easier to get started and follow through without losing track of what you're doing.

6. **Use Visual Organizers:** Look around and see what type of organizers appeal to you. Tools like mind maps, flowcharts, calendars, or simple lists can all help you organize your writing projects as well as your time. You don't have to use a type of organizer that someone else uses. Experiment with a variety of them until you find one that keeps you motivated and moving forward.

7. **Keep a "Disorganized Diary":** The purpose of this is to show you exactly how your disorganization may be derailing your writing progress. Choose a journal and log all of your disorganized moments at least three times a week. Note when you forgot where you put your short story file or misplaced critical notes about your next scene. Include how much time you wasted clearing your messy desk or what other small tasks distracted you from your writing. Try to stay consistent with this diary for at least a month, then go back and review what you wrote.

8. **Dedicate a Day to the Tiny Things:** Though you want to spend most of your writing time on your stories, there's no doubt that the little things can add up if you don't attend to them. If you're starting to feel overwhelmed by the chaos, set aside a weekend day to tackle it. Use that day to clear your desk, organize your files, update your writing tools, and take care of whatever else you need to do to feel good about starting fresh. Then, commit to having one of these days— perhaps every other month—to keep the clutter from piling too high.

9. **Make a "Doesn't Need to Be Organized" List:** Think about everything related to your writing process, focusing on the things you find disorganized. Maybe you have piles of files on your desk or sticky notes posted everywhere. Write it all down on a giant list. Then, take thirty minutes to determine which of these things is *not* slowing you down. Be careful! Make sure to consider any extra time you have to spend looking for things, or when your clutter pulls you away from your writing. It's likely that at least some of your disorganized habits don't need to change, freeing you up to focus on the areas that do need adjusting.

10. **Create a "No-Matter-What" Writing Schedule:** Even if writing is something you do on the side, it's probably one of the most important things in your life. You'll do yourself a favor if you set up a "no-matter-what" writing schedule— one that dictates when you will write, regardless of any other obligations. Even if your desk is cluttered and you can't find your files, you will sit down and write for 15–20 minutes on these days at these times. If you can commit to that and stick with it, you will make progress even amidst disorganization!

Who the Disorganized Can Become: The Creative Navigator

When you're at your best, you become the Creative Navigator. Instead of rigid organization, you go for flexible systems that accommodate bursts of inspiration while keeping your projects moving forward.

THE DISORGANIZED'S BEST SELF

- **Flexible Organizer:** You understand that traditional methods of organization may not work for you. Instead, you adopt a more flexible approach, using tools that integrate seamlessly into your creative process.

- **Embracing Chaos as Creativity:** You realize that disorganization is not *always* a hindrance, recognizing that chaos can sometimes lead to innovative ideas. You continue to experiment to determine when organization is critical to getting your projects done and when your natural disorganization can be a source of inspiration.
- **Prioritization Pro:** You work on setting clear priorities, focusing on your most critical tasks first, and letting the minor stuff go. You've learned to differentiate between what's urgent and what's important, allowing you to tackle your projects more systematically.

In this best version, you use your strengths to come up with unique ideas without slipping into disorganized overwhelm.

Action Plan for the Disorganized Procrastinator

Your attachment to disorganization is holding you back. It's time to find at least some sort of organization that can help you make progress on your stories.

It begins when you give up on the idea that you are "naturally" disorganized or can never learn to be organized. You understand that organization is a skill and that if you're willing to try different ways of doing it, you'll likely find one that works.

Below, I have a sample action plan for the Disorganized procrastination type to finish a novel. If you have a different project in mind—such as creating a new website, starting a blog or YouTube channel, or growing your newsletter audience—you can adapt the plan to fit your goal. The steps will likely be similar, as they're tailored to your specific type.

STEP 1: CREATE A VISUAL TIMELINE
Challenge to Overcome: *I lack organization in my story.*
Use a large piece of poster board or a digital tool like a mind-mapping

app. Start by drawing a horizontal line across the center to represent your story's timeline. Mark key events such as major plot points, character arcs, and significant occurrences along the line. Use different colors or symbols to distinguish character perspectives or subplots.

Below each key event, jot down brief notes or bullet points outlining the scenes or chapters that lead to or follow the event. Regularly revisit and adjust your timeline as your story develops. This method helps you maintain an organized view of your story while making it easy to adapt as new ideas emerge.

STEP 2: CREATE A CHAOS-FRIENDLY OUTLINE

Challenge to Overcome: *I struggle with rigid structures and detailed planning.*

Instead of a traditional outline, create a loose, flexible framework for your novel. Use broad chapter titles, vague plot points, or even random thoughts jotted down on sticky notes or in a notebook.

This outline will give you something to follow and help you keep track of where you are in the story while still allowing creative freedom and reducing the pressure to have everything perfectly organized from the start.

STEP 3: ENGAGE IN "MESSY SPRINT" WRITING SESSIONS

Challenge to Overcome: *I have to get everything in order before I start.*

The practice of trying to organize things before you start can rob you of your writing time. Instead, embrace the mess. Set a timer for 15–20 minutes and write as fast as you can.

Resist the urge to edit or polish. Just get the words down. This creates a sense of urgency that can cut through the disorganization and help you focus.

STEP 4: DESIGN A FLEXIBLE WORKSPACE SYSTEM

Challenge to Overcome: *This space has to be organized like most people do it.*

Don't try to create a perfectly clean workspace like an organized person would.

Instead, set up a flexible space where different areas of your desk or counter are dedicated to specific tasks—one corner for brainstorming, one for writing drafts, and one for editing, for example.

Pile any notes related to these tasks only in the designated areas so you can more easily find them when needed.

STEP 5: EMBRACE MID-NOVEL DISORGANIZATION

Challenge to Overcome: *I hate struggling with the difficult middle of the novel.*

When you reach the middle of the novel, which is notoriously difficult, embrace the disorganization by allowing yourself to write out of order. Pick a scene that excites you and work on that, even if it's not in the right place.

This can stoke your passion for the story and keep you from procrastinating while also contributing to your progress. What's important is that you get some writing done, no matter where it is in your story!

Later, go back and piece the sections together.

STEP 6: KEEP A "STORY IDEAS" FILE

Challenge to Overcome: *I forgot what I was doing on this story.*

Create a file or notebook for each story you're working on, and put everything related to that story in it. You may want to have both a digital file and a physical notebook, as the physical notebook often works better for jotting down ideas or mapping out storylines on the go.

If you get a sectioned notebook, you can label one section "Characters," another "Plot ideas," and another "Setting," etc. Another good section to include is "What's Next?" where you can write down your thoughts on what to tackle next after your writing session.

STEP 7: CREATE A "FINISHING TOUCHES" CHECKLIST

Challenge to Overcome: *I don't think I can get organized enough to finish the novel.*

As you near the end of your novel, create a checklist of all the final touches needed to complete it. This may include editing certain chapters, adding notes for future revisions, keeping a file of title ideas, and more.

Make the list work with your organization system so that you don't succumb to procrastination. You can color-code it if you like, using red for the most urgent tasks and orange for those that can wait. Cross each item off as you complete it so you can see your progress.

The Most Important Thing for Disorganized Procrastinators to Remember

If I were to pick one thing that you must remember as a Disorganized procrastinator, it's this: *You can make progress even if your approach is messy—taking small steps is still moving forward.*

In the past, you may have believed that you had to organize everything before you could write. You absolutely must divorce yourself from that belief, as all it's doing is holding you back.

I hope you will be willing to experiment and try different systems, and that you will allow yourself to learn the skill of organization. Don't worry, you can do it! You just need to embrace the type of organization that will work for you.

Be willing to experiment, and when you find it, you'll feel more empowered to avoid procrastination and restore the joy of writing in your life.

Exercise: Everyday Inspiration Hunt

IT'S TIME TO USE YOUR COMFORT WITH CHAOS TO YOUR advantage. Try this exercise to find new inspiration for a story or novel.

WHAT YOU'LL NEED:

- A stack of sticky notes or index cards
- A place to roam, like your house, a library, or a park

STEPS:

1. **Set a timer for 30 minutes.**
2. **Choose your path:** Decide where you will start and where you will end 30 minutes from now. Plot out your walk.
3. **Take notes:** As you move around the space, observe ordinary items—furniture, decorations, books, food, plants, people, pets, and more. Take a moment to really see them. What stories do they hold? What emotions do they evoke?
4. **Create inspiration prompts:** For each item that catches your eye, ask yourself a series of prompts to generate ideas. For example: *A Chair:* Who might sit there? Which of your characters? What secrets could that chair witness? *A Book:* What genre is it? How does its title or cover inspire a

character or plot twist? *A Pet:* Whose pet is it? What is the character's relationship to the pet? How does it shape the character's life? *A Plant or Tree:* When does the character see this tree? Does it hold some special meaning? Or does something terrible happen under this tree?

5. **Take notes:** Jot down your thoughts on the sticky notes or index cards for each item. Don't worry about writing perfectly—just let the ideas flow.

6. **Stack the pile:** Take your notes or index cards to your writing area. Review them one by one and start grouping them into categories based on similar ideas or themes. For example, some may apply to a certain character or group of characters. Some might be more specific to settings, and others for plot points. Some might fit into multiple categories or no category at all, and that's okay. It doesn't have to be "perfectly" organized.

7. **Make connections:** Once you have your categories, take a moment to analyze the connections. Are there any settings that could enhance your novel's setting? Are there characters that could be added to your plot? See where your ideas take you.

8. **Incorporate a "wild card:"** Choose one sticky note or card that seems completely out of place or unrelated. Challenge yourself to integrate that idea into your story. This can encourage creative thinking and lead to unexpected plot twists.

9. **Set a writing goal:** Based on your generated ideas, set a writing goal. This could be to finish a scene in your novel, expand on your outline, flesh out a character, or explore a new plot direction.

10. **Repeat as needed:** Whenever you feel stuck, revisit this exercise.

fifteen
the overthinker

BASIC FEAR: *I'm afraid I'll make the wrong decision and ruin everything.*
BASIC DESIRE: *I want to find the perfect solution before I take any action.*
SUPEREGO MESSAGE: *My worth depends on making the right choice and avoiding mistakes at all costs.*

AH, *this will work. No, wait a minute. It should be this. Yes. No. Hmm. That may not be right . . .*

As the Overthinker procrastinator type, you get caught up in loops of endless evaluation, analyzing, and second-guessing every part of the writing process. You are the writer who gets lost in researching your story and never writes it. Or, if you do get to writing, you tend to overthink every little paragraph. It's not necessarily perfectionism, but rather the fact that you're thinking about every sentence and every word, and as you think, you come up with "better" ideas.

At the heart of your analysis paralysis is your fear of making the wrong choice. You may get trapped trying to decide which of your ideas to pursue, for example, because you're not sure which one is likely to become a bestseller. Or you may struggle to outline your novel because you can't choose between the various plotlines you've laid out. You're afraid you may end up with the "wrong one" and then waste your time.

The pressure of picking the "right" option can be overwhelming at times, which is another reason you may procrastinate on your project— it's just too much to face. Even when you think you've decided on something, you tend to second-guess yourself, resulting in a type of mental gridlock where no decision feels safe or final.

Another challenge is your tendency to doubt your creative instincts. The writing muse? Mumbo-jumbo. You prefer a definite roadmap. When you sit down to write, you question whether the storyline you've come up with is interesting enough or if the plot has enough twists and turns. This constant self-questioning disrupts your flow, and even small decisions—like choosing your character's name—can derail your progress.

In the end, your biggest hurdle is learning to trust the "process" of writing.

Key Characteristics of the Overthinker

As an Overthinker, you may find that one or more of these habits and characteristics sound familiar:

- **Decision paralysis:** You find it difficult to make decisions, often weighing every option endlessly. Whether it's about plot structure, character development, publishing options, or marketing plans, you struggle to commit, fearing you'll choose the wrong direction.
- **Endless research:** You may get lost in your research, convincing yourself that you need more information before you can start writing. Your desire to be fully prepared becomes an excuse for delaying the actual writing process.
- **Fear of uncertainty:** You crave control and certainty in your writing process. You want to know exactly how the story will unfold before putting pen to paper, making you hesitant to embrace the organic and unpredictable nature of creativity.

- **Overplanning:** You are likely to spend excessive time planning and outlining, striving to prepare for every detail. Planning is essential to many writers, but you may use it as a way to avoid the messy, less predictable act of writing itself.
- **Looping in revisions:** Instead of pushing forward with a first draft, you get stuck revising the same sections repeatedly, nitpicking over small details. Or, you may spend years fixing one book rather than publishing it and moving on to the next one.
- **Overanalysis of feedback:** It's not only your stories that you tend to overthink. If you receive a writing critique from a friend, mentor, editor, or writing coach, you may go over it repeatedly, analyzing every detail and deconstructing every motivation the reader had until you drive yourself into a spiral of self-doubt.
- **Second-guessing:** You regularly question your decisions, even after making them. You worry that you haven't made the right choices and go back to analyze them again. This fuels your procrastination, leading you to postpone your writing in favor of trying to "figure things out" mentally first.

Strengths of the Overthinker

You possess a keen mind and excel at analyzing and reflecting on ideas. You naturally consider multiple perspectives, allowing you to develop a deep understanding of a subject. You can anticipate potential obstacles and devise well-thought-out solutions. When it comes to your writing, these strengths enable you to craft complex plots, characters, and themes that are intricately layered, resulting in rich and fascinating stories.

Another strength is your attention to detail. You rarely miss the little things. Your meticulous approach ensures that if you complete a project, it will be highly polished and thoughtfully crafted. And despite your challenges, you are often remarkably persistent. You are willing to revisit and refine your ideas until they shine, and you are not afraid to tackle problems from different angles.

Challenges for the Overthinker

Your greatest challenge lies in your tendency to get stuck in an endless loop of overthinking. Rather than moving forward on your writing project, you overanalyze every aspect, fearing that you may have missed something or that perhaps there is a better option you haven't yet considered. This can lead to procrastination, where you're unable to make decisions or commit to going in a certain direction. The result is often a lot of mental effort with little to show for it, which can be frustrating and demotivating.

You may struggle to see *action* as the most important step in your career. Ask yourself if you constantly delay writing because you feel the need to prepare more, research further, or develop a clearer plan. The pressure to find the best approach or to be absolutely certain of your next step often keeps you from making any progress at all.

The Overthinker's Limiting Beliefs

- **I need to have everything figured out before I start.** You believe you must have a clear, detailed plan for every part of your writing project before you begin. You spend endless time brainstorming, researching, outlining, planning, and waiting for all uncertainties to be resolved.
- **If I choose the wrong direction, everything will fall apart.** You believe that one wrong decision may ruin the entire project, which makes you afraid to take risks or experiment with new ideas. This fear keeps you stuck in a cycle of second-guessing.
- **There's always more information I need before I can proceed.** You are convinced that you don't yet know enough and that you have to do more research or analysis. You continue seeking more data or resources and never feel ready to take action.

Coping Techniques for the Overthinker Procrastinator

1. **Set Time Limits for Planning:** Give yourself a limited amount of time for brainstorming and planning before diving into the writing process. If you have an hour to write, spend no more than fifteen minutes planning. Use a timer to keep yourself accountable. Another option is to set specific days for planning, while on other days, you focus solely on writing, knowing that your next planning session is scheduled.

2. **Create Analysis to Action Sheets:** Create a simple template with two columns: "Thoughts" and "Actions." Write down all your overthinking thoughts in the first column, then brainstorm quick, action-oriented steps to counter each thought in the second column. Here are some examples: **a) Thought**—This plot is too predictable. **Action**—Brainstorm three unexpected plot twists, choose one, and write a short scene to see how it feels. **b) Thought**—The dialogue in this scene is boring. **Action**—Instead of thinking about it, rewrite the scene and take the dialogue to the extreme just to see what comes up. **c) Thought**—I need to plan out the end of my novel. **Action**—Instead of planning, write three different endings to explore the possibilities.

3. **Write an Overthinking Mantra:** Develop a personal mantra to recite whenever you catch yourself overthinking. Here are some examples: a) *I choose to act, not overanalyze; every word I write brings me closer to finishing the project.* b) *Progress is my priority; I'll embrace the messy journey of creation.* c) *Action fuels inspiration—I'll write freely and see where it takes me.* d) *I'll trust the process. Each written word is a step toward clarity.*

4. **Separate Rumination from Planning and Problem-Solving:** Not all of your planning and problem-solving holds you back; sometimes, it serves you well. The key is to

detect the difference between effective planning and ineffective rumination. *Rumination* involves repeatedly rethinking situations and analyzing them without forming an action plan. *Effective planning*, on the other hand, means weighing options and then coming up with a concrete way to move forward. It may help to keep a journal and regularly record your thoughts about your project. Create two columns on the page, labeling one "rumination" and the other, "effective planning." See where you are spending most of your mental energy and make adjustments as needed.

5. **Watch a Future Failure Forecast:** One of the reasons you're caught up in making the "right" choice is that you fear failure. Take 15 minutes to write down all the possible ways your writing project could go wrong—anything from plot holes to bad reviews to rejections from publishers. Once you've got a comprehensive list written, take some time to reflect. How might you learn from each situation? What might you do if you face that failure? The point is that you can recover from any failure, often much more quickly and easily than you think.

6. **Plan Times to Regularly Get Out of Your Head:** Your tendency to overthink things shows that you likely default to thinking over doing. It can help to get out of your head and into your body so you can see things with a broader perspective. Take a walk or head out for a bike ride. Go camping, rollerblading, or boating. Make a point to schedule these sorts of activities into your week. When you come back, you'll likely be in a more creative mood and want to write without overthinking.

7. **Notice the Present Moment:** Mindfulness (living in the moment) can be a great coping technique for you, as it gives you something to focus on instead of analyzing. As a writer, the best way to practice being in the moment is to be *in your story, with your characters.* Sink into your body. What is your hero feeling? What sensations is he or she experiencing? Describe what it's like to be the character in the scene. This

way, you can stay present and make progress without allowing overthinking to delay you.

8. **Make Your Goals Visible:** You likely have goals related to your writing. Make those visible. Write them on sticky notes and post them around your writing nook, or make a collage with them. Then, whenever you start spending more of your precious writing time thinking, let these visual guides remind you of what's most important.

9. **Embrace Creative Chaos:** Creativity is often messy and chaotic. You are naturally programmed to avoid that, but you can learn to get more comfortable with it. Try scheduling a time once or twice a week that you label your "messy creative session." Limit it to 20–30 minutes. Refuse to allow *any* planning, research, or outlining during this time—it's for writing only. When the time is up, simply put your writing away. The next day, review it without judgment. Highlight the passages or ideas that resonate with you, and focus on the excitement of creation. Do this regularly to help yourself become more at home with the idea that not every piece needs to be perfectly polished to be valuable.

10. **Protect Your Mental Energy:** Overthinking is a huge drain on your mental energy. It's no wonder that it leads to procrastination. When you overthink your project, you're left with no energy to actually do it. Try creating a "mental energy shield" for yourself, designed to set a boundary around your thoughts. Excessive planning, second-guessing, and controlling thoughts are energy thieves that need to be kept outside this boundary. Allow only thoughts that spur action to exist within it. Designate specific times throughout the day to assess your mental energy levels. How are you doing? During these check-ins, ask yourself if your thoughts align with your writing goals. If something feels draining, take a break or shift your focus to something more inspiring or energizing.

Who the Overthinker Can Become: The Insightful Creator

When you're at your best, you become the Insightful Creator. You embrace your ability to research and analyze ideas while also accepting that the creative process can be a little messy. This balance allows you to make progress without getting caught in analysis paralysis.

THE OVERTHINKER'S BEST SELF:

- **Balanced Reflector:** You know the value of contemplation but also know when to shift gears and take action. You can review your ideas thoughtfully without getting bogged down in unnecessary details.
- **Confident Decision-Maker:** You realize that not every decision will be exactly "right" and that there is room for experimentation. You trust your intuition and are less likely to second-guess yourself.
- **Doesn't Fear Failure:** You no longer let failure leave you shaking in your boots. You understand that not every creative project will be a homerun and that failure is part of the writing journey.

In this best version, you find a balance between reflection and action, learning to move back and forth from one to the other as needed to reach your writing goals.

Action Plan for the Overthinker Procrastinator

Your attachment to thinking and planning is holding you back. It's time to get in touch with your adventurous side so you can reconnect to the joy of writing.

It begins when you give up on the idea that you can land upon just the right idea, outline, plan, or theme. You understand that to reach your writing goals, you have to be willing to trust the writing process and actually experience the journey of experimentation.

Below, I have a sample action plan for the Overthinker procrastination type to finish a novel. If you have a different project in mind—such as creating a new website, starting a blog or YouTube channel, or growing your newsletter audience—you can adapt the plan to fit your goal. The steps will likely be similar, as they're tailored to your specific type.

STEP 1: CREATE A "THOUGHT-DISTANCING" TECHNIQUE

Challenge to Overcome: *I get trapped in a loop of overthinking.*

Decide how you will create a physical representation of your thoughts when you start overthinking a scene, character, outline, or plot point. You could write down the thoughts in a journal or on sticky notes or draw a scene representing them. This way, you can see them before you, which will help lessen their power in your mind.

STEP 2: INCORPORATE CREATIVE CONSTRAINTS

Challenge to Overcome: *I tend to get overwhelmed with overthinking.*

It may seem like you can be most creative when your project is wide open, but in truth, creativity thrives within constraints. Setting boundaries on your project can also help you limit overthinking, as you only have so far you can go.

When outlining your novel, create clear limits. Start by choosing a genre. Give yourself only so many characters to work with. Choose to incorporate only two or three tropes (e.g., enemies to lovers or the hero's journey), and limit the setting to a single neighborhood or even one house. Set a word count for each chapter (no more than 3,000 words, for example), and decide to write from only one or two points of view throughout the novel.

The more structure you establish, the easier it will be for you to dive into the writing process as there will be less to consider and analyze.

STEP 3: COMMIT TO A "WRITING-ONLY" FIRST DRAFT

Challenge to Overcome: *I have to overthink every sentence, so I never finish the story.*

For the first draft of your novel, commit to writing only—no editing allowed. If you allow yourself to edit even one sentence, you may fall into the trap of endless revising and never finish your book. Remind yourself that there will be plenty of time to make changes later.

STEP 4: PRACTICE OVERTHINKING OUT LOUD

Challenge to Overcome: *I get stuck in my head and don't write.*

Make it a regular practice to go for a walk while speaking your thoughts about the plot or characters out loud. Use the voice recorder on your cell phone.

Don't censor yourself. Allow the ideas to flow, no matter how disjointed they may seem. When you return from your walk, write down any solutions you came up with, then take action on them as soon as possible.

STEP 5: FOCUS ON THE NEXT STEP ONLY

Challenge to Overcome: *I have to plan out every step before doing it.*

Writing a novel is a huge, sometimes overwhelming project. You'll want to plan it all out first so that you feel certain about what you're doing.

Instead, acknowledge that it's impossible to control everything or to be absolutely certain about every word you'll write over the next 65,000 to 100,000 words. Focus on the next step in front of you, then the next one—the next paragraph, the next scene, the next chapter. That's all. Take the journey step by step. Allow yourself to feel the fear of uncertainty and write anyway.

STEP 6: ONCE-SENTENCE DAILY LOG

Challenge to Overcome: *I focus on creating the perfect plan rather than on writing.*

Try this: At the end of each day, write just one sentence summarizing what you accomplished in your writing that day, or what you learned about your story.

Keep it simple and straightforward. Avoid getting into elaborate explanations. Above all, don't criticize or analyze! Simply reflect without overthinking. This practice can help you to foster a sense of progress that keeps you motivated.

STEP 7: CREATE A WRITING CHALLENGE

Challenge to Overcome: *I allow myself to overthink for way too long.*

To stay on track and finish your novel, partner with another writer for a friendly challenge, such as hitting a weekly word count or completing key plot points by a deadline. Celebrate each other's accomplishments with coffee or a movie night if you're nearby, or connect online for a celebratory Zoom meeting or YouTube live event.

The Most Important Thing for Overthinkers to Remember

If there's one thing you must remember as an Overthinker procrastinator, it's this: *You can take action and make progress without having every detail figured out.*

In the past, you may have believed you needed to plan everything perfectly and have all the "right" ideas before you could start writing. You must let go of that belief, as all it's doing is holding you back.

I hope you'll trust yourself and the creative process a little more, allowing you to move past procrastination and embrace the great adventure that writing can be.

Exercise: The "Wild Writing Prompt Challenge"

IT'S TIME TO EMBRACE THE MESSY PROCESS OF CREATING without overanalyzing. This exercise can help.

WHAT YOU'LL NEED:

- Fun supplies like colored pens, sticky notes, or even art supplies
- Upbeat music (optional)

STEPS:

- **Create random writing prompts:** Write a series of random writing prompts on pieces of paper and put them into a box, bag, jar, or other container. These can be silly, serious, or absurd. For example: Write a scene where your character talks to a talking cat; describe a day in the life of a superhero who loses their powers; write a love letter to pizza or another favorite food; invent a new holiday and explain how it's celebrated.
- **Set a timer:** Give yourself only 5–10 minutes. The goal is to write without planning first and without stopping to think or edit.

- **Draw a prompt:** Randomly draw one of the slips of paper and immediately start writing based on the prompt. Don't analyze or overthink your response. Just write!
- **Switch it up:** After the timer goes off, take a quick break to stretch or grab a drink. Then, draw another prompt and repeat the process if you like.
- **Reflect:** When you're done, take some time to reflect on the experience. Did you have fun? What did you learn? Can you use any of the writing? Even if you can't, did it help you somehow?

sixteen
the tired

BASIC FEAR: *I'm afraid I'll never have enough energy to finish what I start.*
BASIC DESIRE: *I want to feel fully rested and energized so I can pursue my creative work with passion.*
SUPEREGO MESSAGE: *My worth depends on how much I accomplish, even if I'm exhausted.*

"I WANT TO WRITE TODAY, but I'm just so . . . tired."

As a Tired procrastinator, you intend to write, but when you sit down to do it, you're so physically or mentally drained that you struggle to produce anything.

The U.S. Centers for Disease Control and Prevention (CDC) reports that about one-third of U.S. adults don't get enough sleep. Since writers often squeeze their writing in between everything else they're doing in their lives, it makes sense that if they aren't getting enough rest —or are chronically fatigued for other reasons (including potential health issues)—they're likely to delay writing.

This type of procrastination isn't caused by laziness, perfectionism, or any of the other reasons discussed in this book. You simply don't have the energy you need to be creative. You suffer from a type exhaustion that makes even the thought of writing feel overwhelming. While you may experience short bursts of momentum, these are often followed by long periods of avoidance. You might feel guilty about that, which only drains your energy further.

Another challenge is understanding the importance of rest—and not just physical rest, but mental and emotional restoration, too. You may push yourself too hard, thinking you'll tackle one more task before taking a break, only to find yourself completely burned out. Your body and mind desperately need of rest, but your inner critic urges you to keep going, straining your creative process.

Fatigue can also cause problems with focus. When you're worn out, your concentration suffers, and staying on task becomes more difficult. A tired brain is easily distracted, making even simple writing projects seem challenging.

Key Characteristics of the Tired

As a Tired procrastinator, you may find that one or more of these habits and characteristics sound familiar:

- **Chronic exhaustion:** You frequently feel drained, both mentally and physically. This makes it hard to write and leads you to procrastinate.
- **Energy peaks and valleys:** Your productivity often comes in bursts during rare moments of higher energy, followed by valleys of low activity. You struggle to create a consistent writing habit and find it hard to build momentum.
- **Guilt-fueled procrastination:** Feeling exhausted leads to procrastination, which fuels guilt. This cycle further drains your already low energy reserves, making writing seem even more overwhelming.
- **Difficulty focusing:** You may find it hard to concentrate. When you're tired, your thoughts are likely to be scattered, making you vulnerable to distraction.
- **Underestimation of rest:** You ignore or undervalue rest, thinking you need to push through fatigue to get more

done. This can lead to burnout, further reducing your productivity in the long run.

- **Overwhelm from simple tasks:** Your fatigue can make even small writing tasks feel like monumental projects. The blank page looms like an impossible challenge.
- **Poor work quality due to fatigue:** When you force yourself to write through exhaustion, the quality of your work may suffer. When you notice this, it discourages you, making it harder to sit down and write next time.

Strengths of the Tired

You probably possess remarkable perseverance. You have learned to push through fatigue and show up, even when you don't really feel like it, because of a strong sense of responsibility. Though you may struggle to pace yourself, once you set your mind on something, you have a strong desire to see it through. You may have a strong sense of discipline and know how to get things done even when you don't feel like it.

Because you have probably dealt with fatigue for a while, you may have learned how to simplify complex tasks or find efficient shortcuts. If you've managed to get at least some things done even while feeling tired, you've probably figured out how to break down larger projects into manageable pieces and to make progress despite how you may feel.

Challenges for the Tired

Your greatest challenge lies in figuring out how to better manage your energy. You struggle with feeling physically and mentally exhausted, and your creative projects suffer as a result. You may also struggle with time management.

Because your energy fluctuates, you might underestimate how much rest you need or fail to recognize when you're burning yourself out. On a good day, you may push yourself too hard and then crash, making it harder to get back into the writing groove for many days afterward. This inconsistency creates a stop-and-start pattern that isn't conducive to creative flow, making it harder to finish large projects.

It's also likely that you struggle to prioritize self-care while staying productive. Your body and mind may be screaming for a break, but you might ignore them in favor of "pressing on" with some project you want to finish.

The Tired's Limiting Beliefs

- **I can't write unless I feel fully energized.** You may believe that you need to be in an ideal physical and mental state to write well. That can cause you to procrastinate on writing unless you are at the top of your game and feel fully energized and inspired, which means that you may rarely write at all.
- **If I rest now, I'll fall too far behind.** If you are used to pushing through your fatigue to work anyway, you may struggle with the idea of resting. Instead of taking a break, you may worry that any downtime will cause you to lose momentum or lead to some sort of failure or missed opportunity.
- **My writing won't be good because I'm too tired to think clearly.** You are convinced that your writing will be of no value if you try to get something done when you're tired, so you often avoid it instead.

Coping Techniques for the Tired Procrastinator

1. **Break Up Your Tasks:** If you're not doing it already, break up your writing tasks into smaller, more manageable chunks. Instead of aiming to write a complete chapter, for example, set a goal to write a single scene or even just three paragraphs. When the task feels less overwhelming, you'll be less likely to procrastinate.
2. **Create a Restorative Routine:** Establish a daily routine with designated breaks. Give yourself time to relax and recharge. Make each break purposeful. For example, take a

quick walk during one, stretch your muscles during another, and use the third for a power nap. The key is to schedule meaningful breaks that help restore you both physically and mentally.

3. **Prioritize Sleep:** Doctors recommend getting 7–8 hours of sleep per night. Recognize how important this is for your overall well-being and for your creativity. Follow these tips to improve your sleep: a) Go to bed and wake up at the same time every day, even on weekends. b) Keep your bedroom cool, quiet, and comfortable. c) Remove all technology, including cell phones, tablets, computers, and televisions, from the bedroom. These devices emit blue light that disrupts sleep hormones and keeps you awake. d) Avoid caffeine and alcohol at least two hours before bed. Caffeine is a stimulant that can make it harder to fall asleep. Alcohol may make you drowsy initially, but it often wakes you up later in the night, interrupting critical deep sleep. e) Make sure you have a high-quality, supportive mattress. If your mattress is 5–8 years old and feels saggy, it's time for a replacement. f) Plan 8–9 hours for sleep. It usually takes 20 minutes or more to fall asleep, so if you go to bed 8 hours before you plan to get up, you may get only 7 hours or less. Do yourself a favor and give yourself extra time to unwind and fall asleep.

4. **Don't Neglect Daily Exercise:** Exercise is key to feeling more energy. The less you exercise, the more fatigued you will feel. Your body "learns" how much energy you need each day. If you exercise for a couple of days, your body will respond by creating the energy required to exercise for the next few days. Start with a simple 10-minute walk, then build from there. Physical activity also boosts energy and improves mood, making it easier to tackle your writing tasks.

5. **Create an Energizing Workspace:** Set up a writing space that helps chase away fatigue. Natural light is a wonderful stimulant. If that's impossible, use light bulbs that mimic

natural light. Try energizing colors like yellow, orange, and red on the wall or in your hanging pictures. Add revitalizing sounds like a mini-waterfall or upbeat instrumental music. Incorporate houseplants to enliven the space. Use aromatherapy to encourage focus—citrus, peppermint, and eucalyptus are all invigorating scents. Incorporate a standing desk option and extra chairs so you can shift positions.

6. **Practice Meditation:** Meditation is an effective way to clear your mind and create mental rest. There are many guided meditations available on YouTube or on apps like Calm. Take advantage of these to calm your mind and allow it to just *be* without any expectations. The more you do it, the more you'll notice your mental energy picking up.

7. **Add In More Fun Activities:** We often suffer from fatigue because we're slogging through task after task without ever allowing ourselves to have a little fun. Try incorporating more enjoyable activities into your daily life. Engage in your favorite hobbies, get together with fun people, go places you enjoy, and head out of town now and then. Realize that doing these types of things is not self-indulgent, but critical for self-preservation.

8. **Engage in Regular Energy Boost Rituals:** Perform some energy-boosting rituals each day before you write. Try a quick series of stretches, a short walk around your home, a mindfulness meditation, an aromatherapy diffuser, upbeat music, an energizing snack, or a different writing location. The goal is to get into the habit of always doing something energizing before you start writing.

9. **Use Power Naps:** Power naps can be lifesavers when it comes to managing your energy. Just 15–20 minutes of a light nap may be all you need to recharge. If you're afraid you'll fall into a deep sleep, set a timer. Keep the nap brief, but give it a try. You may be surprised at how well it works.

10. **Learn About the 7 Types of Rest:** Dr. Saundra Dalton Smith wrote a book entitled *Sacred Rest: Recover Your Life, Renew Your Energy, Restore Your Sanity,* in which she

described the seven types of rest. These are the types she found lacking in her clinical practice and research: 1) physical rest, 2) mental rest, 3) emotional rest, 4) sensory rest, 5) creative rest, 6) social rest, 7) spiritual rest. It could be that you're neglecting one or more of these types of rest in your life. You can read more about this on my MasterWriterMindset.com blog (search for "7 Different Types of Rest" or find the link in the references section) , or check out Dr. Smith's book for more information. It may be worth taking her quiz (www.restquiz.com/quiz/rest-quiz-test/) to find out what types of rest you may need to get back on track with your writing goals.

Who the Tired Can Become: The Revitalized Creator

When you're at your best, you become the Revitalized Creator. You recognize the importance of rest and self-care, allowing yourself to recharge and approach your writing with new clarity and purpose.

THE TIRED'S BEST SELF:

- **Energized Focuser:** You manage your energy well, allowing yourself to concentrate on the writing projects that matter to you. You have learned to listen to your body and mind, prioritizing self-care to maintain your mental and physical well-being.
- **Adaptable Balancer:** You set realistic goals, allowing yourself the freedom to take breaks when needed without guilt. You adjust your writing schedule to accommodate your energy levels and adapt your lifestyle to always include recharging activities.
- **Resilient Worker:** You are resilient, bouncing back after periods of low energy to attack your schedule again with self-care in mind. You accept that sometimes changes are required, and regularly adjust your routine if needed.

In this best version, you find a balance between productivity and self-care, learning how to incorporate exercise, meditation, naps, and more into your day so that it's easier to reach your writing goals.

Action Plan for the Tired Procrastinator

Your tendency to neglect yourself is holding you back. It's time to recognize how much self-care you need to reconnect with the joy of writing.

It begins when you give up on the idea that you can regularly push through fatigue and exhaustion. To reach your writing goals, you must be willing to change your habits. You also need to accept yourself as you are in any given moment, and not let that stop you from writing, even if you accomplish far less than you planned.

Below is a sample action plan for the Tired procrastination type to finish a novel. If you have a different project in mind—such as creating a new website, starting a blog or YouTube channel, or growing your newsletter audience—you can adapt the plan to fit your goal. The steps will likely be similar, as they're tailored to your specific type.

STEP 1: PRIORITIZE REST AND RECOVERY
Challenge to Overcome: *I feel guilty about taking breaks.*

Writing a novel is a marathon, not a sprint. From the start, you need a mindset that prioritizes rest and recovery. Schedule your sessions during your highest-energy times of the day, and be sure to take breaks to sustain your energy as much as possible.

STEP 2: SET SMALL GOALS
Challenge to Overcome: *I feel overwhelmed by the size of the project.*

Even as you work on boosting your energy, you'll still have low-energy days. Plan for them by breaking your goals into the smallest possible steps. The key to finishing your novel is "momentum." Set small, achievable targets—such as writing 300–500 words a day—rather than focusing on the entire novel at once.

STEP 3: SET A DAILY ENERGY GOAL

Challenge to Overcome: *I'm too tired to write.*

Consider that setting a fixed daily writing time may not work for you. Instead of saying, "I'll write at 6:00 p.m. every day," maybe you should try saying, "I'll write for 15 minutes when I feel most energized."

If this approach doesn't work, adjust your strategy. But if you can take advantage of those high-energy moments—even if they last only 10 minutes—you can make steady progress.

STEP 4: ENGAGE IN STORYTELLING WALKS

Challenge to Overcome: *Sitting exacerbates fatigue.*

On those low-energy days, try taking an easy walk while talking out your story. Use a voice memo app or something similar to record what you say as you go. Check your novel plan before you leave so you know what scene you need to write, then simply speak it while you walk.

Walking not only increases physical energy, it also boosts mental energy and creativity. If you're feeling tired before you start writing, instead of procrastinating, strap on your sneakers and head outside or use your treadmill.

Plan to walk for only five minutes. This can help you overcome any resistance you may feel. You'll find as you go that your energy will pick up, and by the time you get home, you may have a completed scene on your recorder.

STEP 5: HOST "CREATIVE COFFEE" SESSIONS

Challenge to Overcome: *I'm tired and isolated, so who cares if I skip writing?*

You probably already know the power of coffee or tea to help boost your energy levels. Pair that with the energizing company of friends or fellow writers to help you get the writing done.

Plan a weekly or bi-weekly creative session where you meet at someone's house, a local coffee shop, or even online to write for 20-30 minutes and then share your progress. It's fun and energizing and can help motivate you to keep going.

STEP 6: INCORPORATE MINDFULNESS BREAKS
Challenge to Overcome: *I'm too mentally exhausted to write.*

Before you start writing, try a five-minute meditation or simply spend five minutes breathing deeply. Sometimes, your ticket to energy is as simple as bringing more oxygen into your blood. Follow this pattern:

- Take a deep breath through your nose for a count of four, allowing your abdomen (belly) to rise while your chest remains still.
- Hold your breath for four counts.
- Exhale slowly through your mouth for a count of six, allowing your abdomen to fall.
- Repeat for 5–10 minutes.

STEP 7: IMPLEMENT A "SECOND WIND" STRATEGY
Challenge to Overcome: *I'm overwhelmed with fatigue and diminishing returns.*

The farther you get with your story, the more difficult it becomes to overcome fatigue and keep writing.

You may need some coping techniques for this stage of the process. Having friends who support you helps a lot. When you're thinking of quitting or giving up, talk it out with them so they can help energize you again.

Revisit your "why" for writing this story. Why was it important to you in the first place? How can you remind yourself of that? You might set up a huge reward for when you reach "the end." Make it something you really want, like a weekend away, a new computer, or something particularly motivating.

Remember that this is a marathon, and it's natural to feel tired toward the end. Don't give up! Increase your self-care and keep going until you've finished the story.

The Most Important Thing for Tireds to Remember

If I were to pick one thing that you must remember as a Tired procrastinator, it's this: *You must prioritize your well-being and energy, and know that taking breaks and nurturing yourself will fuel your creativity and help you reach your writing goals.*

In the past, you may have believed that you could neglect yourself and still get the writing done. Or you may have been waiting for something magical to grant you more energy so that you could start writing.

Now you know that there is no energy fairy with a magic wand on her way to fix everything for you. You also know that you will have days when it's just impossible to write because your fatigue is too great.

I hope you will love yourself enough to first, take better care of yourself, incorporating all seven forms of rest into your daily life, and second, to find a writing routine that works with your high-energy times, and even allows you to get some writing done on your lower-energy days.

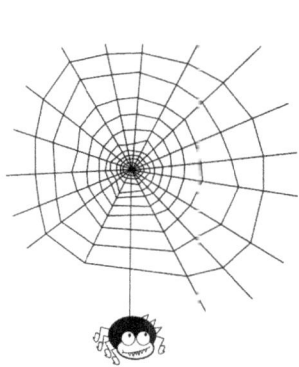

Exercise: The Energy Boosting Brainstorm Walk

It's time to boost your creative energy. This exercise can help.

Steps:

- **Set a timer:** Choose a time frame of 20–30 minutes on a high-energy day.
- **Pick a location:** Choose a nearby park, nature trail, or quiet neighborhood. If it's a cold winter day, consider a shopping mall or museum instead. The goal is to be in a space that inspires you, offers fresh air, or provides new sights to stimulate your creativity.
- **Create a writing prompt list:** Before you leave, write down 3-5 specific writing prompts or questions related to your novel. These may be about certain characters, plot twists, or scenes you need to flesh out.
- **Go for a walk:** Head out for your walk. Take your writing prompts along. As you walk, focus on the prompts and let your mind wander. Record any ideas that come to you on a voice app, text or email, or small notepad.
- **Incorporate energy boosts:** Every few minutes, pause to do an energy-boosting exercise, such as 10 jumping jacks, stretching, or deep breathing. This will help combat fatigue and keep blood flowing to your brain.
- **Reflect and record:** At the end of the walk, find a comfortable spot to sit down and review your notes. Take 10 minutes to write down the best ideas that emerged.

seventeen
the defier

BASIC FEAR: *I'm afraid I'll lose control over my work and creativity.*

BASIC DESIRE: *I want to be free to create on my own terms without anyone telling me what to do.*

SUPEREGO MESSAGE: *I have to prove that no one controls me, and I must do things my own way, or I'm not being true to myself.*

"DON'T TELL me what to do! I'll do it *my* way!"

As a Defier procrastinator, you hate being told what to do. If someone gives you a deadline, you'll probably miss it. Expect you to do something? You may disappoint them. Try to lord authority over you? Um, nope, not going to work. You'll procrastinate before making these people happy!

To you, your creative freedom is what matters most. If anything feels like it's infringing on that, you'll push back, usually by delaying action. This resistance may manifest as avoiding writing projects, missing deadlines, or prioritizing personal projects over assignments from others.

To the outside world, your defiant energy may come across as rebellious or contrary, but in truth, you're simply trying to retain your autonomy and control over your life. You have a strong sense of independence and highly value your freedom, which can make you to balk at anything that feels like an obligation.

You struggle to create structured writing goals or timelines, because you may see them as restrictive rather than helpful. You may want to improve your writing process, but the idea of conforming to someone else's expectations feels like giving up your identity, so you procrastinate as a way of asserting your individuality.

You're also likely to feel frustrated when someone else questions your process. Critiques from colleagues or feedback from editors—no matter how well-intentioned—can make you defensive, especially if you see them as attempts to control your creativity. You may procrastinate on revisions or even abandon projects entirely if you feel too constrained by what others suggest.

You may be a highly creative and original writer, but your strong resistance to outside influence can trap you in a cycle of procrastination that ultimately halts your progress.

Key Characteristics of the Defier

As a Defier, you may find that one or more of these habits and characteristics sound familiar:

- **Resistance to external pressure:** You push back against external deadlines, expectations, or rules. If someone tells you "have" to do something, you delay or avoid it. This resistance can extend to feedback from editors, writing mentors, or even readers, as you may bristle at the idea of conforming to outside "demands."
- **Strong desire for autonomy:** You see yourself as a nonconformist and resist the idea of following anyone else's idea of structure, formula, or plan. You may reject outlining, genre conventions, and story structure simply to "rebel" against the norms, but in the end, this resistance can hurt your writing projects.
- **Reluctance to accept criticism:** Feedback can be hard for you to handle, especially if it comes from someone perceived

as an authority figure. Instead of finding helpful things in a critique, you are likely to interpret the comments as an attempt to control your work, causing you to procrastinate on revisions.

- **Use procrastination as a way to challenge authority:** You aren't likely to tell those in positions of authority (or whom you see as authorities) what you think or feel. To them, you may present an image of cooperation and positiveness. You take the passive-aggressive route, avoiding or procrastinating on the project.
- **Vulnerable to self-sabotage:** Your resistance to being controlled can lead to self-sabotage. When you procrastinate or refuse to meet deadlines, you can undermine your own writing goals.
- **Challenge-seeking:** You are drawn to challenges that allow you to break the rules. That means you're more likely to be motivated by projects that feel rebellious or go against conventional wisdom.
- **Push boundaries:** Your work can be original in that it may push boundaries or challenge accepted norms, whether in genre, prose style, or structure. When you feel fully in control, you can be highly productive and create stories built on unconventional ideas.

Strengths of the Defier

You have a strong sense of independence and self-reliance, driven by a fervent desire to carve your own path. When you're free to operate on your own terms, you can produce original ideas that stand out from the crowd. Your independent mindset also shields you from being swayed by trends or the opinions of others, helping you stay true to your vision.

Your strong sense of personal conviction allows you to push through obstacles, often leading you to take bold risks in your writing. This can result in innovative work that challenges the status quo. You may also use your emotions as fuel for your creativity—your rebellious nature comes with deep feelings of passion and intensity, which, when harnessed effectively, can produce powerful, emotionally driven stories.

Challenges for the Defier

Your greatest challenge lies in resisting external authority and expectations, which can create a self-sabotaging cycle of procrastination. Your strong desire for autonomy makes you bristle at deadlines, structured routines, and even your own goals once they start feeling like obligations. You may delay important tasks simply because they feel imposed on you, even when they align with your own ambitions.

Another major challenge is your tendency to reject conventional methods and systems that may help you achieve your writing objectives. You may be reluctant to outline, set deadlines, adhere to a writing routine, and follow standard story structure. This can cause you to not only be disorganized and unproductive, but may also hurt the writing itself, if you're so unconventional that you lose readers' interest.

Finally, your independent nature may lead to self-imposed isolation. You might hesitate to seek advice, collaborate with others, or ask for help, even when it would benefit you to do so.

The Defier's Limiting Beliefs

- **If I follow the rules, I'll lose my creative freedom.** Some rules— like plot structure and genre standards—can be helpful in storytelling. If you consistently reject them, you can end up stuck. Resisting planning or failing to adopt consistent routines because "that's what others do" can also trash your productivity.
- **I can't trust anyone's advice but my own.** You might feel that relying on someone else for feedback or help means you're giving up your independence. Believing that only you know what's best for your work can ultimately hinder your ability to improve.
- **Others are always trying to control me.** You tend to see the world in terms of what others expect or require you to

do rather than what you want to do. That colors your viewpoint so that whenever anyone tries to help, make suggestions, or give you feedback, you see their actions as attempts to control you.

Coping Techniques for the Defier Procrastinator

1. **Reframe Rules as Suggestions:** Instead of viewing deadlines, guidelines, feedback, and more as rigid rules that you "must" follow, practice reframing them as suggestions. If an editor gives you feedback, for example, see the feedback as "suggestions" for how you might improve the story or make it more understandable or interesting to the reader. If you have a deadline to meet—whether set by you or someone else—try to reframe it as a "suggested" time to complete the project. The goal is to avoid delays and procrastination sparked by a resistance to authority.
2. **Make It Your Own:** Instead of seeing deadlines, goals, and routines as constraining, take ownership of them. Create your own routine that will help you get the writing done. Set goals that work for you. Make your deadlines flexible if you like, or design them in another way that feels less constraining.
3. **Schedule Rebellious Writing Sessions:** Use your rebellious nature to your advantage by regularly scheduling rebellious writing sessions. These are periods where you purposely break conventional rules. Switch genre or create a genre of your own. Start with a wild plot twist. Play around with standard punctuation rules. Write in an unconventional format. Do whatever makes you happy in that session.
4. **Create Reverse Goals:** If regular goals don't work for you, try setting reverse goals, focusing on what you will *not* do. For example: "I will not edit this draft until the chapter is done," or, "I will not check emails until I finish writing this scene." Perhaps, "I will not work overtime until I've finished

my outline." The idea is to allow yourself to be defiant in one area so that you can feel more liberated when it comes to writing.

5. **Write as an Act of Rebellion:** If you've been procrastinating on your writing, try framing it as an act of rebellion. Find a way to make the process feel like a statement of independence rather than a required task. You could write stories that challenge traditional tropes, intentionally breaking the mold. Create a protagonist who rejects the "chosen one" role or craft a story that defies the happily-ever-after ending. Lean into your authentic voice. Make it more pronounced rather than less. Tackle taboo or controversial topics that matter to you. Experiment with non-linear timelines or unusual formats, such as telling a story through text messages or journal entries. You could even use humor to poke fun at traditional expectations or authority figures. The page is your playground. Have fun!

6. **Turn External Expectations Into Challenges:** Let's say an editor has given you feedback or you've been told you need to meet some sort of deadline. Instead of sabotaging yourself by procrastinating, try turning it into a personal challenge. Ask yourself, "How can I make this work in a way that still feels like me?" Or try turning it into a game. Challenge yourself to finish the project before the deadline, for example, but do it in a way that's still fun for you.

7. **Create Your Own Writing Rules:** Instead of spending your time resisting standard writing rules, create your own. Decide how many words you'll write, when you'll write, and when you'll complete your projects. You can take it a step further by developing your own type of story structure. Instead of following a standard plot arc, for example, you might organize your novel by thematic beats—writing a series of emotionally charged moments first, and then filling in the gaps. The more you practice forming your own rules, the more fun you'll have doing it, until you have a system

that helps you complete your work while retaining your autonomy.

8. **Use Reverse Psychology:** If you're starting to see writing as an obligation, you will probably procrastinate on it. Try this: Set aside a block of time where you aren't allowed to touch your writing project. Place your notebook or laptop in front of you and tell yourself, "I'm not allowed to write anything today." You can simply sit there if that works, but your natural rebellious nature may kick in, compelling you to defy your own imposed restriction and get to work!

9. **Create a Rebel Writing Routine:** Building momentum on a writing project is difficult without a regular writing routine. However, that routine may feel too constricting for you, leading to procrastination. Try creating a rebel routine where you write at unconventional times and in unconventional ways. Maybe you write every other day instead of every day. Take your writing to the floor, your bed, or your favorite restaurant. Write in long sessions on Friday and Saturday, giving yourself the rest of the week off. Find a routine that works for you so you can make progress on your project.

10. **Use the "Self-First" Writing Reflection:** To help you focus less on others' expectations and more on your own, start each writing session with a "self-first reflection." Take five minutes to remind yourself why *you* care about the project and what *you* want to achieve. Ask yourself questions like, "What excites me about this story?" or, "How will I feel when I finish this book?" Your answers can help you reconnect with your inner motivations so you're less likely to react to any feelings of being controlled.

Who the Defier Can Become: The Bold Innovator

When you're at your best, you become the Bold Innovator. You use your natural resistance to conformity as a driving source of creativity and originality.

THE DEFIER'S BEST SELF:

- **Confidently Independent:** You embrace your independence without letting it lead to self-sabotage. You no longer reject feedback or deadlines out of defiance but approach them on your terms, choosing how to incorporate them into your vision.
- **Creatively Rebellious:** You challenge norms and push creative boundaries, using your tendency to question conventions as a way to come up with new ideas. Your rebellion becomes a tool for creativity, not procrastination.
- **Purposefully Driven:** You focus on what truly excites and motivates you, aligning your creative process with your personal goals and passions.

In this best version, you find a balance between rebellion and productivity, learning how to incorporate others' expectations into your process so that you no longer have to procrastinate as a way to challenge authority.

Action Plan for the Defier Procrastinator

Your fear of losing control is holding you back. It's time to learn how to channel your desire for independence in a positive way.

It begins when you give up on the idea that your procrastination is hurting someone other than yourself. Understand that to reach your writing goals, you have to be willing to accept that you are always in control of your own writing process. Further, learn to manage your rebellious nature so that it fuels your creativity, while allowing others to help guide you when needed.

Below, I have a sample action plan for the Defier procrastination type to finish a novel. If you have a different project in mind—such as creating a new website, starting a blog or YouTube channel, or growing your newsletter audience—you can adapt the plan to fit your goal. The steps will likely be similar, as they're tailored to your specific type.

STEP 1: CLAIM YOUR PROJECT AS YOUR OWN

Challenge to Overcome: *I feel disconnected from the project because of external pressure or expectations.*

From the very start of this project, it's important to establish ownership. Make a declaration—something like, "This novel is mine, and I'll write it on my own terms." Write down why this story matters to you, ignoring what anyone else may think.

Connect with your inspiration and focus on what excites you about the story. It may also help to create a visual representation of your ownership—a collage, chart, or graphic design—then put it somewhere you can see it before you write.

STEP 2: SIGN A "DEFIER'S CONTRACT"

Challenge to Overcome: *I'm struggling to finish my novel.*

Write a personal contract with yourself in which you lay out specific terms for completing your novel. Include what rules you will follow and which ones you will reject.

For example, you may commit to writing three times a week, but refuse to follow any word count goals. Or you may commit to completing the novel by the holiday season, but refuse to do any editing as you go.

STEP 3: SET REBELLIOUS DEADLINES

Challenge to Overcome: *I resist deadlines imposed by others.*

It's easy to procrastinate on your novel if you don't set deadlines. But deadlines can feel constraining to you and may lead to procrastination. Try getting a little creative with them. Instead of the usual, "I'll finish my book in six months" deadline, try something like, "I'll finish the first chapter by the next full moon," or "I'll write 1,000 words by sunrise."

For the novel as a whole, again, try to think outside the box. Maybe you'll finish it before the kids are out of school for the summer, or by the time the first snow falls. Deadlines are important, but they don't have to feel dull or rigid. You could even give yourself a range— such as "between May and August of this year"—to allow for more flexibility.

STEP 4: CREATE A RULE-BREAKER OUTLINE

Challenge to Overcome: *I reject traditional structures.*

Even if you're a discovery writer (or "pantser," as they're sometimes called), you can still benefit from having some sort of roadmap to follow. It doesn't have to be the traditional step-by-step outline.

Instead, try using mind maps, sketches, colored lines, rooms in a house, or stops along a journey—anything that sparks your creativity while still giving you direction. Focus on capturing the key moments in the narrative in a way that feels fun and free-flowing.

STEP 5: ADD CREATIVE CHAOS TO YOUR PROCESS

Challenge to Overcome: *I lose interest or feel restricted if I follow a predictable story path.*

If you tend to lose interest in your story as you go, try injecting random writing prompts or challenges into your process. Every week, pull a "chaos card" from a jar you made with prompts like, "write a flashback," "introduce a new character," or "create a new and exciting setting that the reader won't expect."

These random disruptions can help prevent boredom while still allowing you to make progress on the story.

STEP 6: GET HELP ON YOUR TERMS

Challenge to Overcome: *Getting help will cause me to lose creative control.*

A novel is a monumental project. You'll likely need help along the way, but your rebellious nature may resist that. Try setting up a collaboration that is strictly on your terms. When asking for feedback or guidance, be very specific.

For example, say, "I want feedback only on character development in this story," or "I'm looking for big-picture thoughts, not line edits."

This allows you to get the needed help without feeling like someone else is taking over your project.

STEP 7: THE DEFY DISRUPTION RULE

Challenge to Overcome: *I feel like my writing is being overtaken by external forces.*

Create your own defy-disruption rule, where you rebel against life's interruptions (which always occur) by committing to writing for just five minutes whenever life throws you a curveball.

Let's say someone in your family gets sick, the car breaks down, or you have to change your schedule at your day job. This can throw a big wrench in your writing progress. This is when the rule kicks in.

You find five minutes somewhere—anywhere—in your day and use it as an act of defiance against the chaos. Jot down thoughts about the next scene in a notebook, dictate dialogue into your phone, or sketch out a quick scene wherever you are. Show life that you're still in control and can move your story forward, no matter what.

The Most Important Thing for Defier to Remember

If I were to pick one thing that you must remember as a Defier procrastinator, it's this: *True freedom comes from creating on your own terms, not from resisting everything.*

In the past, you may have believed that by showing defiance—through procrastination or other means—you were preserving your independence and control when all you were doing was hurting yourself.

I hope you will focus less on what others think and more on creating your own processes and structures that will help you build momentum and complete your projects.

Exercise: The Custom Rulebook Challenge

IT'S TIME TO TAKE OWNERSHIP OF YOUR OWN RULES AND structures. This exercise can help.

STEPS:

- **Create a rulebook template:** On a piece of paper or digital document, create a "Custom Rulebook" for your writing life. Divide it into three sections: "My Writing Rules," "Rules I Break," and "Rewards."
- **Set your writing rules:** Write 5–7 personalized rules for how you will approach writing. These rules must *work for you* and make you feel in control. Here are some examples: a) *I will write 500 words every other day, but only between 9:00 p.m. and midnight.* b) *I will never start a writing session without playing my favorite music, going over my personal commitment contract, remembering *why* I'm doing this, or whatever else works.* c) *I can write in any order I like as long as I'm making progress.*
- **Break the traditional rules:** In the "Rules I Break" section, list the standard writing or productivity rules that you reject. Here are some examples: a) *Outlines don't have to be boring. I'll decide what sort of roadmap to create for my story.* b) *I won't force myself to write at the same time every*

day. c) *I'm not sticking to genre conventions.* d) *I will skip sections that bore me and come back later.*

- **Define your rewards:** In the "Rewards" section, set up small, enjoyable rewards for following your own rules. Choose activities that feel fun to you, such as binge-watching your favorite show or heading out to the park with your dog.

- **Make it official:** Print out your rulebook and sign it. This reinforces the idea that you are in control of your writing process. Place it somewhere visible so you can refer to it when you like.

- **Experiment with your rules:** Over the next few weeks, follow your custom rulebook. If you feel like something isn't working, update the book. The goal is to create a structure supporting your productivity while still allowing you to feel fully in control of the process.

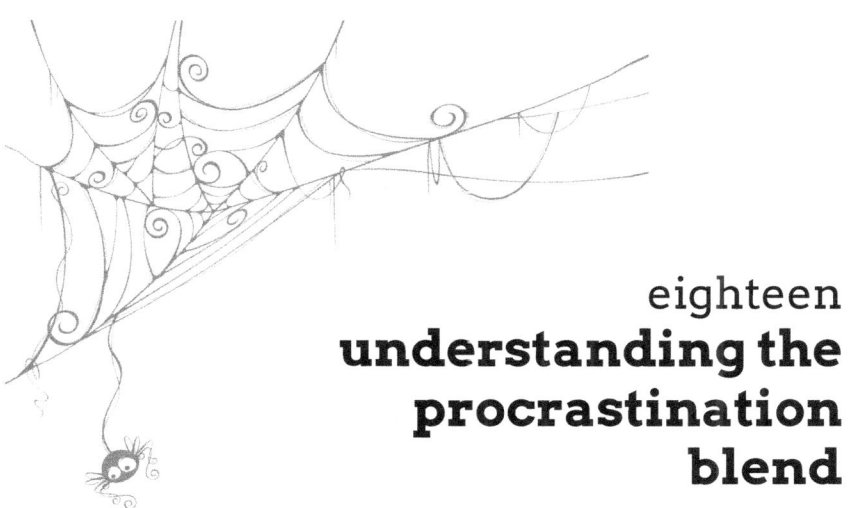

eighteen
understanding the procrastination blend

IDENTIFYING your primary procrastination type is a great first step. It can offer key insights into how your current habits may be slowing you down while providing various strategies to help you overcome delays and boost your writing productivity.

Through my research with writers, I discovered something interesting: many identified with three primary types—sometimes even four or five—particularly if they had two or more with a score of 20 or above. Rather than fitting neatly into a single category, they found that a blend of multiple types best described them, creating a chain reaction that hindered their progress.

You too may find that while your top one or two types strongly reflect your procrastination tendencies, it's the combination of all of your higher-scoring types that reveals your unique set of challenges and your most effective solutions.

In this chapter, we'll explore blended procrastination types to see how they may interact to slow your progress. Then I'll share some examples of tailored coping techniques for various combinations. I can't cover them all—that would take several books!—but I hope to demonstrate the process so that even if your unique combination isn't included, you can still analyze your blend and develop the best approach to manage it.

How Multiple Procrastination Types Work Together

Procrastination is rarely a one-dimensional issue. When you have more than one type working in your writing life, each can interact with the others in a way that intensifies the effects.

If you're both a Worrier and an Avoider, for example, your anxiety about potential problems (Worrier) may cause you to steer clear of writing tasks altogether (Avoider). Each type feeds the other. The more you avoid writing, the more you worry about falling behind, but that worry, in turn, leads to more avoidance.

Sometimes, different procrastination types can pull you in opposite directions. If you're a Fun Seeker, for example, you might crave enjoyable and stimulating writing sessions. But if you're also a Perfectionist, you may want to meticulously edit every sentence, which will make the writing process feel tedious—exactly what your Fun-Seeking type doesn't want. This conflict can result in your feeling torn between wanting to write and dreading the process, ultimately causing you to procrastinate.

Understanding how your types work together is essential because it shows you why traditional strategies may not have worked for you in the past. When you look at all of your highest-scoring types together, you can see how this interaction may take place, allowing you to create a customized plan that addresses *all* facets of your habits.

Examples of Combined Procrastination Types and Possible Coping Techniques

In each example below, I've included a few possible coping techniques you can use to get around these combined patterns. Don't stop with these, however. Once you discover your procrastination blend and start to figure out how it's operating in your writing life, re-examine each of the types in the preceding chapters and see if you can come up with your own blended coping techniques.

EXAMPLE 1: OVERDOER + GUILTY + AVOIDER

When the drive to take on too much (Overdoer) meets the burden of guilt (Guilty) and the tendency to avoid (Avoider), it creates a perfect storm that can halt your writing progress. The combination often leads to overwhelming stress and a cycle that's hard to break.

- **Burnout:** Overcommitting to a variety of things drains your energy and may lead to physical and/or emotional and mental exhaustion.
- **Paralysis by Guilt:** Feeling guilty over those things you couldn't do or haven't done yet increases your feelings of inadequacy, which may make you withdraw further.
- **Cycle of Inaction:** Overwhelm leads to avoidance, which then increases guilt, reinforcing a negative cycle that can be difficult to break.

COPING TECHNIQUES

- **Set Realistic Boundaries:** As long as you continue to overcommit, the cycle will repeat itself. Learn to prioritize those tasks that align with your major goals and dreams in life. Before accepting any new commitments, ask yourself whether they fit into your schedule and support your primary objectives. Practice saying "no" politely but firmly to any additional requests that may overwhelm you.
- **Practice Self-Compassion:** Soothe your guilty feelings by acknowledging that it's impossible to do *everything* perfectly, particularly all the things you had piled in your schedule. Celebrate small achievements and recognize your efforts rather than focusing on any supposed shortcomings.
- **Break Tasks Into Smaller Steps:** The last step is tackling avoidance. You do that by starting with the smallest possible task. All you have to do is stick your toe back into writing. Each small step completed boosts your confidence and feeds your momentum.

EXAMPLE 2: OVERDOER + PERFECTIONIST + TIRED

When an insatiable desire to do more (Overdoer) combines with a relentless pursuit of perfection (Perfectionist) and culminates in exhaustion (Tired), productivity grinds to a halt. This trio creates a high-pressure environment that's simply unsustainable.

- **Chronic Fatigue:** A continuous overexertion without proper rest and recovery drains your energy, affecting your health, creativity, and well-being.
- **Decreased Productivity:** Exhaustion diminishes your focus, creativity, and efficiency, making it harder to produce quality work or to produce anything at all.
- **Increased Stress:** The pressure to perform perfectly in all areas heightens stress levels, further eroding your productivity and ultimately, your enjoyment of writing.

COPING TECHNIQUES

- **Prioritize and Delegate:** Look at everything that's on your plate, prioritize the most important, and then either eliminate, reduce, or delegate the rest. Focus your energy on your most important tasks, like writing.
- **Set "Good Enough" Standards:** Not everything you do has to be perfect. Pick three priority projects—maybe your novel, your next book launch, and your book cover. Then, allow other things, such as your blog post, email newsletter, website, etc., to be "good enough." Don't let your Perfectionist type rule you. Allow it only minimal access.
- **Schedule Rest Periods:** Practice rest in multiple areas of your life. Prioritize sleep, but also consider taking time away to recharge. Find a spiritual outlet to center yourself, and consider taking up meditation or journaling to give your mind a break.

EXAMPLE 3: DREAMER + AVOIDER

The combination of big dreams (Dreamer) along with a reluctance to take action (Avoider) can leave you stuck in the realm of ideas without tangible progress. This pairing can be particularly frustrating, as your aspirations can seem perpetually out of reach.

- **Lack of Progress:** This is the biggest roadblock for this combination. Without actionable steps, your writing projects stagnate.
- **Self-Doubt:** The more you fail to make progress, the more you will doubt yourself. When you follow through and get the writing done, you feel more confident.
- **Fear of Implementation:** Your avoidance tendencies prevent you from taking the steps you need to take to bring your ideas to life. Starting feels overwhelming and risky, so you prefer dreaming instead.

COPING TECHNIQUES

- **Set Actionable Goals:** The key is to set goals based on what you will *do* rather than a specific outcome. Instead of saying, "I'm going to write my novel," commit to writing 100 words a day for the next 30 days. Setting small, manageable goals makes it easier to take some sort of action.
- **Start with Low-Risk Tasks:** Take away the intimidation by making your goals super small. You want to get some positive momentum going, so edit just one page, outline just one scene, or commit to taking one workshop to better learn story structure.
- **Find an Accountability Partner:** As a Dreamer, you really need someone else to bring you down to earth. Find a partner who can encourage you to take action and follow through on your ideas. Schedule regular check-ins.
- **Reward Yourself for *Doing:*** Instead of praising yourself for your great ideas, reward yourself *only* when you get

something done. Reward even for the smallest task completed!

EXAMPLE 4: PERFECTIONIST + WORRIER

When the demand for perfection (Perfectionist) meets persistent anxiety (Worrier), moving forward can feel impossible. This combination often leads to overanalysis and fear-driven paralysis, hindering any meaningful progress.

- **Analysis Paralysis:** Worried about making mistakes, you overanalyze everything, trying to make it mistake-proof. This can cause huge delays and make it impossible to move forward until everything feels perfect.
- **Fear of Starting:** You may avoid getting started on your writing project because you fear failure or inadequacy.
- **Anxiety-Related Issues:** The more you overanalyze and avoid starting, the more your anxiety increases. This could cause other problems like insomnia, chronic self-doubt, and a feeling of never being able to be the writer you want to be.

COPING TECHNIQUES

- **Set Time Limits for Tasks:** Give yourself only so much time to plan your project before you start working on it. Similarly, give yourself only so many drafts to polish a work. Knowing you have a deadline can prevent excessive analysis or editing and encourage you to focus on progress.
- **Embrace Imperfection:** No work is ever perfect. Read some of the bestselling books. You'll find typos in most of them! Allow yourself to make mistakes. What matters in the end is your body of work—not just one specific book. See yourself as a lifetime artist, not a one-hit wonder.
- **Use Meditation and Positive Affirmations:** Put habits into place that will help you cope with your anxiety. Use the

10-minute guided meditations on YouTube. Post positive affirmations around the house. Exercise regularly. Allow yourself to rest and relax at least once a week.

EXAMPLE 5: DISTRACTED + FUN SEEKER

When you're constantly seeking enjoyment (Fun Seeker) yet easily sidetracked (Distracted), staying focused on your writing can feel nearly impossible. This combination can lead to inconsistent work habits and difficulty meeting deadlines.

- **Inconsistent Focus:** When you have trouble focusing on a task, you may end up with a lot of writing fragments around but no completed work.
- **Preference for Immediate Gratification:** Choosing entertainment or more enjoyable activities over writing results in missed deadlines, stalled progress, and a lack of momentum.
- **Difficulty Establishing a Productive Routine:** The regular pursuit of fun and vulnerability to distractions can make developing and maintaining a consistent writing schedule challenging.

COPING TECHNIQUES

- **Create a Stimulating Work Environment:** Indulge your desire for fun by making your writing nook more stimulating. Incorporate things you love like inspiring music, comfortable seating, ambient lighting, colors, art, and more.
- **Use Timed Intervals:** To get around distraction, work in short, focused bursts. Give yourself 10–25 minutes per writing session, then grant yourself a "distraction break," wherein you allow yourself 5–10 minutes to peruse social media or YouTube videos. This can keep your writing

225

sessions productive while indulging your desire for variety.

- **Set Rewards for Completion:** Motivate yourself by promising a fun activity after reaching a specific milestone or completing even a small task. Give yourself a reason to stay focused.

EXAMPLE 6: OVERTHINKER + PERFECTIONIST + AVOIDER

When meticulous planning (Overthinker) and a demand for perfection (Perfectionist) meet a tendency to avoid challenging tasks (Avoider), moving forward becomes near impossible. This combination can result in extensive preparation without execution and a reluctance to start or finish projects.

- **Delayed Action:** This is your biggest problem—you're not getting your work done because your three types are feeding into each other.
- **Fear of Imperfection or Failure:** The fear of your projects being less than perfect leads to further delays.
- **Avoidance of Challenging Tasks:** You may put important projects off indefinitely, leading to missed opportunities and stagnation.

COPING TECHNIQUES

- **Realize that Delays Are the Problem:** Face the truth that your procrastination types sabotage your progress and lead you to doubt your abilities. Journaling about this can help. Look back on what progress you've made over the last year and examine how your types are stopping you.
- **Set Decision Deadlines:** Give yourself only so much time to plan each step of the process. Thirty minutes to outline a chapter before you write, for example, or two weeks to outline a book before you either write or reach out for help.

- **Let It Be Less than Perfect:** Challenge yourself to start before you feel ready. Realize that the process of writing and rewriting brings you to your best work. You simply can't foresee everything before you start.
- **Get More Help:** Instead of trying to make everything perfect yourself, employ beta readers, editors, writing coaches, and others to help you. Get your story to a certain point, then hand it off and get started on your next project. Doing this regularly can help you get used to making progress rather than staying stuck in one area.

EXAMPLE 7: DEFIER + OVERDOER

Balancing a desire for autonomy (Defier) with a tendency to over-commit (Overdoer) creates a lot of inner turmoil. This combination can lead to resistance against your own goals and a feeling of being trapped by your obligations.

- **Conflicting Priorities:** You commit to these tasks but then resist them because you don't like feeling controlled. This creates internal conflict, stress, and inaction.
- **Rebellion Against Your Own Goals:** Tasks you initially chose yourself may start to feel like obligations, leading you to sabotage your own projects.
- **Burnout Due to Self-Imposed Pressure:** Taking on too much while resisting outside help, guidance, or schedules can lead to physical and emotional exhaustion, making it harder to get your writing done.

COPING TECHNIQUES

- **Align Tasks with Personal Values:** Choose projects that genuinely interest you and align with your passions while allowing you to maintain at least some control. This can reduce your resistance and make you more likely to finish these projects.

- **Set Personal Challenges:** If you take on a commitment that involves others' rules or schedules, try to add some self-imposed challenges that will allow you to feel more in control. The idea is to reinforce your feelings of autonomy wherever you can.
- **Limit Your Commitments:** Ultimately, if you're resisting some of your commitments, you probably made too many of them. Be more selective about the projects you take on. Prioritize quality over quantity.

EXAMPLE 8: DISORGANIZED + CRISIS-MAKER + GUILTY

When disorganization (Disorganized) meets a tendency to create crises (Crisis-Maker) and is compounded by feelings of guilt (Guilty), productivity suffers. This combination can lead to last-minute scrambles, chaotic workflows, and emotional burdens that leave you exhausted.

- **Chaotic Workflow:** You may feel your stress levels go up whenever you tackle your writing work, maybe because you have misplaced notes, unclear priorities, or no way to track your progress.
- **High Stress Levels:** Constantly working under tight deadlines increases your stress and may reduce the quality of your work.
- **Emotional Drain:** Guilt over repeatedly finding yourself in crisis mode can eventually affect your self-esteem, motivation, and energy levels.

COPING TECHNIQUES

- **Find Simple Ways to Organize**: Find basic, easy ways to bring some organization into your writing process. Try a calendar, a to-do list, or even a project management app. Start with minimal structure so you don't feel overwhelmed.

- **Set Incremental Deadlines**: Instead of waiting until the last minute, break your project into smaller parts, each with its own deadline.
- **Practice Self-Forgiveness and Reflection:** Give yourself time to reflect on the process that leads to crises and guilt. Avoid criticizing yourself; instead, try to identify gaps in your process where you can make positive changes.

EXAMPLE 9: OVERTHINKER + DEFIER + TIRED

When excessive analysis (Overthinker) combines with resistance to external expectations (Defier) and is worsened by fatigue (Tired), initiating and sustaining your writing can feel extremely challenging. This trio can lead to mental exhaustion and a reluctance to write at all.

- **Decision Paralysis:** The more you overanalyze, the less likely you are to make a decision and move forward. This stalls your progress, resulting in a lot of unfinished projects.
- **Lack of Motivation:** Resistance to outside obligations can reduce your drive to work on writing projects, especially if you're already tired.
- **Increased Fatigue:** As this cycle continues, you may find yourself experiencing chronic fatigue, or at least coming to every writing session feeling worn out.

COPING TECHNIQUES

- **Simplify Decision-Making:** Limit your options to reduce overthinking. For example, choose between two writing prompts instead of considering many. Or review two types of plotting techniques before choosing one rather than reviewing several. Make a decision and move forward.

- **Set Self-Determined Goals:** Decide what you want to achieve in your writing over the next three months. Make sure these goals align with *your* values and interests, not someone else's.
- **Prioritize Rest and Self-Care:** Recognize that you need more rest to maintain productivity. Schedule breaks and activities that replenish your energy.

EXAMPLE 10: PERFECTIONIST + DISTRACTED + CRISIS-Maker + Avoider

This combination is common in the writing world. You have the pursuit of perfection (Perfectionist) intersecting with a vulnerability to distraction (Distracted), a tendency to create crises (Crisis-Maker), and avoidance behaviors (Avoider). Ultimately, this leads to chronic procrastination and unmet deadlines.

- **Incomplete Work:** You may have a desk or file full of unfinished projects. These do *nothing* for your writing career! Don't think of their "potential." Think of them as lost opportunities.
- **High Stress Levels:** Your last-minute efforts to get things done create stress and result in subpar work—something your Perfectionist type definitely won't like.
- **Avoiding Writing Altogether:** As the pressure mounts, you may throw up your hands and avoid writing altogether. This can significantly slow you down, as it takes a lot more time to recover from this step than if you had kept going.

COPING TECHNIQUES

- **Start Small:** Start with an extremely small goal—re-read what you've written, for example. Make it a priority to get back into your writing.

- **Make Writing Fun Again:** Realize that the high pressure you're putting on yourself—both from your Perfectionist and your Crisis-Maker types—is making writing feel like a drag. Return to why you started writing in the first place. Take one day to just go somewhere and write for the fun of it.
- **Establish a Distraction-Free Environment:** Don't allow distractions to deter your focus. Turn off notifications, put your phone in the other room, and create a dedicated workspace with noise-canceling headphones if necessary.
- **Set Realistic Standards and Deadlines:** Break your projects into smaller tasks with individual deadlines to prevent last-minute rushes. Practice short, focused writing sessions (20-30 minutes) to avoid distraction and create high-quality work that will be "good enough" for moving forward.
- **Engage in Regular Mindfulness Practices:** Try deep breathing exercises, meditation, or short walks before writing to help yourself relax and approach writing with an accepting, no-judgment attitude.

Strategies for Managing Blended Procrastination Types

Hopefully, these examples will give you some additional things to think about when you're examining your procrastination blend. To create your own coping techniques, combine those from each of the types (found in the previous chapters) in a way that makes it more likely you'll want to get your writing done.

Remember that it's okay to experiment! Try something for a week or two, then see how it works.

Now that you've looked at how your various types may combine to affect your writing, let's examine some additional strategies for addressing this complexity.

RECOGNIZE THE INTERACTIONS

Start by developing a keen sense of self-awareness. Pay close attention to how your different types interact on a day-to-day basis. Notice specific triggers and patterns that lead you to procrastinate. You may find that your Perfectionist type causes you to Overthink details, for example, which causes you to Avoid starting a task for fear that you won't do it "right." The key is to watch for patterns and then get them down, either in a dedicated file or journal.

Action Tip
Throughout your day, pause to reflect whenever you feel the urge to procrastinate. Ask yourself which of your types may be influencing this feeling or how your various types may be interacting to cause it.

KEEP TRACK

As mentioned above, it's best to keep track of your observations, at least for the first few weeks. Commit to a regular schedule when you document your experiences—every night, maybe, or at least a couple of times a week. Over time, your observations can reveal new insights into how your blended types are affecting your productivity and creativity.

Action Tip
Set aside a few minutes every day to jot down moments when you procrastinated or felt the urge to do so. Note what you were doing, how you felt, what happened right beforehand, and any other thoughts that seem related.

Develop Customized Coping Techniques

Once you've observed your behaviors, patterns, and tendencies for a couple of weeks, move to the next phase of developing your own coping techniques.

COMBINING STRATEGIES

Since your procrastination is influenced by multiple types, you'll likely need coping techniques from each. Customize your plan by selecting those strategies from the relevant chapters that address different aspects of your procrastination.

For example, if you're both an Overthinker and a Perfectionist, you might set decision deadlines to curb overanalysis while embracing imperfection to ease the pressure of producing flawless work.

Action Tip
Make a list of coping techniques that resonate with each of your types. Then, combine those that seem like they would work together in your daily routine. Feel free to experiment with different combinations.

FLEXIBLE APPROACHES

Be willing to adjust your strategies as you go. Some will work for you and others won't. Flexibility is key, as what helps overcome procrastination in one situation may not be as effective in another.

You may also notice that certain procrastination tendencies become more prominent at different stages of your writing process. For example, perfectionism might not appear until you start editing, while your fun-seeking tendencies could play a bigger role during the drafting period.

Stay open to different techniques and be patient with yourself as you navigate this process.

Action Tip
Regularly review and assess your coping techniques. Set a schedule—perhaps twice a month—where you spend 30 minutes on a Saturday morning jotting down notes about what is working and what isn't. If something isn't helping, try a new combination for the next two weeks. Then at your next review, check in with yourself to see if more changes are necessary.

SEEK SUPPORT

If trying to manage your blended types seems overwhelming, consider seeking support from a writing coach or other professional. Sometimes all you need is someone providing guidance, feedback, and support to get you over the hump. An outside perspective can help you untangle what's really holding you back so you can create a path forward that actually works for you.

Action Tip
Research professionals who specialize in procrastination or creative blocks. Schedule an initial consultation to see if it's a good fit.

PEER GROUPS

Sharing your experiences with other writers who are facing similar challenges can foster a sense of camaraderie and help you stay motivated. Look for online groups that exchange coping strategies and offer accountability support.

Action Tip
Be selective about whom you choose to share your work with. Some writing groups are less beneficial than others. Even a single supportive writer is more valuable than a group that offers little real help.

Embrace Your Complexity!

Understanding that you may have to face multiple obstacles hindering your writing progress is crucial to overcoming the barriers between you and your writing goals.

If you're still feeling a little confused or uncertain about tackling your challenges, that's okay. I have more help on the way, and we're going to begin with something especially important: mindset shifts.

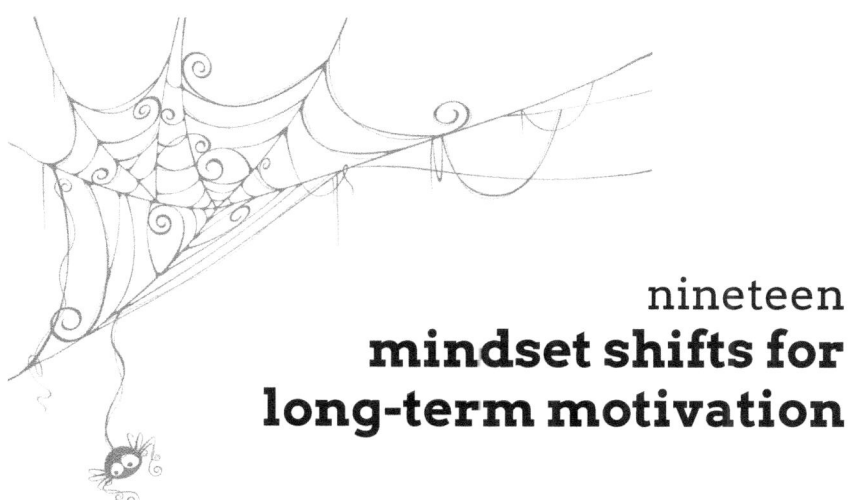

nineteen
mindset shifts for long-term motivation

YOU MAY HAVE NOTICED that in each of the procrastination-type chapters, there was a list of three limiting beliefs. These are beliefs that each particular type tends to have about what they can and can't do as writers.

It's easy to assume that the problem of procrastination comes from outside circumstances—or from an internal personality flaw—but it's often just a mindset that we've fallen into by habit. When you dig a little deeper, you may discover that "why" you procrastinate is rooted in how you think about your writing, yourself, and the creative process, in general.

Changing your mindset is one of the most powerful things you can do to break free from procrastination as it can help shift the limiting beliefs that are holding you back. You may be tempted to skip past this step, thinking it doesn't matter much, but I'd encourage you to at least try it. After over 25 years of writing, I've learned that mindset is much more important than I used to think it was!

We'll start with three general mindset changes that can work for all types, and then I'll give you some specific guidance for your unique type as well. Between the two sections, you will gain new tools that you can use to change your thinking when it comes to getting your writing projects done.

Three General Mindset Changes that Can Work for All Types of Procrastinators

No matter what type of procrastinator you are, you likely struggle with three limiting beliefs. Let's tackle these one at a time.

Mindset Change 1: From "Have to" to "Get to"

Think about how you feel when it comes time to write. Are you excited that you get to spend time doing something you enjoy? Or do you feel that writing is a chore you "have to" complete?

We usually start out writing because we like it, but it can be easy to fall into the "have to" mindset after a while. Maybe you have a deadline that feels overwhelming, or you're dealing with a lot of other things in your life that make writing seem like just another task on the to-do list.

When you see it as an obligation instead of something you *choose* to do, your mindset puts you in a losing position. Most of us don't want to do things we feel we "have" to do.

Changing the way you talk to yourself can help. Instead of saying, "I have to write," say, "I get to write" or "I'm looking forward to writing." You may not imagine such a small change would make a difference, but give it a try—it can be really effective.

How to Put it Into Practice

- **Start with Gratitude:** Each time you sit down to write, take a minute to think about why writing matters to you. Why did you decide to do this, anyway? Tap into the things you like about writing—the joy of creating something from nothing, the fun of telling stories, or the satisfaction of holding your own book in your hands. Realize that not everyone has the opportunity or freedom to write, and see yourself as fortunate that you have this creative outlet. *Example:* "I get to create worlds, explore ideas, and share my voice with others. Writing is a gift, and I'm glad I have the chance to do it!"

- **Reframe Tasks that Feel Like Obligations:** Not everything we do as writers brings joy. Each of us has aspects of the craft that aren't as fun as others. Maybe for you, it's editing, meeting deadlines, or updating your website. Whatever it may be, try to reframe that task—not as something to dread, but an opportunity to improve your writing life. *Example:* Instead of "I have to revise this chapter," think, "I get to improve this chapter and make my story more engaging to readers."

- **Use Positive Affirmations:** For those times when writing feels like a burden, try using positive affirmations to remind yourself of the privilege of creating. By shifting your mindset, you change your emotional connection to the task. *Examples:* "Today, I get to express my creativity and I'm excited to see where it leads." Or "I get to bring my new idea to life today!" Or, "I can't wait to see where my story leads me."

Mindset Change 2: From All-or-Nothing to Small Steps

Sometimes, you may fall into all-or-nothing thinking. You feel like you have to "finish this novel," for example, instead of just writing a single scene. This mindset makes you believe you must complete a monumental task or you're not making any progress. If you're tired that day or feeling unfocused, you're more likely to avoid it altogether.

It's better to shift to a mindset that embraces small steps. Nothing has to happen all at once. By focusing on small wins, you reduce feelings of overwhelm and start building momentum that leads to long-term success.

Here's how it works: once you experience a small win, you'll want to experience it again, which is how you use this mindset to motivate yourself to return to your project again and again.

How to Put It Into Practice

- **Set Smaller, Achievable Goals:** Break everything down
  into its *smallest* steps. If you're feeling tired or uninspired,
  break it down even further! The trick is to tackle the
  smallest possible goal that will move you forward. *Progress*,
  no matter how small, is the key to maintaining motivation
  over the long term. Imagine you've set a goal of writing 500
  words five days a week. But one of those days, you're wiped
  out. You didn't sleep well, you had to work overtime, and
  you just don't feel like you can do 500 words, so break it
  down. How about 200 words? Or even 50? Make it feel
  manageable, and you'll be less likely to procrastinate.
  Example: "I'm tired today, so I'm going to write 50 words
  and be happy with that accomplishment."
- **Break Large Projects Into Smaller Tasks:** This idea
  follows the same logic—breaking big jobs down into their
  smaller components. This applies particularly to writing a
  novel, creating a new website, or self-publishing a book. On
  the surface, these projects seem huge and intimidating.
  Break them down into steps and then break those steps
  down again and again until you have a series of tasks you can
  easily accomplish. With a novel, for example, you could start
  with the major sections—Acts I, II, and III—then break
  those down into chapters and the chapters into scenes.
  Knowing that you only need to write just one scene today is
  much easier than thinking you have to write an entire
  chapter, and certainly better than feeling like you have to
  tackle the entire novel at once. *Example:* "Rather than
  tackling the whole novel today, I'm just going to focus on
  outlining the opening scene."
- **Celebrate Micro-Wins:** Setting smaller goals is not
  enough. You must celebrate when you achieve them! If you
  don't, you train your brain to stay in the "all-or-nothing"
  thinking. Plus, you miss out on the opportunity to build up
  your excitement and momentum on the project.

Acknowledge *every* small victory that you achieve. *Example:* "I finished writing my 50 words today! I'm now 50 words closer to a finished draft than I was yesterday. I'm going to enjoy my favorite cup of tea (or coffee or whatever you enjoy)."

Mindset Change 3: From Fear of Failure to Curiosity

The last common mindset authors have is a fear of failure. It makes sense. Writing isn't easy, and the market is extremely competitive. It's a small step from thinking about a difficult task to imagining you will probably fail at it.

You can get around this defeating mindset by changing the thought of *I'm afraid I'll fail* to *I'm curious about how this will go*. Creativity is all about exploration.

Remember how you felt as a child when you made something? You did it just for the fun of it and to see how it might turn out. Try to approach your writing with a curious mindset. What will happen in this story? What may come up as you're writing it? This can help you get away from worrying about outcomes and refocus your thoughts on the process instead.

How to Put It Into Practice

- **Experiment with Your Writing:** You may be working hard on your novel, but try setting aside time here and there to experiment. Find a prompt that inspires you or try writing something different, like a poem or short story. Approach these writing sessions as gifts you're giving yourself to see what else your creativity may have in store for you. *Example:* "I saw an opening for a flash-fiction contest. I'm going to give it a try just for fun!"
- **Focus on What You Can Learn:** We fear failure because we imagine it to be a terrible experience where others look down on us. But it's rarely that way in the writing world.

Stories come and go. Some succeed, some don't. Ask yourself what you can learn from your failures. How can you improve? Instead of seeing failure as a sign of defeat, view it as a stepping stone on your journey. *Example:* "I'm disappointed that my editor thought my main character lacked depth, but now I have a chance to learn how to create more nuanced, emotionally compelling characters, and that will make my stories stronger in the future."

- **Adopt a Playful Approach:** Always aiming for that perfect story can be exhausting! Lighten up and have more fun by shifting your mindset to one of play. Most likely you started writing in the first place because you thought it was fun. Let the act of creating be more about enjoying the process of discovery than hitting any specific mark. *Example:* "This new plot structure I'm trying may not work perfectly, but I'm going to pursue it just for fun. I'm excited to see where it takes me."

Mindset Shifts for Each Procrastination Type

Now that we've reviewed the three mindset shifts that can benefit all writers, let's look at those specific to each procrastination type.

WORRIER: FROM "WHAT IF?" TO "WHAT IS?"

You are often preoccupied with worrying about what could go wrong. Shifting your thoughts from "what if?" to "what is?" grounds you in the present moment where you can focus on what's happening now rather than what may go wrong later.

- When you find yourself spiraling into "what if" scenarios, stop. Remember that these are just imagined fears. They haven't happened yet and probably won't happen. *Example:* "I'm worrying about what might happen if my book isn't successful, but that hasn't happened yet. I don't need to solve that problem right now."

- Then reframe those thoughts by asking yourself, "What is happening right now?" This allows you to focus on what's right in front of you, which almost always erases worry from your mind. *Example:* "Right now, I'm writing this scene. That's all I need to focus on today—not the outcome, not the future feedback."

AVOIDER: FROM AVOIDANCE TO OWNERSHIP

You tend to procrastinate to avoid uncomfortable feelings associated with writing, such as self-doubt, uncertainty, and fear of criticism. If you can shift your mindset from avoidance to ownership, it can help you claim your writing as your own—your choice, your passion, and your responsibility.

- The next time you feel like skipping your writing routine because of negative emotions, take a step back and remind yourself that this is *your* story. You don't have to share it with anyone if you don't want to. Writing it was something you wanted to do in the first place. Reconnect with that feeling.
- *Examples:* "I'm avoiding this chapter because I'm afraid it won't be good enough, but I can't improve it if I don't write it first." | "I'll write for 10 minutes today and feel good about my progress no matter how it turns out." | "I'll write today in safety, knowing I don't have to show my work to anyone until I'm ready."

DREAMER: FROM IDEAS TO ACTION

You love the world of big ideas, but you struggle to turn those ideas into tangible products. Shifting your focus from *ideas* to *action* encourages you to make real progress toward your goals rather than staying stuck in your imagination.

241

- Pick one project and break it down into its smallest parts. Then start with the first task. Maybe you'll write 200 words of your first chapter, or outline a single scene. The key is to shift from dreaming about the project to actually working on a piece of it. *Example:* "Today, I'll write the opening scene of my novel. All I have to do is this one small part."
- Gradually this will turn into a daily habit, where you will practice taking action on some small part of your project. If you do it nearly every day for at least two weeks, it will get easier! *Example:* "Each morning I'll write for 15 minutes, knowing that each word gets me closer to making my dream a reality."

Fun Seeker: From Instant Gratification to Self-Made Fun

You may procrastinate on your writing because you don't think it will be fun in the moment or immediately rewarding. Try shifting your mindset to one where *you* create the fun, rather than simply wait for the fun to come to you. If you can do that, you'll start to look forward to it more often.

- View each writing session as an opportunity to explore and create something new. Appeal to your desire for fun by imagining where your story will take you next and being willing to go on that adventure. Or see how you can turn your writing session today into a type of game or exploratory outing. *Example:* "Today, I'm going to play around with a new character idea. This is my time to explore!"
- Then, be sure to reward yourself for any progress you make with something immediate and tangible. This will help train your brain to see writing as something it wants to return to again and again. *Example:* "After writing for 30 minutes in my favorite cafe, I'll head out to a movie for fun."

PERFECTIONIST: FROM PERFECT TO PROGRESS

You are likely to procrastinate because you're afraid your work won't live up to your high standards. It's time to stop focusing on making it perfect and start focusing on making progress. Think about moving forward rather than getting everything right the first time.

- Set goals that prioritize progress—like writing a rough draft or completing a certain word count, no matter how "good" it is. Remind yourself that you can always fix it later. *Example:* "Today, I'm going to write 500 words, even if they're messy. I'll worry about perfecting them during the revision process."
- Then, focus on celebrating what you accomplish progress-wise rather than worrying so much about quality. *Example:* "I finished drafting my chapter today! It's not perfect, but it's on the page, and that's what matters right now."

CRISIS-MAKER: FROM LAST-MINUTE STRESS TO STEADY Momentum

You thrive on last-minute deadlines, which creates a lot of pressure and stress and often results in sub-par work. Try focusing more on steady momentum instead. You can create the urgency you crave throughout the writing process if you set smaller, regular deadlines.

- Instead of seeing your project as one thing ("I will complete my novel by the end of the year"), break it down into many smaller sections, then set deadlines for each of those. Create several situations that are urgent before the ultimate deadline. *Example:* "I'll finish drafting this scene by Thursday evening, then finish the chapter by Sunday morning."
- You can also create timed writing sessions where you push yourself to complete as much as possible within a set period. *Example:* "I'll set a timer for 30 minutes and try to finish this chapter by then. This will help me feel the pressure to

get it done quickly, even though there's no major deadline today."

DISTRACTED: FROM SCATTERED FRENZY TO SHORT-TERM FOCUS

You likely to feel pulled in many directions and find it hard to focus on your writing. Embracing a short-term focused mindset can help you stay on task and resist the temptation to get sidetracked.

- Set a timer for 15–20 minutes where your only goal is to write without interruptions. Put your phone in another room, use noise-canceling headphones if you need to, and turn off email and internet access. Commit to staying focused during this short period, knowing that the session is easily manageable. *Examples:* "I'll put my phone in another room and turn off notifications on my computer so I can stay focused on my writing session." | "I'll write for 15 minutes without checking my phone or looking at emails. Once the timer goes off, I'll take a break and check my phone if I want to."
- Whenever you manage to work for a short time without succumbing to distractions, reward yourself—perhaps by perusing your social media feed for a little while.

OVERDOER: FROM SAYING "YES" TO SAYING "NO"

You often procrastinate because you've made too many commitments, leaving little time for your own creative work. The mindset shift from *saying yes* to *saying no* helps you to set boundaries that prioritize your writing over other obligations.

- Get into a new habit of checking in with yourself before agreeing to *anything*. Before saying you'll take on a new task, for example, ask yourself if it aligns with your current goals and priorities, of which your writing should be one. If it doesn't, practice saying "no" or at least postpone your commitment until after you've met your writing goals. *Example:* "I have too much on my plate this week. I'll decline this new project and focus on finishing my chapter instead."

- It may also help to set regular, non-negotiable writing times. *Example:* "From 8:00 to 9:00 a.m. five days a week, I'll say *no* to other meetings or requests."

GUILTY: FROM SELF-BLAME TO SELF-COMPASSION

When you procrastinate, you carry the guilt of not getting things done around with you. This can compound the problem and lead to even more procrastination. Shifting your mindset to one of self-compassion encourages you to treat yourself with kindness, which is more likely to lead to productivity.

- When you catch yourself feeling guilty for not writing enough or meeting your other writing-related goals, pause and reframe the thought. Instead of saying, "I'm failing at this," try saying, "I'm doing the best I can, and every step counts." *Example:* "I didn't write as much as I wanted to today, but that's okay. I'll celebrate what I did accomplish and try again tomorrow."
- If necessary, reduce the size of your goals to make them more manageable and help you avoid guilt. *Example:* "I'll aim to write 300 words today, but I'll be happy with 200."

DISORGANIZED: FROM CHAOS TO SIMPLICITY

You often feel overwhelmed by the messiness of your writing process or area. Shifting your mindset from chaos to simplicity encourages you to streamline your process, prioritize what is essential, and create small structures that bring a sense of order to your work.

- Simplify! Choose just one task or section of your project to focus on for the day. Don't worry about organizing everything else. Just bring clarity to one piece at a time. *Example:* "Today, I'll focus on drafting one scene. I don't need to organize all my notes right now—just this scene."
- It may also help to create a flexible writing framework. Use a rough outline or bullet points to organize your thoughts. *Example:* "I'll write a loose outline of the next three chapters using bullet points, sticky notes, or index cards so I can see where I'm going without feeling fenced in."

OVERTHINKER: FROM ANALYSIS TO ACTION

You tend to underestimate the importance of taking action on your ideas. Change your mindset to embrace action, which will encourage you to focus on taking small steps forward rather than getting stuck in endless planning and thinking.

- Start by setting a time limit for the planning stages of your project—say, no more than two weeks overall or no more than 10–15 minutes a day. Once the time is up, stop planning and take action (writing or otherwise), even if you don't feel fully ready. *Examples:* "I'll spend 10 minutes outlining this scene, then I'll dive in and write, even if I haven't figured everything out yet." | "For the next 20 minutes, I'll write without worrying whether I'm following the perfect plan. I can always revise later, but today I'm focused on taking action."
- Consider setting up experimental periods where you write without planning *at all.* Sometimes all you need is to practice this process a few times to start enjoying it!

TIRED: FROM EXHAUSTION TO ENERGY MANAGEMENT

You often struggle with low energy and fatigue, making it difficult to stay focused on your writing. Shifting your mindset from exhaustion to energy management can help you to work with rather than against your natural energy levels.

- Pay attention to when you feel the most energy during the day, then schedule your writing sessions during these high-energy times if at all possible. *Example:* "I'm usually alert in the morning, so I'll write for 15 minutes after breakfast when I'm still feeling fresh."
- Plan short, timed writing sprints of only 10–20 minutes, followed by a break. *Example:* "I'll write for 20 minutes, then take a 5–10-minute break to recharge before the next session."
- During your "down times," engage in activities that restore your energy rather than drain it. *Example:* "After writing, I'll step outside for a nice walk to clear my head."

Defier: From Resistance to Autonomy

You hate feeling like someone else is telling you what to do and when to do it. Shifting your mindset from resistance to autonomy helps you recognize that you have the power to set your own creative path, making the process feel more like self-expression.

- If traditional structures and deadlines feel restrictive to you, create your own system. Decide to write only at certain times, and set flexible deadlines that allow for creative freedom. *Example:* "I'll write for 15-45 minutes today, depending on how the creativity flows."
- You may also want to reframe your writing as a form of rebellion. Focus on projects that are risky or "against the rules" so that you feel more excited and energized to work on them. *Example:* "I'm going to add some letters and diary entries into this mystery novel just to shake up the usual genre rules and create something unexpected."

Embracing New Mindsets for Lasting Change

Shifting your mindset is one of the most powerful things you can do to overcome procrastination. In fact, if you're a little overwhelmed about how to start tackling your procrastination habit, this is a good first step.

The key to making these mindset shifts happen is practice. Be aware of your thoughts and regularly reframe them. If you fail one day, that's okay. Try again the next.

These changes won't happen overnight, but with each writing session, you have the chance to reinforce your new thinking patterns. Over time, you'll notice that procrastination is losing its grip and that writing has become a more joyful part of your daily life.

twenty
the power of
small wins

NO MATTER what type of procrastinator you are, you probably delay writing at least some of the time because the task in front of you feels overwhelming. We tell ourselves we have to "finish the novel," "design the website," or "create the book launch plan"—all projects that feel intimidating and difficult. This leads us to avoid them entirely, which, of course, is a surefire way to never get them done.

We touched on this in the last chapter. But now, we're diving deeper into why "small wins" are so critical to writing success, and offering you more ways to incorporate this powerful strategy into your new writing routine.

Why Small Wins Are So Effective

When you're facing a large writing project—and by "large," I mean anything that feels like more than you can accomplish in about twenty minutes—your brain sees it as overwhelming and "hard." That means you'll likely procrastinate if you're feeling anything but 100 percent that day.

Be honest: how many days do you really feel at 100 percent? Most of us are running anywhere from 50 to 75 percent most of the time, and sometimes lower than that. Life happens, and we can't expect everything to be perfect for our writing time. I'd say that it's best to expect that you will *not* feel at 100 percent most days when it's time to write, but you can't let that stop you.

When you focus on small wins, you do yourself and your writing a huge favor. Small wins give you quick gratification and a sense of accomplishment. Each time you complete a small, manageable task, you experience a release of dopamine, which is one of the brain's feel-good neurotransmitters. This dopamine boost makes you feel good in the moment and helps fuel your motivation to keep going.

Like a snowball gathering speed, each small-win success leads to another, and pretty soon, you've finished your novel, published your book, completed your website, or whatever you were going for. Pursuing small wins helps you reinforce positive habits and build your confidence.

15 Small Achievable Writing Goals for Procrastinating Writers

To get started on setting smaller goals, try the following 15 approaches. These will work for most writers, no matter their procrastination type. Then, in the next section, we'll focus more on tips that will specifically apply to each type.

1. **Write 100-200 Words a Day:** Having a word-count goal can be a great way to establish and maintain a writing routine. Often, however, we bite off more than we can chew, feeling we have to write 2,000 words or a complete chapter in one session. If it's not working for you to write a lot every day, give yourself a much smaller goal. You can always write more if you like, but if you set the bar low, you'll be much less likely to procrastinate, and getting *something* done is always better than nothing.

2. **Outline a Single Scene:** If you want to outline your novel but have been delaying it, break it down. Maybe you can outline just Act I, a single chapter, or even a single scene. You may believe doing something so small will be useless,

but that's not true. There is great power in getting started! Outline one scene and then go from there. You'll be much more likely to come back and do the next one the following day.

3. **Edit One Page or Paragraph:** Some writers find editing particularly difficult. If you're one of them and you've been putting it off, break it down. Instead of thinking, "I need to edit my story," think, "I need to edit one page," or "I need to edit one paragraph." Make it easier for yourself. Once you get going, you may want to stay with it, but you don't have to. One paragraph is enough for today.

4. **Write for 10 Minutes:** If you don't respond well to word-count goals, try using time instead. A short time frame can feel like a small commitment—something you can handle even when you're tired or uninspired. You'll write for 15 minutes, tell yourself. If that still seems overwhelming, lower it to 10 or even 5. It works.

5. **Jot Down Character Notes:** On those days when you just can't face the blank page, try playing around with your characters instead. Develop their backstories or personality traits. Find pictures of celebrities that appear similar to what you imagine your characters will look like. Determine their astrological signs and biggest flaws. Get creative and you'll soon find that you're drawn into your story.

6. **Write the First Sentence:** One sentence. That's all you have to do. Sound silly? It's not. Think of all those days that you don't write anything at all. If you had written just one sentence on each one, you could have a complete chapter by now! And remember—*it's the getting started* that's the hardest.

7. **Free-Write for 5 Minutes:** This works in a couple of ways. First, you've reduced your time commitment to just five minutes. Second, you're giving yourself permission to free-write. That takes the pressure off. You don't have to worry about structure, what scene you're in, or what your characters are supposed to do. You don't have to worry

about anything at all. Just set the timer and type away, recording whatever comes to mind. This will help you reconnect to the joy of writing. You may want to work on your project after that or you may have discovered the seeds of a new one. Either way, you exercised your writing muscles, which is so much better than not writing at all.

8. **Make a List of Five Plot Points:** If you're working on a novel, think about five main plot points in that novel and simply list them one after the other. These may include your hook, inciting incident, mid-point, climax, and resolution, or any other plot points you want to include based on the story structure you're following. Keep in mind that you're just playing around with these points for now. Nothing is written in stone. Making a simple list is an easy task and can inspire more brainstorming once you get started.

9. **Review and Highlight Favorite Passages:** If you aren't up to writing today, look over what you've already written instead. That's easy, right? Just read some of it and highlight those passages or sentences where you think you nailed it. What seems really good to you right now? What would you like to improve? As you go back through, don't be surprised if you decide to start writing again!

10. **Update Your Author Website with One New Element:** Updating your author website might feel so daunting that you keep putting it off. To stop procrastination in its tracks, commit to making just one small update today. Add a recent book review, list an upcoming event, or write a short, two-paragraph update on your progress with your next book. Don't worry about overhauling the entire site—just take small steps.

11. **Post One Social Media Update About Your Book Today:** It can feel overwhelming to juggle writing and maintaining your author platform at the same time, but it doesn't have to. Commit to posting just once a day. It could be a quote from your book, a quick update on your

progress, or a question for your readers. It takes only about five minutes but keeps you present in your readers' minds.

12. **Write One Email to Your Mailing List:** If you have a subscriber list (and I hope you do!), you might find yourself procrastinating when it comes to sending out emails. But they don't have to be long. A short note from you is often enough to stay connected with your readers. In fact, a brief, engaging email can often be more effective than a lengthy one. Your readers are busy, too, and they'll likely appreciate a quick, uplifting message from you.

13. **Create One Graphic for Your Book:** Using Canva, Book Brush, or another design program, create one simple graphic related to your book. It could include your cover and a short review or your cover and the first sentence of your synopsis. Use the templates available to make it easy. Then share that graphic for the rest of the week on all your social media channels.

14. **Draft a One-Page Book Launch Plan:** Launching a book can seem like a daunting project. Break it down by deciding that you'll start with just the first page today. On that page, outline the basic strategy for launching your book. Include things like your launch date, a list of promotions you'll do, and your target audience. Just that much is enough to get you started. Then come back the next time and expand on what you've got.

15. **Reach Out to One Fellow Writer:** Partnering with other writers can help boost your book's visibility. Start by making a list of potential authors you could team up with for a joint promotion or newsletter swap. Just creating the list is enough for one day. Next time, choose the top three authors that you think would fit best. The following day, draft the email you plan to send subscribers. Then, a day or two after that, send the emails out.

Time to Set Your Own Small, Achievable Goals!

The previous 15 small goals are meant to serve as examples to help you get used to breaking things down. Now that you've got the hang of it, start creating your own. Think of every writing project as a big pie that needs to be sliced into its smallest pieces. Take just a bite each day, and you'll find it much easier to avoid procrastination and stay productive.

Small Wins for Each Procrastination Type

While small wins, in general, are beneficial for breaking through procrastination, each procrastination type faces unique challenges that can make even small goals feel daunting. In this section, I give you some suggestions for how each type can integrate small wins in a way that addresses their individual tendencies. Use the "ultimate goal" for each type as a guide when deciding how to break up your large projects into smaller goals.

Worrier
Focus on small tasks that reduce pressure. Ask yourself, "How can I make this less intimidating or anxiety-producing?" Consider bite-sized revisions that lower the stakes, such as teeny-tiny word-count goals. *Your ultimate goal:* Create a small win that helps you feel more *relaxed* and *in control* of the task ahead of you.

Avoider
Diminish any negative emotions you may feel by focusing on the smallest step forward. Ask yourself, "How can I encourage my own confidence?" Write just a paragraph or a few sentences that excite you about your story.
Your ultimate goal: Create a small win that helps you feel *empowered* and *capable* when approaching the task ahead of you.

Dreamer
Tap into your love of big concepts while still taking small, meaningful action. Ask yourself, "How can I use my imagination on this task and

still get something concrete done?" Spend 15 minutes sketching out a scene from the story you've been dreaming about, for example, or explore three story ideas by writing the first scene of each to help decide which one to pursue next.

Your ultimate goal: Create a small win that gives you the satisfaction of *seeing your vision begin to take shape.*

Fun Seeker

You want your small wins to be playful challenges. Ask yourself, "How can I make this fun to do?" or "How can I make this more exciting?" Turn the project into some sort of game, then reward yourself afterward.

Your ultimate goal: Create a small win that helps you feel *energized* and *engaged.*

Perfectionist

Allow yourself to play on the page without feeling like your words have to be perfect. Ask yourself, "How can I make progress while feeling less pressured to be perfect?" Write a chapter without editing it, for example.

Your ultimate goal: Create small wins that are *progress-focused.*

Crisis Maker

You tend to avoid doing a task until the last minute. Ask yourself, "How can I make this small task feel more urgent right now?" Maybe you can create several deadlines to meet between now and the final deadline.

Your ultimate goal: Create small wins that help you feel *a sense of urgency.*

Distracted

Understanding your tendency to succumb to distraction, keep your small wins short. Ask yourself, "How can I increase the likelihood that I'll be able to focus on this task for a short time?" Writing in 10-minute bursts can help, as might writing with other writers who encourage you to focus.

Your ultimate goal: Create a small win that helps you feel *focused* and *productive.*

Overdoer
You have a tendency to take on too much at once. Ask yourself, "How can I lower my sense of overwhelm when thinking about this project?" Decide to do just one small task, for example, or say "no" to another task so you have more time to work on your writing.
Your ultimate goal: Create a small win that helps you feel *balanced* and *calm.*

Guilty
You tend to feel bad about everything you haven't accomplished so far. Instead, ask yourself, "How can I feel good about this project today?" Maybe you review and highlight your favorite passages from past writing, or write just 100 words to regain a sense of forward momentum.
Your ultimate goal: Create a small win that helps you feel *proud* and *self-compassionate.*

Disorganized
When you're feeling overwhelmed by the chaos in front of you, try narrowing your focus to just one thing. Ask yourself, "How can I bring a sense of order to one small part of this today?" Maybe you create a list of three key tasks for your project or review your outline and make a few refinements.
Your ultimate goal: Create a small win that helps you feel *clear-headed* and *in control.*

Overthinker
You often spend too much time planning and analyzing. Ask yourself, "How can I actually *make prog*ress on the project itself?" Write one scene for 10 minutes, for example, or outline the next chapter without allowing yourself to worry about the rest of the book.
Your ultimate goal: Create a small win that makes you feel *decisive* and *confident* moving forward.

Tired
You're often too tired to work on your writing projects. Ask yourself, "How can I adjust this so it takes less energy?" Brainstorm a chapter

title, free-write for five minutes, or write 100 words during the time of day that you feel most energetic.

Your ultimate goal: Create a small win that helps you feel *energized* and *accomplished*.

Defier

You are all about making your own rules, so get creative with your small wins. Ask yourself, "How can I make this uniquely my own?" Set rebellious goals or allow yourself to break conventional rules.

Your ultimate goal: Create a small win that helps you feel *independent* and *empowered*.

Building Your Own Small Wins

Creating small wins that work with your procrastination type is a skill you can develop with practice. As you get used to recognizing your specific tendencies—whether wanting everything to be fun, worrying about being perfect, or struggling with energy levels—you can start pivoting with small, achievable goals that will help you move forward.

You may want to keep a journal as you go through this process to track the types of small wins that work for you. The more you focus on breaking down your writing tasks into manageable chunks, the better you'll get at turning even those big intimidating projects into a series of easy-to-do tasks that lead to motivating milestones.

Keep practicing, and before long, you'll find that small wins are not just a tool for overcoming procrastination but a habit that fuels your writing success.

Exercise: Create Your Own Bite-Sized Goals

OKAY, IT'S YOUR TURN TO CREATE SMALL, ACHIEVABLE writing goals tailored to your unique procrastination type (or blend) and your current writing project.

STEP 1: BRAINSTORM QUICK WINS

Set a timer for five minutes and brainstorm a list of tiny writing tasks that feel achievable and low-pressure. Some examples:

- Write 100 words
- Edit one paragraph
- Make a list of plot points
- Sketch out one character's main traits
- Outline Act I

The goal is to come up with bite-sized tasks that move your project forward and feel really easy to do. Try to aim for at least 10 ideas.

STEP 2: PICK YOUR TOP 5

Review the list you made and highlight the five tasks that seem to be the most fun, easy, or motivating right now. If you find it hard to choose, start with those that feel doable within a few minutes.

STEP 3: SET A TIMER AND START SMALL

Choose one task from your list of top five and set a timer for just 10 minutes. Tell yourself that this short session is for finishing this one small task—no more. Whether you finish early or the timer goes off, celebrate that win!

STEP 4: REFLEECT AND BUILD ON

Once you're done, jot down a few notes about your experience. Did that small win make writing feel more manageable? Did you feel a sense of accomplishment? Did it energize you to keep going? Use these reflections to inspire more small wins in the future.

twenty-one
creating accountability

WRITING IS OFTEN A SOLITARY ENDEAVOR, which is why it can be so easy to put it off. No one knows whether you wrote today or not, so it's no skin off your nose if you delay. Without any external structure or encouragement, even the most dedicated writers can lose momentum.

Creating accountability—whether it comes from others or self-imposed challenges—helps you break through this kind of isolation-induced procrastination. Inviting others into your creative progress increases your motivation to push through procrastination and get the work done. Likewise, participating in structured challenges or setting public goals can create a sense of commitment that provides just the pressure you need to stay the course. Someone else—or something else—will be making it harder to put off working on your project.

And that's what we want—to make it harder.

Accountability can come in three main forms: writing buddies, groups, and timed challenges. Each offers a way for you to connect, encourage, and push yourself forward. When you're surrounded by others who are showing up, or you've entered a challenge with clear expectations, it becomes easier to show up yourself.

In this chapter, we're going to focus on the value of each account-ability method and how they can help you build productive habits so you can stay on track while feeling more supported in your creative journey. Then, I'll give you some tips on building accountability for each procrastination type.

Why Accountability Is Essential for Writers

Internal motivation isn't always enough to carry you through to the finish line, which you probably already know or you wouldn't have picked up this book! It's easy for self-doubt, distractions, fatigue, busy schedules, and more to interfere along the way, making it harder to stick to your long-term goals.

Think of accountability as an added layer of support. Knowing that someone is expecting an update on your progress—or simply knowing that you've publicly committed to a goal—can create a sense of responsibility that gives you just the push you need to keep moving forward.

Once you set up an accountability program that works for you, don't be surprised if you feel less isolated as a writer and that you experience more energy around the work of writing. Regularly building accountability into your process can also help you develop more productive writing habits over time, keeping procrastination from getting in your way.

Benefits of Accountability for Writers

Here are a few of the clear benefits of building accountability into your writing world.

- **Keeps You On Track:** Regular check-ins or progress updates prevent you from drifting away from your objectives, even when you don't really feel up to working on them. Knowing you have to report on what you've been up to adds that extra push to work on days when procrastination would otherwise take over.
- **Offers Emotional Support:** Writing isn't just a mental activity. It's emotional, too. Having a support network gives you somewhere to vent your frustrations, brainstorm

solutions, and celebrate your achievements. Knowing that others understand your struggle can also make a big difference in your ability to stick with it and keep going.

- **Provides Feedback and Perspective:** You may want to get feedback on your writing from your accountability partners, as they can offer fresh insights and ideas. Being part of a positive, supportive writing group can help you grow as a writer and build confidence in your abilities. Other writers may also help you put a problem into perspective, so it doesn't seem larger than it actually is, giving you the strength to tackle it.
- **Builds Accountability Habits:** If you have regular check-ins with your accountability buddy or group, these can become part of your writing routine over time, making your goals feel more structured and achievable. Integrating accountability into your regular process will reinforce the habit of consistent writing, goal-setting, adjusting, and writing again, leading to higher productivity and motivation.

Types of Accountability

Each option gives you a way to connect with others, share progress, and tackle goals together. We'll look at how each approach works so you can decide which may be best for you.

1. WRITING BUDDIES

These are your one-on-one accountability partners. They provide personalized support and motivation. Together, you set goals and check-in with each other regularly, typically weekly or biweekly. During these check-ins, you share your progress, talk about any challenges you're having, and celebrate your small wins. This is more of a personalized form of accountability and works great for introverts and those who prefer keeping their writing network small.

How to Use Writing Buddies

Start by looking for writers who share your goals and values, either in local communities or online. You could attend local writing events, workshops, or book clubs where other writers may gather. Libraries, bookstores, and community centers also host writing meet-ups, which can be an ideal place to network.

Online, look to platforms like writing-focused subreddits, writing communities on Facebook, or dedicated sites like Scribophile and Critique Circle, where writers actively seek critique partners and accountability buddies.

Try to find someone who is working toward similar goals and could use some support. Once you've connected with that person, aim for a trial period to see how it goes. Schedule regular check-ins, and during each session, discuss what you've accomplished and share any road-blocks. Exchange feedback on each other's work if you like, but know that it's not required. Then, set clear, achievable goals for your next session. (Remember to go for small wins!) This last part is especially important—you want it to be clear what you're both expected to accomplish by your next check-in.

When you find someone who works well with you, you may be amazed at how much having a writing buddy helps you stay on task!

2. Writing Groups

Writing groups are made up of multiple writers who gather to share goals, progress, and feedback. These groups may meet in person or online, depending on the members' preferences and schedules. They often offer a broader community of support and a variety of perspectives, which can be helpful if you're looking for diverse insights.

Keep in mind that writing groups can vary widely depending on who is leading them and what their general guidelines are. Some may be unproductive or even discouraging, especially if the group dynamics are negative or not aligned with your goals. To avoid getting into a situation like that, hold off on sharing any of your writing until you can get a good sense of how the group feels to you. If members are overly critical —particularly if they lack experience in writing and publishing—be extremely cautious. Do the same if some members seem overly competitive or if the group, as a whole, lacks structure.

The best groups have clear guidelines about feedback and a focus on mutual respect. You may want to seek out a group that offers support only, without feedback, as that may be more in line with what you need initially. When you're ready for feedback, in many cases it's better to hire a qualified book coach or editor than to take your piece to a writing group where a variety of people with differing backgrounds may only confuse you with their comments.

Prioritize groups that share your values and, above all, support each member's creative journey. Remember that you can always start a group of your own. That way, you'll be sure that it aligns with your goals.

How to Use Writing Groups

Effective writing groups hold regular meetings—at least once a month, but preferably more often—where members can share their goals and progress, participate in group writing activities, and, when appropriate, provide thoughtful feedback on each other's work. They also give members the chance to tackle shared goals, such as hitting specific word counts, finishing a short story to submit to a contest, or reaching milestones like completing a book.

Ultimately, a writing group should support your progress and help build excitement and momentum around your work, making it easier for you to stay on track. If it's not doing that, get out of it and try again.

3. Writing Challenges

Writing challenges give you a time-bound way to stay accountable. National Novel Writing Month (NaNoWriMo), though defunct now, was a well-known example. It set a specific goal—writing a novel of at least 50,000 words—in 30 days. Challenges like this help push writers to maintain a high level of productivity within a limited time. Other examples include StoryADay—a free, month-long creative challenge—and Shut Up and Write!, a free community-driven nonprofit initiative designed to help writers get their writing done.

Writing challenges can be group-based, but you can also set them up with your writing buddy or even on your own. They have clear start and end dates (or times) and are paired with a focused goal, such as reaching 50,000 words. These elements work together to help writers overcome procrastination, at least during the challenge.

How to Use Writing Challenges

You can join an official challenge or create one of your own with your writing buddy or writing group. Set clear, time-limited goals and create a schedule that works for you. The combination of a tight deadline and a shared purpose helps reduce the chances that you'll succumb to procrastination, allowing you to get more done in less time.

Some examples of writing challenges you can do yourself or with writing friends include the following:

- **7-Day Story Challenge:** Set a goal to write a complete short story within seven days. Each day, focus on a specific element, like brainstorming, outlining, characters, plot, writing, editing, and polishing. This type of challenge can help you better manage your time while encouraging you to break the project up into manageable pieces.
- **Flash-Fiction Daily Challenge:** Set a challenge to write one 100- to 500-word flash fiction piece every day for a month. Choose a different theme, prompt, or genre each day to keep things fresh and fun. By keeping the word count low and the writing window short, this challenge helps build discipline while still allowing for flexibility.
- **Genre Exploration Month:** This is a great option for writers who aren't sure which genre to choose. Over 30 days, challenge yourself to write a short piece—no more than 500 words—in a different genre each day. You might tackle romance one day, science fiction the next, then horror, fantasy, mystery, supernatural, thriller, and more. The variety pushes you to experiment with new styles, tones, and techniques. By the end of the 30 days, you may

discover new genres you want to explore further, along with fresh ideas you can later expand into longer projects.

- **One-Line-A-Day Story Challenge:** Set aside 30 days. On each day, write just one line of an ongoing story. The idea is to build gradually on this story without overwhelming yourself. Tap into your love of words and play around with each sentence. Make sure that each line moves the plot forward so that by the end of the 30 days, you have a unique, organically grown story you can share. Then take some time to reflect on the process. Is there something about it you can use in the future to get your novel finished?

Accountability Tips for Each Procrastination Type

By this point in the book, you probably understand your top procrastination type(s) pretty well. Using what you know, you can create the type of accountability that works best for you. To get you started, I've added some dos and don'ts below.

Worrier

Do: Find a supportive writing buddy or group where you feel safe sharing your progress without fear of judgment. Start small with achievable goals so you don't feel overwhelmed by the pressure to perform.
Don't: Don't choose a partner or group that fuels your anxiety. Sharing worries can amplify your fears rather than help you focus on making progress.

Avoider

Do: Use a buddy or group that provides gentle, consistent check-ins. You want to be sure you feel comfortable with this person or group so you have no reason to avoid meetings.
Don't: Don't choose a partner who won't check in regularly. That will only help you avoid accountability, defeating the purpose. In other words, don't choose another Avoider! You need someone who will help you stay on track—someone who will hold you accountable without judgment.

Dreamer

Do: Join a group with a set structure for sharing progress or completing small tasks. You can still dream big, but regular check-ins will keep you grounded in action.

Don't: Choose a group that goes overboard on productivity. You want to feel compelled to produce, but if the demands are too intense, they could burn you out, so avoid groups that focus solely on output. Similarly, avoid a writing buddy who only wants to talk about ideas without producing anything. That won't help you either. You need people who enjoy brainstorming, but who get the work done.

Fun Seeker

Do: Make accountability fun by joining a group that knows how to celebrate each other's small wins. Even better if the group has regular challenges and rewards. If you prefer to choose just one or two writing buddies, you can set up your own challenges and rewards that may work just as well.

Don't: Don't set up accountability with someone who is very rigid or too focused on goals. This can lead to you feeling stifled and soon you'll be back to procrastinating. Look for partners and groups that encourage a sense of play in their progress.

Perfectionist

Do: Partner with a person or group that encourages progress over perfection. You're looking for people who will celebrate your work rather than criticize it too harshly. The focus should be on getting the words down and making progress toward your goals.

Don't: Don't join groups or link up with partners that overemphasize critique and feedback. Getting too much criticism too soon will be demotivating for you, so choose those who focus mostly on encouraging progress, perhaps with the occasional constructive feedback, but only at the right time!

Crisis-Maker

Do: Find a group or partner that schedules short, intense sprints or daily check-ins. Use writing challenges to give yourself and your partners that sense of urgency that you crave.

Don't: Don't wait until the last minute to check in with your accountability partner or group. Delayed check-ins put you right back into your bad habit of procrastination. You want to have regularly scheduled check-ins so you create urgency outside of the deadline.

Distracted

Do: Use timed group writing sprints or focused sessions with a writing buddy to write without succumbing to distraction. Set clear guidelines before each challenge to put your phones away, shut down search engines, etc. Be sure that your buddy or group stays focused on short, achievable tasks.

Don't: Resist the temptation to join too many groups or take on too many buddies at once. This is a reflection of your distracted type and will only exacerbate the problem. Choose one group or buddy and stick with that for at least a certain amount of time to see how it works for you.

Overdoer

Do: Use your accountability partner or group to help you prioritize tasks and set boundaries. Have your buddy check in, for example, on whether you're focusing on your writing rather than overcommitting to other projects.

Don't: Don't agree to multiple overlapping accountability commitments. In other words, don't agree to do too much! Choose a partner or group that understands your need for balance and achievable goals.

Guilty

Do: Join a supportive writing group where you can celebrate your small wins. Use check-ins to recognize the progress you've made, even if it feels like you haven't done enough. Find people willing to help you focus on what you have done rather than what you haven't.

Don't: Don't choose a partner or group that adds pressure or judgment. You'll benefit more from those that encourage self-compassion, rather than those who focus more on what you've missed.

Disorganized

Do: Find a partner or group that offers clear, structured check-ins, tasks, and timelines that help you stay on track. It also helps if they have very clear guidelines of what's expected of you, which can help you focus on just one task at a time.

Don't: Don't rely on informal accountability without structure. You benefit from specific meeting times (that don't change often) and defined goals. A loosey-goosey group is not for you.

Overthinker

Do: Choose a writing group or partner that helps push you to action while pulling you away from overthinking and planning. Find a buddy who encourages action over analysis and will call you out if they see you're delaying your actual work on the project.

Don't: Don't choose a partner or group that indulges in too much planning and discussion. If this group just loves to get together and talk about what their novels are going to be like without actually writing those novels, that is not the group for you.

Tired

Do: You need a low-pressure accountability buddy or group to help you set bite-sized goals. Avoid those with heavy expectations. Look for something that will help you make slow but steady progress.

Don't: Don't join a group or partner up with someone with overly demanding schedules or expectations. That is just setting yourself up for failure. Look for something that offers gentle, energy-sensitive goals with members who value finding a healthy balance between rest and productivity.

Defier

Do: Choose a group or buddy that allows you to set your own rules. Find something that encourages creative freedom and non-traditional approaches to writing—that will help you make progress without feeling rebellious against group rules or standards.

Don't: Avoid any writing buddies, groups, or challenges that impose rigid rules or micromanage. You will benefit from partners who encourage creative autonomy while gently promoting progress on your terms.

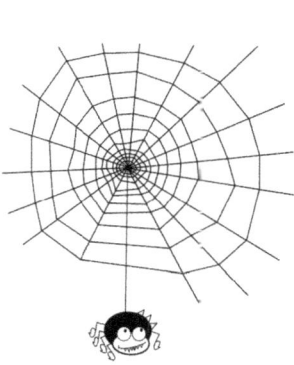

Exercise: Find Your Ideal Accountability Partner

USE THIS EXERCISE TO IDENTIFY THE IDEAL PARTNER OR group to support your writing goals.

STEP 1: REFLECT ON YOUR ACCOUNTABILITY PREFERENCES

Grab a piece of paper or open a document on your computer and answer these questions. Keep your procrastination type in mind as you do! Remember that your regular preferences may lead to procrastination, so answer based on what you need to get your work done.

- Do you need frequent check-ins or work better with less frequent, bigger updates?
- What level of feedback feels best to you—light encouragement, constructive critique, or a mix?
- Do you want a partner, a group, or a writing challenge? (Choose just one for now. You can change it later if you like.)

STEP 2: DEFINE YOUR IDEAL ACCOUNTABILITY QUALITIES

List the qualities you think your accountability partner or group should have to support you effectively. Focus on what you know about your type. Do you need someone who is organized, disciplined, caring, encouraging, flexible, reliable, fun, energetic, laid-back, or driven? Write down at least three qualities that you think will best help you succeed.

If you're focused on finding a writing challenge, list the qualities the challenge needs to have. How long should it last? How much will you need to get done in that time? Think about your schedule right now to find one you can manage. Remember—if you can't find one that already exists, you can always make your own!

STEP 3: TEST THE WATERS

Find a low-pressure way to test your accountability setup. Join a short-term writing challenge, for example, attend just one meeting of a writing group, or have a trial check-in with a potential writing buddy. Afterward, ask yourself how you felt: Was it motivating, or did it add pressure? Did you feel connected, or was it a mismatch?

Use your answers to refine or change your approach. Don't give up if the first attempt doesn't work out. If you keep trying, you'll find a motivating accountability structure that helps you reach your writing goals.

the power of fear in procrastination

ONE THING I heard over and over while researching the thirteen types of writers was this: many of us procrastinate because of fear.

No matter what our main type or blended type, fear often rears its ugly head and chases us away from our writing work. Because it's so pervasive in the writing world, I wanted to dedicate a separate chapter to address it.

The danger is that fear can disguise itself. It whispers doubts and uncertainties in our ears, and we procrastinate without fully realizing what's happening. Instead of sitting down and enjoying the next scene in our stories, we delay or distract ourselves with less important tasks, only to regret those choices later.

This book is all about discovering what's at the root of your procrastination, and as we've learned, it's usually a combination of factors. Understanding how fear fits into the picture can go a long way toward helping you find workable solutions.

In this chapter, we'll explore how fear influences procrastination across the thirteen different types. By identifying the specific fears that tend to be associated with your main types (and your blended type), I hope to offer strategies you can use to overcome these barriers and get back to writing.

How Fear Fuels Procrastination

Procrastination often serves as a coping mechanism, helping us to avoid the uncomfortable emotions associated with fear. Think about how you feel right before you sit down to write. Are you relaxed and looking forward to the session, or do small fears bubble up in your belly, making you feel uneasy?

Fear can show up in many forms. We may fear failure, success, criticism, or even the unknown. We might worry that we're not capable of telling the story we want to tell or that we'll invest time in something people won't like or that will never sell.

We can put fear in its place by confronting it directly. Sit down and write despite the discomfort, and the fear often disappears pretty quickly. But we don't always do that because we *aren't fully aware* that fear is sabotaging us in the moment. All we notice are vague, uncomfortable feelings, so we choose to do something else or distract ourselves, convinced that we'll be better prepared to write "later."

Ultimately, procrastination is often not about poor time management or laziness—it's about *feeling better*. It gives us a way to avoid the negative emotions that can surface when we think about writing or a writing-related task. Anxiety, insecurity, self-doubt, worry—all of these can come up when we face the writing chair. By putting off the work, we escape the discomfort. But the underlying fear remains, now compounded by guilt, disappointment, and a sense of failure.

Common Fears Among Writers

Below are some of the most common fears writers experience at different times in their careers.

1. **Fear of Failure:** Perhaps the most pervasive of all is the fear of failure. We worry that our work won't live up to our expectations, that it will be rejected by an agent or editor, or that it won't sell. Often, before we've even written a few chapters, we're already imagining fearful future scenarios that hold us back.

2. **Fear of Success:** Most of us long for success. We work hard for years and years to achieve whatever our version of success may be. But often, just as we're on the cusp of reaching it, we get scared. We pull back. Sometimes, we sabotage ourselves completely. If you've ever had a publisher request the full manuscript of your story and you missed the deadline, you know what I mean. Or maybe you were invited to do a reading at an event and you backed out. Success brings its own set of challenges. Some of the scariest include increased visibility—maybe we're not ready to be "seen," even though we have wanted it for so long. Or we may fear that success will come with higher expectations that we won't be able to meet.

3. **Fear of Criticism:** Sharing our work exposes us to the judgments and opinions of others. If we want to become successful writers, there's no way around that part of the process. Yet the fear of receiving negative feedback from readers, peers, judges, editors, or critics can discourage us from putting our writing out into the world. When this kind of fear creeps in, we often avoid writing, obsessively edit the same piece again and again, or abandon projects altogether, convinced they won't be good enough.

4. **Fear of Imperfection:** Similar to the fear of criticism, we may fear imperfection. Perfectionist types are especially prone to this, but other types—such as the Worrier, Avoider, and Overthinker—can experience it as well. These types strive to produce flawless work, which often leads to spending an inordinate amount of time editing, refining, polishing, redoing, and editing again, never feeling satisfied enough to consider the story complete.

The Cycle of Fear and Procrastination Leads to Avoidance

Unfortunately, fear is one of those things that "feeds" procrastination. We feel fear, we procrastinate, and that reinforces the fear, and around and around we go. When we dodge a writing project to escape uncomfortable emotions, we inadvertently strengthen those emotions. The more we avoid writing, the more daunting it becomes, making it even harder to begin.

FEAR'S IMPACT ON CREATIVITY

Fear can also stifle your creativity by fostering self-doubt and limiting your willingness to take risks. To produce original and impactful work, you need confidence in what you're doing and a willingness to stick your neck out a little. That's what creativity is about.

But when we're consumed by fear, our mental energy shifts away from creative exploration and toward coping with anxiety. This shift results in:

- **Reduced Innovation:** As you hesitate to experiment with new ideas or styles for fear of making mistakes or producing subpar work, your creativity drops.
- **Self-Censorship:** If you're worried that you may be writing about controversial topics or unconventional concepts that others will criticize, you may find yourself censoring your writing, again, reducing your creative spark.
- **Loss of Authentic Voice:** If you let fear alter your writing to fit perceived expectations rather than expressing your genuine self, the originality of your work will suffer.

If we let it, fear will diminish the richness and authenticity of our writing. It keeps us confined within safe boundaries, preventing us from discovering our unique voice and forming a deep connection with our readers.

Coping with Fear: Tips for Each Procrastination Type

Fear is a universal saboteur for writers, but it tends to show up a little differently depending on your procrastination type or blend. Below are some common scenarios for each, along with some possible coping techniques and exercises that may help.

This list isn't absolute, meaning that you may experience fear in ways that differ from what's shown below. Use this information as a starting point, but be prepared to do some detective work in your own writing life to uncover how fear might be messing with you.

1. The Worrier: Fear of the Unknown

You are concerned about all the things that could go wrong, which can lead to inaction. *To cope:* Address your fears directly through calming techniques and proactive planning.

- **Set Contingency Plans:** What will you do if the worst happens? How will you handle it? Determining this in advance can help. For example, "If I get bad reviews on my work, I'll realize that all authors get bad reviews from time and time, and remind myself that I can't please everyone."
- **Meditate Before Writing:** Spend 5-10 minutes before writing to calm your mind with a guided meditation. Let your anxieties go so you can have fun on your story.

Exercise: The Worry Jar
Place a jar or a small box and a stack of sticky notes on your writing desk. If you find that you're about to procrastinate on your writing task, take a sticky note and write down what's worrying you or making you feel anxious. Put it in the jar or box and forget about it. Then, spend at least 5-15 minutes writing.

2. The Avoider: Fear of Failure and Judgment

You see failure and criticism as the worst possible things that could happen to you. You can't imagine facing up to them. You'd rather avoid the task altogether. *To cope:* Make the task feel more approachable so that fear is less intimidating.

- **Create a Supportive Environment:** Surround yourself with supportive people who can provide positive reinforcement and accountability. Find these people in local reading and writing groups or in online writing groups.
- **Visualize Positive Outcomes:** Focus on the benefits of simply finishing the story rather than thinking so much about potential negative outcomes.

Exercise: The "5-Minute Start"
Set a timer for five minutes and work on your writing during that time. When the timer goes off, you can choose to stop or keep going. The point is to give yourself an easy way to get past the fearful emotions and dive into the story itself rather than thinking too much about how you might fail.

3. THE DREAMER: FEAR OF IMPLEMENTATION

You prefer imagining over doing, fearing that reality won't match your vision. *To cope:* Embrace the creative process as a journey rather than a destination.

- **Start with Low-Stakes Projects:** Begin with tasks that feel less intimidating to build confidence in your ability to bring your ideas to life. Outline your first chapter, for example, or start working on a character profile.
- **Use Visualization:** Imagine the process of working through your writing tasks—not just the end result. Try visualizing each step along the way. See yourself writing each chapter, outlining the story and then writing each scene, or deciding what you're going to focus on with each subsequent draft. Train yourself to "see" the process.

Exercise: The "Idea to Action" Map
Choose one idea and create a colorful mind map, drawing the steps you need to take to make this story happen. Use images and colors if you

like. The point is to move yourself from brainstorming into action, while leaving the fear behind.

4. The Fun Seeker: Fear of Boredom or Discomfort

You may procrastinate because you fear the discomfort associated with less enjoyable or more difficult tasks. *To cope:* Integrate "fun" into your work more often.

- **Incorporate Fun Into Your Tasks:** Make writing more enjoyable by adding elements you think are fun, like writing in a favorite café or with colorful pens.
- **Use Gamification:** Turn tasks into games with rewards to keep yourself motivated, such as earning points for each writing session. Invite other writers to join you and make a competition out of it.

Exercise: Exploring the Fun

Take 15–20 minutes to explore all the ways you can make your writing more fun. Think about how you can spruce up your writing nook, what programs or apps you may use, what props you could add (like Tarot cards or letter boards), what treats you could have only after writing, who may be fun to work with, what types of stories may be more fun to write, and more. Once you have a robust list, see if you can put at least some of those things into action. As you do, your fear will lessen, as you'll realize you can always control your own level of fun.

5. The Perfectionist: Fear of Criticism

You fear that if your work isn't perfect, you'll be opening yourself up to humiliating criticism. *To cope:* Reframe your mindset to value progress over perfection.

- **Seek Constructive Feedback Early:** Head off fear by sharing your second or third draft with a trusted professional to gain feedback. Work with beta readers,

editors, and book coaches to improve your work so you feel less afraid of making mistakes.
- **Map Out Your Writing Career:** Instead of focusing too much on one book or one project, see your writing career as a whole. Imagine yourself at 80 years old perusing a bookshelf that holds all of your published books.

Exercise: The Imperfect Poem Challenge
Set a timer for 10 minutes and write a short poem. Don't worry about grammar, punctuation, or any rules—the goal is to create something imperfect on purpose. When you're done, be brave and share your poem with someone. Remind yourself that a little criticism isn't enough to stop you.

6. The Crisis-Maker: Fear of Losing Motivation
You may worry that without the urgency of a deadline, you won't be productive or that your work won't be any good. *To cope:* Find other ways to motivate yourself to get the work done sooner.

- **Find Alternative Motivators:** Look into other ways to motivate yourself outside of time pressure. Accountability partners, rewards, writing challenges, and other sources of inspiration may work just as well to get you going. These can also help you forget about your fears, at least for a short time.
- **Set an Automatic Early Deadline:** Start treating every deadline like a "false" deadline and set your deadline two weeks (or whatever time frame feels right) earlier. If your edits are due in four weeks, set a deadline for two weeks from now. Get into a pattern that you can regularly keep to help avoid last-minute chaos.

Exercise: The "Beat the Clock" Challenge
Set a timer for a specific period—like 30 minutes—and challenge yourself to complete a task before it goes off. Finish a chapter, an outline, a

blog post, or any other type of writing-related task. For more fun, invite other writers to join you.

7. THE DISTRACTED: FEAR OF MISSING OUT (FOMO)

You fear missing out on something important, so you may regularly check notifications or multitask, thinking you can keep track of more than one thing at once. *To cope:* Take control of your distraction time.

- **Set Specific Times for Distractions:** To assure yourself that you won't miss out, set certain times during the day when you will allow yourself to check social media, read emails, peruse the Internet, etc. This can help keep you from feeling deprived when you shut down distractions while writing.
- **Practice Mindfulness:** Realize that your anxiety about missing out could be tied to a general underlying anxiety. Practice mindfulness techniques like daily meditation to help calm and quiet your mind.

Exercise: The "Distraction Vault"
Write down distracting thoughts or things you want to check on and place those notes in a "vault" (box or drawer). Promise to revisit them during your designated break time.

8. THE OVERDOER: FEAR OF LETTING OTHERS DOWN

You fear disappointing others or missing opportunities, so you over-commit, stretching yourself too thin. *To cope:* Set priorities and boundaries.

- **Practice Saying "No:"** You may fear telling people "no" for many reasons—you don't want to disappoint them, you're afraid they will resist or argue, or you're afraid of what others think about you. Start small. When someone asks to help you in the store, say "no" politely. Gradually increase the difficulty until you get better at honoring your own priorities with a simple "no."

- **Set Boundaries:** Establish limits on your time and energy to improve your focus on your writing.

Exercise: The "Yes/No" Boxes
For each new request or opportunity, write it down, and after thinking about it, place it in either a "yes" or "no" box or jar. Limit the number of "yes" slips you allow per week. Remember that your priorities matter as much or more as others' priorities.

9. The Guilty: Fear of Not Doing Enough

You fear letting yourself and others down, which can prevent you from attempting new projects. *To cope:* Practice more self-compassion and focus only on your present actions rather than those in the past.

- **Focus on the Present Moment:** Concentrate on what you can do now—in the next 5-10 minutes—rather than dwelling on the past.
- **Talk to Yourself in Third Person:** Talk to yourself as you would a good friend. "It's okay, Bob. Everyone struggles at times. You can start over today. Let's write for just 10 minutes." It may feel silly, but it can really help!

Exercise: The "Clean Slate" Ritual
Write down all your guilty feelings on a piece of paper, then tear it up or safely burn it to symbolize letting go. Allow your fear of letting people down to dissipate.

10. The Disorganized: Fear of Structure

You may worry that too much organization will limit your spontaneity and the natural flow of ideas. *To cope:* Instead of avoiding organization altogether, try adopting more flexible organizational methods that feel good to you.

- **Organize in Small Increments:** Tackle organization in short sessions to reduce resistance and prevent overwhelm. Take just five minutes to organize your writing desk as much as you can, for example, before writing. Or spend 10 minutes of your writing time organizing your notes before actually writing.
- **Adopt Flexible Planning:** Alleviate your fear of too much structure by adopting "just a little" organization or remaining flexible in how you approach your planning. Use a loose outline for your story that can be changed, for example, or a flexible schedule for completing your next writing task.

Exercise: The "Creative Chaos" Board
Put a cork board up in your writing nook, then use it to pin notes, images, and ideas freely without a set structure. If you regularly review it, replacing those things you don't need anymore, it may soon serve as a helpful organizational tool for you. Focus on this and other ways you can ease the pressure you feel around organization.

11. THE OVERTHINKER: FEAR OF CHOOSING WRONG
You fear making the wrong choice or selecting the wrong path, so you overanalyze, procrastinating on the actual writing. *To cope:* Accept that not all your decisions will be perfect, and that's okay.

- **Set Decision Deadlines:** Give yourself only so much time to make decisions. Stick to your deadlines to build decisiveness. Remind yourself that your fear is holding you back.
- **Focus on Action Over Thought:** Prioritize taking action to build momentum and reduce anxiety. Doing is often better than deliberating.

Exercise: The "Coin Flip" Decision Maker
For small decisions—such as what to name your character or which

plotting method to use—flip a coin to choose between two options. Then, commit to acting on the result no matter what. Face your fear that you've ended up with the "wrong" decision and act anyway. Keep in mind that decisions about our stories and writing processes are often much less important than actually *doing* the writing itself.

12. The Tired: Fear of Inadequacy Due to Fatigue

You may worry that your tiredness will result in poor-quality writing, so you delay. *To cope:* Work on managing your energy levels and setting more realistic goals.

- **Work During Peak Energy Times:** Spend some time identifying your peak energy times, then see if you can fit at least a short writing session into those times. Set your fear aside by telling yourself you're just practicing for now.
- **Set Realistic Expectations:** Adjust your goals to match your energy levels. You may not be able to write a full chapter today, but you could potentially get in a couple of paragraphs. Remind yourself that it doesn't have to be award-winning. You just need to get something down.

Exercise: Make an "Energy Boost" Playlist
Music has a way of tapping into the nervous system to stoke energy. Take a few minutes to create an energy-boosting playlist of tunes that lift you up. Listen to it before or during your writing session.

13. The Defier: Fear of Losing Autonomy

You fear losing control of your own projects, so you may procrastinate, preferring to assert your independence. *To cope:* Change the way you look at your writing tasks.

- **Practice Self-Reflection:** Explore your underlying fears about control. Where are they coming from? Did you have an experience as a child that made you want to keep control no matter what? See if you can better understand and address this resistance to losing control.

- **Reframe Tasks So They Reflect Your Autonomy:** If you're resisting getting the edits done on your story because your editor gave you a deadline (and you'd rather make your own deadlines, thank you very much), remember that publishing this book is *your* goal and that *you* are in control of what edits are to be made. Reframe the editing process as something you have control over, then choose to meet the deadline so the publishing process goes smoothly.

Exercise: The "Challenge Accepted" List
Write down the tasks you need to complete as personal challenges, reframing them as things you want to get done. For example, you may break your editing project down into how many pages you need to edit per day, then challenge yourself to meet those goals. Remember that these tasks are fully within your control. This can put the ball back in your court, helping you feel less resistant.

Embracing Courage to Move Forward

Fear doesn't have to control your writing journey. If you can start to figure out how it may be influencing your procrastination types, you can determine solutions that will work for you.

The main goal is to confront your fears head-on, or at least distract yourself so you're not focused on what you fear. It's natural for us to be afraid of all sorts of things related to writing, so you don't have to feel like you need to completely eradicate fear. Instead, just think about how you can prevent it from causing you to procrastinate.

twenty-three
embracing change

OVERCOMING PROCRASTINATION IS no small feat. Often, we don't even realize that it's working on us. We just succumb to the urge to delay and off we go.

I imagine that since you picked up this book in the first place, you have the desire to change. You want to break free from this thing that's slowing you down, and now you know why it's there and what you can do about it.

Actually *doing it*, though, is a whole other thing.

You may want to change but still find yourself returning to the same patterns again and again. They're comfortable, after all, and familiar. But ultimately, they'll stall—or even kill—your writing dreams.

In this chapter, we're going to look at this idea of creating change in our lives and why it can be so difficult. Then, I'm hoping to empower you to *want* to change so much that you overcome your own resistance to it.

Keep this in mind—you *will* resist change, because we all do. It's a human trait. We prefer things to stay the same, so making changes takes extra effort. I hope you won't stop with what you've learned so far; instead, embrace this chapter and the change you're hoping to make in your writing life.

Why Is Change So Difficult?

Human beings, as a whole, aren't big fans of change. Our brains are wired to seek the familiar, even when we know it isn't good for us. This tendency is rooted in our survival instincts. Familiar patterns and routines create a sense of security, helping us feel safe in an unpredictable world.

Our routines, particularly in writing, can become like safety nets, offering a sense of predictability in the otherwise uncertain—and often intimidating process—of creation. Change can lead to progress, but it also requires stepping out of our comfort zones, so our brains resist.

This is especially true when it comes to procrastination. The brain is used to avoiding the writing work by focusing on something more immediately enjoyable or gratifying. It doesn't want to try anything different. Observe your own behavior. Notice how you feel when you begin making some of the changes suggested in this book, or even when you just *think* about changing. Do you feel a little anxious? Worried that you'll fail? Afraid that you'll make mistakes or disappoint yourself?

If so, that's okay. It's normal to avoid taking steps toward change, because then you can protect yourself from new or unfamiliar feelings of disappointment, which may seem even scarier than the old, familiar ones.

But staying within those old familiar habits and routines only reinforces your existing procrastination behaviors. It strengthens those patterns in your brain, making it even harder to change later on. *Understand this: the longer you wait to start changing, the harder it becomes.* Each repeated behavior carves deeper neural pathways in the brain, making those actions increasingly automatic. The more you procrastinate, the more likely you are to continue procrastinating. Before long, you've become a professional procrastinator.

That's why you need to break through—now.

Breaking Through and Moving Forward

To move past your ingrained tendencies, you have to create a new narrative in your mind—one that makes change feel *good*. This is where those small, achievable goals we've talked about come in. By setting tiny, non-threatening goals—like writing for five minutes—you can bypass your brain's resistance to change.

It's like fooling yourself, and that's exactly what you want to do. You need to work around the pathways you've already built so you can start forming new ones.

The moment you accomplish a small task, your brain gets a dopamine boost. That's positive reinforcement for your new habit. Keep giving yourself those hits.

The more of these small wins you achieve, the more dopamine you release, the more motivation you feel, and the more you reinforce those new routines. Over time, this gradually reshapes your habits.

This is how you make change—step by tiny step, repeated over and over again.

What If I'm Not Excited About Changing?

You probably picked up this book because something inside you wanted change in your life. But how much do you want it?

This is an important question to ask yourself. You may reach this point and feel a sense of apathy or indifference. That might indicate that your writing dreams aren't as important to you as you thought. Maybe you'd prefer to pursue something else. Only you can answer that, but I encourage you to think carefully about it.

Understand that whatever you decide, it's okay. Just do yourself a favor and *decide*. There's nothing worse than feeling stuck and being unable to move forward. Whether you set your writing dreams aside or buckle down and do something about them, you'll free yourself from that stuck place where you feel confused and discouraged.

It's possible that this book has helped you realize you're only torturing yourself with these writing dreams, and that, in truth, you might be better off letting them go so you can move on to something more likely to bring meaning to your life.

On the other hand, indifference or apathy might be a shield protecting you from discomfort. After all, if you don't try to change, you won't have to face the pressure of potential setbacks. It's also possible you could be disheartened by past failures or simply over-whelmed by the idea of change, and all of it might manifest as apathy.

At the end of the day, what matters is determining where you stand in your approach to change—and why.

What Do You Really Want?

Consider asking yourself the following questions to uncover your deeper motivations and clarify what kind of writing life you envision for yourself.

WHAT WOULD I GAIN BY FINISHING?

The brain tends to cling more tightly to what it thinks it will lose than to what it might gain. To truly understand what you want, you must shift your focus to what you stand to *gain* by making a change.

Your brain is already well aware of the potential losses, but what are the possible rewards? These might include finishing your book, making book sales, or gaining a devoted readership.

Take 10–15 minutes to reflect on what you could gain in your life by changing your procrastination habits. List at least five potential rewards before moving on to the next question.

What could I gain by changing my procrastination habits?

1. _____
2. _____
3. _____
4. _____
5. _____

WHAT AM I GAINING BY NOT WORKING ON MY WRITING?

Now, it's time to get crystal clear on the payoff you're getting from holding on to your procrastination habits. And don't kid yourself—there are rewards, or you wouldn't keep doing it.

Maybe it's helping you avoid fear or anxiety. Perhaps it's protecting you from judgment or criticism, or allowing you to stay in the dream-world you've created of what being a writer is like without having to face the tough reality.

Take 10–15 minutes to list the benefits of procrastination. Write down at least five before moving on to the next question.

What are the benefits I experience when I procrastinate?

1. _____
2. _____
3. _____
4. _____
5. _____

WHAT WILL HAPPEN IN FIVE YEARS IF I DON'T CHANGE?

Finally, try to get real with yourself about where your current habits are leading you. Take 10–15 minutes to write down where you will be as a writer in five years if you continue to allow procrastination to slow you down. Write three to four sentences about what your life may look like then, and then write three to four more sentences describing how you will feel about that.

What will my life look like if I don't change now?

_____
_____
_____

How will I feel about that?

_____
_____

REFLECT ON YOUR ANSWERS

Once you finish this little exercise, give yourself some time to reflect on your answers. Pay close attention to how you feel emotionally, and try to view your answers with compassion. Do you have a better idea of what you truly value? Can you see through your own protective shields to determine what you really want?

Your First Steps Toward Change

If you've decided to set your writing goals and dreams aside for now, follow through on that decision and see where it takes you. Don't feel guilty about it. Simply accept how you feel and live your life. You may find that this is the right choice for you and that in three months or so, you feel more at peace with it.

If, on the other hand, you've discovered that you truly want to pursue your writing dreams, it's time to start working toward change.

LET GO OF GUILT

The first thing you'll want to do is let go of any guilt you may be feeling over your perceived failures. If you're holding onto guilt, it's easy to feel defeated, making it seem pointless to try again. Forgive your past mistakes and give yourself permission to start over with a clean slate.

Action Step: List three writing achievements you're proud of, no matter how small. Reflect on what these accomplishments say about your potential for future success. Start focusing on the positive!

Writing achievements I'm proud of:

1. _____
2. _____
3. _____

CREATE A PERSONAL "WHY" FOR CHANGE

If you don't have a concrete reason to change, it will always feel optional in your life. You don't want optional, here. You want urgent. Necessary! To connect to your own drive to change, link your goals with something deeper that matters to you personally.

What do you want your writing to achieve? How will overcoming procrastination bring you closer to that goal? Developing your own personal "why" will help make change feel more purposeful.

Action Step: Take 5–10 minutes to write down your reason for wanting to overcome procrastination. Keep asking yourself "why" until you get to a deep, emotional reason. Here's an example:

Why do you want to overcome procrastination?
I want to complete my novel.

Why?
Because I've been working on it for a long time.

Why?
Because I care about the characters and I like the story.

Why?
Because it feels important to me. It comes from me. I feel connected to it.

Why?
I feel it may be the best expression of who I am.

So why do you want to overcome procrastination?
Because if I can finish this novel, I'll have expressed myself in the best way I know how, which feels important to me. I think I'll feel more "whole" if I can do that.

Let the question of "why" take you to your own emotional core when it comes to change.

Visualize Future Success

Imagining a future where procrastination no longer controls your writing life can help you feel more excited about the possibilities change might bring. It also serves as a reminder of the rewards waiting on the other side—something especially helpful for a brain that tends to cling to the familiar.

Picture what it will feel like to complete your manuscript, compile a collection of short stories, or simply maintain a consistent writing practice that leaves you feeling creatively fulfilled.

Action Step: Take 5–10 minutes to visualize two future scenarios—one where procrastination continues to hold you back and one where you've found a way to break free of it. Then list the emotions that are tied to each option.

For example:

Scenario 1 | *Scenario 2*
I'm still working on the same novel. | *I've finished my novel.*
Discouraged. Disappointed. | *Elated. So proud of myself!*
Still struggling and stressed. | *Feeling stronger and empowered.*

CREATE SMALL, CONSISTENT HABITS

As we mentioned in Chapter 19, lasting change isn't about massive, sweeping shifts. It's about small, doable changes. Small wins are easier to accomplish and help you build confidence and motivation over time.

Action Step: Look over your top procrastination types and choose one small change you can commit to this coming week. Follow through and reflect on how it affected you by the time the week is over. Then repeat the process for the next week.

BUILD ACCOUNTABILITY

As mentioned in Chapter 20, building accountability into your writing practice will help you stay on track with your changes. Having some type of support from a challenge, partner, or group gives you positive pressure and encouragement, making it easier to stick with your new habits even when you don't feel like it.

Action Step: If you haven't already, find an accountability partner, group, online writing community, or challenge to try. (Remember, you can always create your own.) Give it a go for about a month, then step back and see how it's working for you. Feel free to try another type of accountability if your first one is ineffective.

Practical Tips for Making Change Stick

Making change stick can be tricky. We often start out with the best of intentions, but then slip back into our old habits after the initial enthusiasm fades. Lasting change requires consistent application of your new habits, along with clear strategies that will support you over the long haul.

We've talked about a lot of these throughout this book, but I want to give you a few things you can do to reinforce your new habits as you go. Think of it as building a new foundation supporting this new approach to your writing life.

SCHEDULE REGULAR REFLECTION SESSIONS

This is super important, and it's something most people don't do. Create scheduled times to sit down and take a look at where you are, how far you've come, and where you want to go next. Regularly taking stock of your achievements and challenges allows you to make adjustments as needed, which in turn, will prevent you from sliding backward.

Action Step: Schedule a regular reflection session at least once a month, though once a week may be better when you're first getting started. Set aside 20 minutes or so to list what went well, what challenges arose, and what you want to improve upon next time. Before you finish, write down three specific actions you're going to take to keep moving forward.

IDENTIFY TRIGGERS AND CREATE BOUNDARIES

This is also really important when you're first starting to address your procrastination. Knowing your top types gives you a lot of information about why and when you procrastinate. But you can take it a step further by paying close attention to your "triggers"—those things that happen right before you delay taking action. By identifying and remembering these triggers, you can create boundaries for yourself that will make it easier to stay on track.

Action Step: Keep track of your triggers in your procrastination journal or a dedicated document. Whenever you catch yourself procrastinating, ask yourself why and write that trigger down. Maybe you were tired, so you put off working on a project. Or perhaps your workspace was cluttered, and that led you to avoid writing altogether.

Examples
I was worried I wouldn't write very well.
I didn't get much sleep the night before and I was tired.
I just got some negative feedback and I wasn't feeling very confident.
I've been stuck on my story and I doubt my ability to get unstuck.

As your list grows, write down one boundary or response for each trigger to reduce the chances of getting sidetracked again. If you delayed because of a cluttered workspace, for instance, your response might be to clear off a corner of your desk so it's ready for next time. If you were tired, your response could be to make a cup of coffee or tea, stretch for five minutes, or play some energizing music to help you get into the writing mindset.

REWARD PROGRESS, NOT JUST RESULTS

It's easy to get discouraged if you celebrate only the big milestones. This is particularly true in writing, where the rewards are often few and far between. Find ways to reward yourself frequently. Small, consistent celebrations make the writing process more fun and provide reinforcement for your new habits.

Action Step: Make a list of rewards you'll give yourself for achieving small goals. They can be anything. Indulge yourself! This is something I've learned to do over time, and it makes a big difference in how I feel about my writing.

Remind Yourself of the Benefits of Change

The mind clings to what it knows, especially when it comes to patterns and habits that feel comfortable or familiar. You might feel like you're making progress, but then something happens—a setback in your writing or another area of your life—and suddenly those old habits feel like comfy blankets. You'll wrap yourself in them and drop back to square one.

It's okay to experience these setbacks, and it's probably best to expect them. You can get around them by regularly reminding yourself of the benefits of change. Especially in the first few months, it's important to spend time during your weekly reflections visualizing what a changed writing life will look like and what benefits you'll enjoy. Picture the satisfaction of finishing your project or the pride you'll feel when sharing it with others.

The key is to consistently counter the brain's attachment to familiar habits. Doing it once won't be enough. To train your mind to do what you want, you have to regularly remind it of why change is a good thing. "Looky here!" you say. "This is what you can get if you keep going this way!"

Action Step: Keep a working document of all the ways your changes are going to make your writing life better. List one benefit after the other and regularly review this list!

Embracing the Path to Change

Change can be intimidating, but as you know, it's also the key to unlocking your full potential as a writer. If you go into it knowing it probably won't be easy, you'll already be ahead of the game. Be compassionate with yourself. Expect to make mistakes. Every day offers a chance to start again. Small changes. Little wins. Step by step, you'll make it happen.

twenty-four
the magic of today

WELL HERE WE ARE—THE final chapter. You've come a long way since we started. I trust you've learned a lot about yourself, the types of procrastination that tend to hold you back, and how you can manage them so you can get back to what matters—your writing!

The journey to overcoming procrastination isn't a quick one, though. You now have a clearer understanding of the obstacles that may trip you up and some useful coping strategies, but that doesn't mean everything will be smooth from here on out. Procrastination will still creep in now and then, and you may start and stop a few times before finding your rhythm.

In this chapter, I want to help you prepare for the road ahead. Too often, we read a helpful book, nod along in agreement, and then set it aside, only to go right back to doing what we were doing before. I *really* hope you won't let that happen. Instead, let this book be your catalyst for making meaningful, lasting changes in your writing life.

The Ongoing Fight Against Procrastination

Procrastination is a mighty foe and won't disappear just because you've finished reading these pages. I wish it were that easy! But chances are, before diving in, you had already developed a strong procrastination habit. It may be your go-to response when you feel uncomfortable. Over time, it's probably become deeply ingrained, which means overcoming it will take real, consistent effort.

Even with all this knowledge and the right strategies in place, there will still be times when you struggle with the urge to put things off. The keys to lasting change are patience and persistence. Most likely, you'll need to confront procrastination more than once. I'd recommend doing that with the following three steps.

1. BE AWARE

Before, you probably put things off without much thought. Now, I want you to become aware of when and why you do it. Each time you catch yourself procrastinating, take a moment to journal about it.

Why did it happen? What was going on just before? What were you thinking about?

Do this every time it occurs for at least a month. This practice will train your brain to recognize procrastination's sneaky patterns, and before long, you'll start catching it in the act. When that happens, you're ready to take the next step.

2. GET TO THE EMOTION OF IT

When you catch yourself about to procrastinate, pause and ask, "What are you *feeling*?" Try to identify the emotion beneath the urge to delay.

For example, if you're an Overdoer, you might say, "I don't have time right now and I feel overwhelmed." If you're a Fun Seeker, your response might be, "I don't want to do it because it feels like a chore and I'll feel bored." If you're a Tired procrastinator, it could be, "I feel exhausted."

Use what you know about your procrastination type to guide this self-questioning before you put off your writing. Tap into the emotion, then move on to the next step.

3. Ask, "How Can I Make This Easier to Do Today?"

Once you identified the emotion, it's time to ask the final question: "How can I make this *easier to do today*?"

In the introduction to this book, we talked about the "curse of tomorrow"—how we gradually chip away at our writing lives by always assuming we'll get to it tomorrow. Now that you know how damaging procrastination can be, it's time to start thinking differently. Instead of putting things off for tomorrow, train yourself to ask, "How can I make it easier to get this done *today*?"

Let's say you're a Perfectionist, and you're about to delay working on your next chapter. You recognize the urge and ask yourself, "Why?" You might say, "Because I don't feel up to it today. I'm afraid I'll write badly." Your emotion is: *fear*.

Next, ask, "How can I make this easier to do today?" You could go back and check your type chapter for potential solutions, or—since the emotion is tied into fear—review Chapter 22. Then, you might remind yourself, "The writing doesn't have to be perfect. I could write something bad and it would still be better than writing nothing at all. If I allow myself to write badly, could I manage 15 minutes?" That should make it easier.

Or maybe you're a Guilty procrastinator. When you ask yourself "Why?", you respond, "I feel guilty about not writing yesterday, and I don't think I can catch up today." Your emotion is: *guilt*.

Then ask, "How can I make this easier to do today?" You might check your type chapter and decide, "I'll forget about yesterday and start with a fresh slate. All I have to do is write 100 words and I'll feel proud of myself." That should make it easier.

Use this simple pattern every time.

1. Be aware.
2. Ask yourself why—get to the emotion.
3. Ask yourself, "How can I make this *easier to do today?*"

Over time, this approach can help you gradually overcome the habit of procrastination. It will take repeated applications, though, before you'll begin to notice a substantial difference. I'd say give it about six months of regularly practicing this three-step process.

In the meantime, put safeguards in place, as outlined in your type description and in the later chapters. These will help reduce the chances that you'll procrastinate in the first place. Write out your mindset change and tape it to your refrigerator. Set up your bite-sized goals, and decide how you'll reward yourself for achieving them. Get an accountability partner and schedule a sample check-in. Identify the fears that may be holding you back and determine how you'll face them.

Try taking one small step forward each day. Start by writing and posting your mindset change. Tomorrow, begin breaking down your project into smaller, manageable goals. The next day, tackle one of those goals and see how it goes. If procrastination shows up, notice it and write about it in your journal.

Bit by bit, day by day, you will start to make real progress. The most important step you can take right now is this: *Decide that procrastination is no longer your master.*

Decide that Procrastination Will No Longer Be Your Master

Up until now, procrastination has had at least some control over your writing dreams. It's gotten in the way, slowed you down, and perhaps even stopped you altogether. You have allowed it to do that, as you were unaware of what was really happening. But now you know. So you have a choice.

On the one hand, you can continue to let procrastination derail you. You can understand that it will keep showing up and decide you're okay with that. Maybe your writing isn't important enough to push back, so you figure you'll find fulfillment in other ways.

Or you can choose the opposite approach: now that you know what procrastination is doing to your writing dreams, you can decide to fight it. It won't be easy, but it will be worth it. Taking control of your writing destiny begins with that choice.

There is great power in choosing to break through to creative freedom. This isn't necessarily about eliminating procrastination from your life forever (though you can do that if you want to!), but about freeing yourself from the blocks that keep you from moving forward. It's about declaring to yourself that you *are* a writer, you *intend* to realize your writing dreams, and that you will *no longer* allow procrastination to stop you.

Make that decision and follow through. You'll be amazed at what you can accomplish. I wish you the very best on your journey.

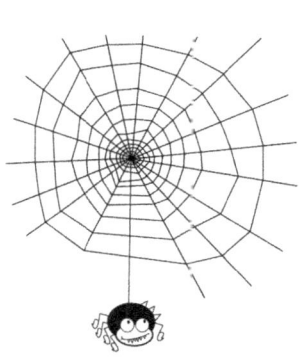

Exercise for the Road Ahead

1. **Reflect on your journey:** Spend 10 minutes reflecting on what you've learned about your procrastination habits. Write down three key insights from this book that have resonated the most.
2. **Set your creative intentions:** Write a short paragraph about the type of writer you want to be in six months. What projects do you want to complete? How do you want to feel about your writing and yourself? What mindset will you carry forward? What will be your relationship to procrastination by then?
3. **Create a small-wins checklist:** List 5–10 small, achievable writing goals you will tackle in the next 30 days. Examples could be setting up a new writing routine that works for your type, putting into place certain coping techniques,

303

making a certain amount of progress on your writing project based on your new approaches, or completing 30 days of journaling about your procrastination. Then, check off each goal as you achieve it, and reward yourself with something that inspires you.

thank you!

Thank you for reading *Escape the Writer's Web!*

It took me over a year to finish this book. I was thrilled to see it in its final form, and happy that you've read it all the way to the end. :)

If you've enjoyed reading about the 13 different types of procrastinators, please consider rating and reviewing the book on Amazon.com, Goodreads.com, or wherever you regularly purchase your books. The review doesn't have to be complicated—just share your honest thoughts about the book. I'd be grateful!

And if you haven't grabbed the workbook yet, this is the perfect time. The *Escape the Writer's Web Workbook* is designed to help you take everything you've learned here and turn it into real, lasting transformation. Inside, you'll find personalized exercises, mindset shifts, practical plans for your procrastination type, and tools to help you stay free when life pulls you back. It's available wherever books are sold.

Get the scoop on future releases and behind-the-scenes insights at **www.masterwritermindset/newsletter.**

acknowledgments

First and foremost, thank you to my family for your unwavering support of my writing. I'm especially grateful to Gerald for your help with the book cover production, and to Mary for your sharp eye during the proofreading process.

Heartfelt thanks to Alisha Sanders for your thoughtful and thorough edits—my sentences are stronger and smoother because of your expertise.

I'm also grateful to Miblart for designing such an original cover.

To the many authors who contributed to my research for this book, I so appreciate you lending your time to this project!

A big shout-out to my newsletter subscribers—it's a joy to share this journey with you. I hope those of you who struggle with procrastination gained some insights from my work here.

And to every reader who's picked up one of my books and taken the time to leave a review, thank you.

about the author

Photo by Ellibean Photography

Colleen M. Story writes award-winning historical fantasy, supernatural thrillers, and motivational books for writers. She grew up on a Colorado ranch making up stories on horseback, which probably explains a lot. A life-long musician, she still plays French horn in the local symphony and teaches music on the side. With 25+ years as a freelance health writer, she's the unofficial "medical hotline" for friends and family. When she's not typing away, you'll probably find her at the movies—sci-fi, fantasy, action, or anything with a good chase scene. Find her books at colleenmstory.com or masterwritermindset.com.

consider these other titles by colleen m. story

OVERWHELMED WRITER RESCUE: Stop drowning in your to-do list and start living a more joyful creative life! "If you read only one self help book this year – grab this one! It is not just for writers. This book is very motivating and so easy to read quickly." ~Laura's Reading

WRITER GET NOTICED!: Stop feeling invisible and start attracting the attention you deserve! "Colleen M. Story does an awesome job, sharing valuable information in a down-to-earth genuine voice. A Five Star must have in your library as an invaluable guide for writers. I found her information and self-discovery processes applicable in other aspects of my life as well!" ~Susan Violante, Reader Views

YOUR WRITING MATTERS: You start to wonder if you're wasting your time. Does your writing even matter? "I wish I'd been able to read this book when I was a beginning writer. . . . It would have helped me vanquish my self-doubts, ignore naysayers, and encouraged me to develop the craft of writing." ~Joe Wisinski for Readers' Favorite

THE CURSE OF KING MIDAS: This captivating tale of King Midas begins the new mythological fantasy series. "A gripping fantasy that blends classic myth with contemporary storytelling finesse . . . a standout in the genre." ~Foram Vyas for Readers' Favorite Book Awards

THE GIMIRRI INVASION: The gripping saga that began in *The Curse of King Midas* continues: "A vivid, engrossing tale . . . thoroughly absorbing, unpredictable, and powered by strong forces that both enlighten and create an incredible page-turner." ~D. Donovan, Sr. Reviewer, Midwest Book Review

THE BEACHED ONES: He came back, determined to keep his promise . . . "A poignant tale of forgiveness and redemption that reaches beyond the grave . . . will have you staying up late to accompany Daniel on his journey to the end." ~Melissa Payne, bestselling author of *The Secrets of Lost Stones* and *A Light in the Forest*

LOREENA'S GIFT: A blind girl's terrifying "gift" allows her to regain her eyesight—but only as she ferries the recently deceased into the afterlife. "This book sucked me in and I couldn't turn the pages fast enough . . . I absolutely loved this story and I will be on the lookout for future books from Story." ~JBronderBookReviews

references

Intro

Ferrari, Joseph R., Kelly L. Barnes, and Piers Steel. "Life Regrets by Avoidant and Arousal Procrastinators." *Journal of Individual Differences* 30, no. 3 (2009), 163-168. doi:10.1027/1614-0001.30.3.163.

Foroux, Darius. "When Procrastination Turns Into Regret (and How to Avoid It)." Darius Foroux. Last modified November 14, 2022. https://dariusforoux.com/procrastination-regret/.

Pychyl, Timothy A. "Living Well & Dying Well: Some Reflections on Regret, Grief and Procrastination." *Psychology Today*. Accessed August 4, 2024. https://www.psychology today.com/us/blog/dont-delay/200807/living-well-dying-well-some-reflections-regret-grief-and-procrastination.

Chapter 1

Blouin-Hudon, Eve-Marie C., and Timothy A. Pychyl. "Experiencing the temporally extended self: Initial support for the role of affective states, vivid mental imagery, and future self-continuity in the prediction of academic procrastination." *Personality and Individual Differences* 86 (2015), 50-56. doi:10.1016/j.paid.2015.06.003.

Burka, Jane, and Lenora M. Yuen. *Procrastination: Why You Do It, What to Do About It Now*. Boston: Da Capo Lifelong Books, 2007.

Jaffe, Eric. "Why Wait? The Science Behind Procrastination." Association for Psychological Science - APS. Last modified March 29, 2013. https://www.psychologicalscience.org/observer/why-wait-the-science-behind-procrastination.

Jochmann, Anna, Burkhard Gusy, Tino Lesener, and Christine Wolter. "Procrastination, depression and anxiety symptoms in university students: a three-wave longitudinal study on the mediating role of perceived stress." *BMC Psychology* 12, no. 1 (2024). doi:10.1186/s40359-024-01761-2.

Johansson, Fred, Alexander Rozental, Klara Edlund, Pierre Côté, Tobias Sundberg, Clara Onell, Ann Rudman, and Eva Skillgate. "Associations Between Procrastination and Subsequent Health Outcomes Among University Students in Sweden." *JAMA Network Open* 6, no. 1 (2023), e2249346. doi:10.1001/jamanetworkopen.2022.49346.

Rozental, Alexander, David Forsström, Ayah Hussoon, and Katrin B. Klingsieck. "Procrastination Among University Students: Differentiating Severe Cases in Need of Support From Less Severe Cases." *Frontiers in Psychology* 13 (2022). doi:10.3389/fpsyg.2022.783570.

Steel, Piers. "The nature of procrastination: A meta-analytic and theoretical review of quintessential self-regulatory failure." *Psychological Bulletin* 133, no. 1 (2007), 65-94. doi:10.1037/0033-2909.133.1.65.

Stodola, Sarah. "Procrastination Through the Ages: A Brief History of Wasting Time." Mental Floss. Last modified May 11, 2015. https://www.mentalfloss.com/article/63887/procrastination-through-ages-brief-history-wasting-time.

References

Tice, Dianne M., and Roy F. Baumeister. "Longitudinal Study of Procrastination, Performance, Stress, and Health: The Costs and Benefits of Dawdling." *Psychological Science* 8, no. 6 (1997), 454-458. doi:10.1111/j.1467-9280.1997.tb00460.x.

Zeigler-Hill, Virgil, and Todd K. Shackelford. "Procrastination." In *Encyclopedia of Personality and Individual Differences*, 4046–4053. Basingstoke: Springer, 2020. https://link. springer.com/referenceworkentry/10.1007/978-3-319-24612-3_2272.

Chapter 2

Blouin-Hudon, Eve-Marie C., and Timothy A. Pychyl. "Experiencing the temporally extended self: Initial support for the role of affective states, vivid mental imagery, and future self-continuity in the prediction of academic procrastination." *Personality and Individual Differences* 86 (2015), 50-56. doi:10.1016/j.paid.2015.06.003.

Ersner-Hershfield, Hal, M. T. Garton, Kacey Ballard, Gregory R. Samanez-Larkin, and Brian Knutson. "Don't stop thinking about tomorrow: Individual differences in future self-continuity account for saving." *Judgment and Decision Making* 4, no. 4 (2009), 280-286. doi:10.1017/s1930297500003855.

Froese, Arnold D., Sheryl J. Nisly, and Roxanna M. May. "The Effects of Task Interest and Difficulty on Procrastination." *Transactions of the Kansas Academy of Science* (1903-) 87, no. 3/4 (1984), 119. doi:10.2307/3627847.

Sirois, Fuschia M. "'I'll look after my health, later': A replication and extension of the procrastination–health model with community-dwelling adults." *Personality and Individual Differences* 43, no. 1 (2007), 15-26. doi:10.1016/j.paid.2006.11.003.

Sirois, Fuschia, and Timothy Pychyl. "Procrastination and the Priority of Short-Term Mood Regulation: Consequences for Future Self." *Social and Personality Psychology Compass* 7, no. 2 (2013), 115-127. doi:10.1111/spc3.12011.

Wieland, Lena M., Johannes D. Hoppe, Anett Wolgast, and Ulrich W. Ebner-Priemer. "Task ambiguity and academic procrastination: An experience sampling approach." *Learning and Instruction* 81 (2022), 101595. doi:10.1016/j.learninstruc.2022.101595.

Chapter 3

Chun Chu, Angela H., and Jin N. Choi. "Rethinking Procrastination: Positive Effects of "Active" Procrastination Behavior on Attitudes and Performance." *The Journal of Social Psychology* 145, no. 3 (2005), 245-264. doi:10.3200/socp.145.3.245-264.

Hossain, Nishat N., and Monirul A. Hossain. "The Relationship between Big Five Personality Traits and Procrastination among Students of International Islamic University Malaysia (IIUM)." *International Journal of Business and Management Research* 10, no. 3 (2022), 71-81. doi:10.37391/ijbmr.100302.

Rist, Fred, Margarita Engberding, Anna Hoecker, Johanne Wolf-Lettmann, and Eva-Maria Fischbach. "Diagnostic criteria to differentiate pathological procrastinators from common delayers: a re-analysis." *Frontiers in Psychology* 14 (2023). doi:10.3389/fpsyg.2023.1147401.

Rozental, Alexander, Erik Forsell, Andreas Svensson, David Forsström, Gerhard Andersson, and Per Carlbring. "Differentiating Procrastinators from Each Other: A Cluster Analysis." *Cognitive Behaviour Therapy* 44, no. 6 (2015), 480-490. doi:10.1080/16506073.2015.1059353.

References

Steel, Piers. "Arousal, avoidant and decisional procrastinators: Do they exist?" *Personality and Individual Differences* 48, no. 8 (2010), 926-934. doi:10.1016/j.paid.2010.02.025.

Watson, David C. "Procrastination and the five-factor model: a facet level analysis." *Personality and Individual Differences* 30, no. 1 (2001), 149-158. doi:10.1016/s0191-8869(00)00019-2.

Yan, Bo, and Xiaomin Zhang. "What Research Has Been Conducted on Procrastination? Evidence From a Systematical Bibliometric Analysis." *Frontiers in Psychology* 13 (2022). doi:10.3389/fpsyg.2022.809044.

Zohar, Ada H., Lior P. Shimone, and Meirav Hen. "Active and passive procrastination in terms of temperament and character." *PeerJ* 7 (2019), e6988. doi:10.7717/peerj.6988.

Chapter 12

What is important is seldom urgent and what is urgent is seldom important. (2014, May 9). Quote Investigator[β] – Tracing Quotations. https://quoteinvestigator.com/2014/05/09/urgent/

Chapter 13

Wohl, M. J., Pychyl, T. A., & Bennett, S. H. (2010). I forgive myself, now I can study: How self-forgiveness for procrastinating can reduce future procrastination. *Personality and Individual Differences*, 48(7), 803-808. https://doi.org/10.1016/j.paid.2010.01.029

Chapter 16

Dalton-Smith, S. (2017). Sacred rest: Recover your life, renew your energy, restore your sanity. FaithWords.

Han, A., Kim, J., & Kim, J. (2021). A study of leisure walking intensity levels on mental health and health perception of older adults *Gerontology and Geriatric Medicine*, 7. https://doi.org/10.1177/2333721421999316

Sacred rest. (2020, July 3). Dr. Dalton-Smith - I Choose My Best Life - Live Fully, Love Boldly, Rest Intentionally. https://ichoosemybestlife.com/sacred-rest/

Sleep. (2024, August 14). Chronic Disease Indicators. https://www.cdc.gov/cdi/indicator-definitions/sleep.html

Stanford study finds walking improves creativity. (2014, April 24). Stanford Report. https://news.stanford.edu/stories/2014/04/walking-vs-sitting-042414

Story, C. M. (2022, December 6). 7 different types of rest writers need to restore creativity. Master Writer Mindset. https://masterwritermindset.com/2022/12/05/7-different-types-of-rest-writers-need-to-restore-creativity/

www.ingramcontent.com/pod-product-compliance
Lightning Source LLC
Chambersburg PA
CBHW070546130626
46556CB00001B/40